FATHER DOES KNOW BEST

LAUREN CHAPIN
WITH ANDREW COLLINS

BERKLEY BOOKS, NEW YORK

This Berkley book contains the complete
text of the original hardcover edition.
It has been completely reset in a typeface
designed for easy reading, and was printed
from new film.

FATHER DOES KNOW BEST

A Berkley Book / published by arrangement with
Thomas Nelson Publishers

PRINTING HISTORY
Thomas Nelson edition published 1989
Berkley edition / May 1990

"IT TOOK ME A LONG TIME
to share this often unsavory story, and when the pieces of
my bizarre life begin to fall into an understandable
perspective, you will know why it has taken me as long as it
has to grasp it for myself, much less to tell it."

—*LAUREN CHAPIN*

"I WATCHED LAUREN GROW UP ON THE SET OF
Father Knows Best.
I loved and respected her then, and I do now. Although she
has gone through extremely difficult times, she has once again
come out on top."

—*ROBERT YOUNG*

"LAUREN WAS MY DELIGHTFUL TV CHILD.
After that, life was not kind to her. I'm sure it
took courage to write *Father Does Know Best.*"

—*JANE WYATT*

"LAUREN'S LIFE WAS NO FAIRY TALE,
but I can think of no one who better deserves to live happily
ever after."

—*ELINOR DONAHUE*

"WITH WHAT I KNOW OF LAUREN'S EARLY LIFE,
I'm not surprised she became 'Peck's Bad Girl' for a time.
This should be *some* read."

—*BILLY GRAY*

To Matt and Summer, my beloved children.
If we make mistakes,
there is no shame. But if we fail
to learn from our mistakes,
shame on us.

Lauren Chapin

• Lauren's Introduction •

LAUREN ANN CHAPIN was born on Wednesday, May 23, 1945, in Los Angeles Hospital of the Good Samaritan. Like most newborns, this eight-pound baby with big brown eyes was little more than an empty vessel waiting to be filled with the knowledge and the experiences that would make her whole. Yet, when I look back over this child's life, I realize that, while she received in her formative years a great deal of information and lived through a wide variety of both wonderful and not-so-wonderful experiences, she never gained access to what she needed to discover her own worth. So it was only natural that she would come to spend most of her life searching for who or what she was. Tragically, hers was a very long search.

Lauren's life began just a few miles from the Hollywood studios. She would soon have an association with these "dream factories," and at least one of them would allow her to escape the nightmare of her home-life for a short time. Yet, even in the very beginning, show business would at once touch her life and warp her values, values which often emphasized the result over means, money over love. I know so much about this girl's life because I was the infant who would do so much and gain so little from my childhood. I would become the teenager and then the adult who would search for love, acceptance, and truth in so many places and find them in so few. I was the person who should have died from drug overdoses or in suicide attempts, only I lived to try both again and again. Even though there is so much of which I am not proud, this is *my* story.

I have not lived a particularly long life, but when I put my activities into perspective, there is a great deal to tell. In retrospect, I'm sure my life would have been far simpler had I been raised in a normal fashion and taken a smoother road to where I now find myself. But even before I could walk, a path had been set for me, and I followed this course through both success and failure. Had I known how, I would have changed directions. Opportunities for change were always present, but I wasn't bright or enlightened enough to understand the ways to turn my life around. When I was very young, it was probably impossible. As I grew older, bitterness often ruled my judgments; it was far easier to run away from problems than to stop and face them.

So, for years, I avoided looking at my past. I wanted to forget much of what had happened to me. I spent my time trying to erase all signs of who I had once been, even denying what I had done. Now I know what wise men have long known: to completely understand why I became what I became and to realize my future potential, I had to go back and put my past in perspective, no matter how painful the experience.

It took me a long time to share this often unsavory story, and when the pieces of my bizarre life begin to fall into an understandable perspective, you will know why it has taken me as long as it has to grasp it for myself, much less to tell it. But if you begin the book, don't give up on my story until it's done; otherwise you will only feel my pain and fail to understand the real joy I now feel about life and living.

• One •

THE FIRST EIGHT days of my life must have been a frantic time for my parents. I spent them in the hospital suffering from a unique stomach condition called *piloric stinosis*. Piloric stinosis is caused by a shrinking at the bottom of the stomach that prevents the stomach from processing and flushing food. Hence, any person suffering from this disease displays little appetite and grows increasingly weak because of the inability to absorb nutrients. Given time, the condition cures itself, but my family was mightily concerned as the doctors' assurances that I would be fine proved misleading; they were confused by the fact that I was not better and couldn't go home. This delay was made even worse with a big nursery full of toys, furniture, and new clothes waiting for me when I was released. Having a sick newborn is every parent's nightmare.

During this time probably no one suffered more than my mother. I am her third child, and the first not to be perfectly healthy from day one. Therefore, my initial *trepid* steps into the world must have been harder on her than anyone, including myself. I am sure that when she finally was allowed to take me home, a massive rush of relief flooded her soul. Now looking back, for my mother's own sanity, it might have been better for her not to have gone through her third pregnancy and the suffering of my first few days. For her, it would have probably been better to have had only two children. Because of her future health problems and the time constraints of my two brothers' careers, she never knew me as well as she might have. Her contribution to shaping my early years was far less intensive than I needed and she would have wanted. Doubtless this lost time contributed to what became a long-term personality clash. Still, at the moment of her baby girl's homecoming, I know that the only thing on her mind was me, and I am equally sure that her heart was full. For a few moments, I was all that mattered.

My first home was a very comfortable, but not ostentatious, house in a then-exclusive section of Los Angeles known as "Miracle Mile." Once out of the car and inside, I was met and surrounded by my father's parents, Gee Gee and Frank, my mother's mother, Laura or as I would later call her, Nonnie, my two brothers, Michael, almost nine, and Billy, sixteen months, and the family Irish setter, Shawnee. Within seconds the boisterous welcoming committee was joined by Mom and Sterling Settles, our maid. A queen could not have had a more wonderful coming-out party.

At that time, everything promised the most wonderful of childhoods. I had a mother who was loving and kind, two brothers who were obviously proud to have a little sister, a father who was becoming very successful in business, and an assertive black housekeeper to keep everyone in order. Yet, unforeseen events set in motion a generation before would soon change the nature of my house and shake the very fabric of my life. As would soon become evident, the timing of my birth was all wrong.

Sterling, Gee Gee, and my brothers have told me that I was a good baby. I cried and complained very little and was extremely easy to care for; yet, I must have been a most insecure infant. Even before my toddler stage, I spent a great deal of time either with Sterling or various relatives; rarely was I with my parents. With my brother Michael's established acting career and my other brother Billy just getting started in the business, Mom was eternally on the move, and my Dad, a man who made a good living in banking, was more absent than present. Therefore, my early rearing was largely done by third parties. Then, to separate me further from my family, a major illness hit my mother.

In early 1947, I was turned over to my Uncle Edward and Aunt Helen on a full-time basis while my Mom, sick with tuberculosis spent over a year in a sanatorium. I don't remember much about the next eighteen months, but I am sure that a deep impression of not belonging had been made on me. By the time Mother was well enough to be released, I was three and had been moved from my aunt's home and given to another couple who were friends of my parents. I now had no recollection of ever having lived with my own family. So, in July 1948 when my mother and father picked me up to take me to their home, I cried. I must have believed that I was being kidnapped by strangers. I didn't want to leave my home. Dolls, food, hugs, and kisses all failed to calm me. I was traumatized. I felt like a misplaced stranger, out of step with everything that was around me. It took me weeks to get used to my own parents, my brothers, and my home again. I just didn't feel as if I belonged, so very early I was insecure.

My time away from my parents, particularly my mother, apparently had erased our early bonding experiences. We were now strangers to each other. All the things that we should have shared in the intervening years, we hadn't. I had changed a great deal during the time she and I were separated, and nothing could have prepared her for this change. I was no longer a baby. I ran and talked, with a personality and a will that was not at all what she remembered. I had developed differently from my brothers because of the different environment I had just experienced. In many ways I probably seemed like someone else's child, which must have been a shock to her. Besides, because she had been sick for so long, a certain fear had come over her that served to push the two of us even farther apart. Mother was now reluctant to get close to people. She didn't hug and kiss as much as she once had, frightened that she would give us her disease.

She was also on a great deal of medication, and this sometimes affected her moods. She could still be a loving person, but just not as often as she had been. T.B. had taken away a piece of her soul and robbed her of some of her zest, and she seemed unable to recover it completely. Much more than anything else, I know that it had stolen my chance to get to know the mother my brothers had known before my birth. That was the saddest part of all.

After a few hard weeks, I finally adjusted somewhat to my home, and once again I settled into a fairly normal childhood. I don't recall too much about those early days; they all blend together into a routine of playing, eating, and sleeping. My father, Roy, was at work most weekdays, so the only time I really saw him was on weekends. I do remember looking up to him and wanting to be around him when he was home. He was at times very loving and very playful, but at other times he seemed stern and unforgiving. Dinner was when the harshest facets of his personality usually appeared.

He enforced strict rules at the table, and these rules made mealtimes most unpleasant. He demanded that we eat every bite of food on our plate. We also had to sit erect with napkins in our laps, backs straight, and mouths silent, unless we made an important contribution to the polite conversation he allowed. Childish behavior was unacceptable. If we broke any of these rules, Dad would fly into a rage, sometimes even whipping the guilty before the meal continued. Needless to say, even at a preschool age, my stomach was often churning before I got to the table, and I was constantly praying that I could just get through the meal without making a mistake.

Dad usually sat at the head of our dinner table, Mom at the other end. Billy and I sat together with Michael on the other side facing us.

"Well, Michael, how was your day? What did you learn at this school of yours?" Dad asked one day.

Clearing his throat, Michael looked at Dad and started to talk. But Billy and I wanted to be noticed too, so we chimed in before Michael could get a word out. When Daddy glared at us, Billy and I fidgeted but shut up quickly. Michael proceeded cautiously, explaining what catechism lesson he had learned that day. As Michael talked, I leaned over to Billy and asked him to pass the salt. Billy stretched over the table and spilled the milk with his arm. Michael abruptly quit talking, then Dad's temper broke loose.

"————! Can't either one of you kids ever behave properly? That's it! I've had it! We can't even have one dinner without one of you————kids misbehaving."

With that, he got up, pushing his chair back until it fell over. He seized us by the napes of our necks, grabbed us out of our chairs, and pushed us into the other room for a whipping.

"But, Daddy, we didn't mean it. It was an accident," we pleaded.

After our whipping, everyone sat in complete silence, afraid to say a word.

Mother's given name was Marquerite Alice Barringer Chapin, but everyone called her Megs. She was a four-foot, eleven-inch, ninety-six pound redhead whose green eyes always seemed to be filled with energy and life. She was pretty bordering on beautiful, with perfect manners and posture. Her attractive face, highlighted by an English nose, was always held high, and she walked with a long, confident stride. She was obviously petite, and in some people's eyes, frail. Despite her small stature and her illness, however, she possessed a great deal of dynamic passion. When she needed to be, she was forceful, bright, and charming. Because of these qualities, people were always drawn to her. She possessed a charisma that even as a young girl, I recognized. She made people laugh, and she knew how to make visitors feel comfortable. At the time, I wanted to be like her.

No one who ever knew her could say that Mother wasn't

resourceful. Even as a child she had always made the most of what she had. The daughter of a barely middle class school-teacher, she had still managed to fit in at the exclusive Hollywood High School, and despite having little money and no real star connections, she had affected the other students. She learned during this time what she believed all of her life: that wealth and respect fit hand in hand. She couldn't earn the latter without having the former. All of her energies and imagination went into this endeavor. Money and what it could purchase was at the center of her every thought, and her whole moral pattern reflected this thinking. In her mind, to be poor was to be dirty.

When she met Roy Chapin, Mom found a man who fit all of the categories that were needed in a mate. For starters, Dad's parents had money, and as an added bonus, he was handsome, smooth, and full of life. She would later tell me that she had never loved my father. As a matter of fact, she would say that she hadn't even liked him. But he had offered her a way up the social ladder, a way to be somebody in society, and that was more important to her than love. With position and money, love could be bought.

In retrospect, I honestly believe that Mom really did love and felt a strong attraction for Dad in those early years of marriage. Maybe she hadn't wanted to, and maybe it was his money that had first attracted her, but my older brother informed me that when he had been small, they had seemed happy for a long while. So, even though she would later spew words of hate when it came to remembering her times with Dad, it may have been simply the pain caused by her drinking that was already, even when I was a toddler, beginning to cloud her judgment and control her thoughts and actions.

Mom's plan to capture Daddy had worked beautifully to a point. She made it down the aisle, and she got the name of a well-to-do family, but what she hadn't foreseen was that just because Dad came from money didn't mean she was going to get it. As circumstances would have it, Roy Chapin was forced to go out and get a job just like most other people. His folks believed money was to be earned, not given away. My grandparents were not going to elevate the lifestyle of their only child simply because his wife wanted to live in a finer fashion.

After several years, Mom got wiser and gave up on getting money from Dad's parents. Now a mother and even more tired of living such a "normal" life, she began searching for another way to gain status and respect. While she knew she couldn't trade on her own talents, perhaps, she thought, she might be able to find a way to use her children to raise her social level. After all, there were lots of places for children in the movie business, and she was at least somewhat familiar with opening a few of Hollywood's doors.

Her mother had been a schoolteacher for over twenty years. Some of her teaching time had been spent at various Hollywood studios. Grandmother Laura had taught the likes of Micky Rooney, Judy Garland, Elizabeth Taylor, and a host of others. Through these associations, she had gotten to know the agents and casting directors, and these connections helped Mom arrange for Michael first, and then Billy, to get auditions and agents. Thus, my brothers were introduced to show business. Through my brothers' work, Mom in turn entered the Hollywood social scene, and because of the treatment she received from studio directors and executives, she thought she had gained some respect. This newfound attention was almost a drug to her, something she had sought all of her life. She wasn't satisfied with just a little taste, of course; she always wanted more.

Within months of my moving back in with my family, Mother had become so involved in Michael's and Billy's professional lives that she spent most of her time developing their acting careers by taking them to radio, modeling, and movie auditions. This simply didn't leave her with very much time for me. So Sterling took on a great deal of my mothering. At a time when a special bond should have been growing between Mom and me, it was actually Sterling who was gaining my trust and confidence.

Sterling was a large, heavy woman with sparkling brown eyes and a chocolate brown complexion. As years passed, she would be the one who would always reach out to me when I cried and laugh with me when I was happy. More than anyone else, she would be the one person who would freely offer her love with not a single string attached. Heaven knows who I would have run to all those times I needed a hug and comforting word if she hadn't been there.

But even though Mother wasn't always on top of things at home, she was a great "Stage Mother." She always found work for her kids. Michael worked in scores of films, reaching his zenith playing the title role in a Western movie serial for Republic Pictures. By the time I was born, Billy had already played a child in Gary Cooper's "Casanova Brown." Many other parts would follow. Because of who my brothers were and the success they had already experienced, my own birth was duly noted by the two major Los Angeles daily newspapers. Nonetheless, though my family already had attained a certain amount of "star" power, and we lived in a very upper middle class lifestyle, Mother still was not satisfied. As much as my brothers worked and as much money as they made, she wanted more.

Mom probably didn't even understand the reasons she so desired success for her kids. Deep down, she probably rationalized it as providing something essential in their lives. But the fancy doors and the excitement, as well as the fact that she was no longer poor, probably turned her on most and challenged her to do even better. They fueled the passion that drove her forward, regardless of the odds or the obstacles. She felt she could move heaven or hell and still have enough left to do it again. If it had required her to do so, she would have gone to war to get a shot at a part for her boys.

First and foremost, Mom was a fighter, and those who underestimated her always lost. She did her research, learned her business, and had an instinctive knowledge as to how to play the studio's political games. She knew when to use people, and when to let people use her. When push came to shove, few people could move her. So my brothers were almost always busy, due in no small part to their considerable talent, but due even more to my mother's perseverance.

Somewhere in her search for fortune, a normal life, normal desires, and a normal marriage were forgotten. Show business had consumed her. She was just too busy ushering her kids onto movie sets or attending social gatherings to need or miss the simple elements of a happy home-life.

As my brothers became more famous in the inner circles of the industry, she attended as many social gatherings as possible. Being at a party, drinking pretty drinks, and eating delicate foods while rubbing elbows with important people made her feel like she had status and respect. So if she found a social event or a club that could give her another day or night on the town, she became a part of it. To her the membership was another medal, a mark of her arrival and acceptance. No one realized then, but these social gatherings were also turning into opportunities to drink.

I doubt very little that throughout her whole life, Mother was searching for love and respect. The way that she lived life was the only way she knew how to pursue it. The environment in which she was brought up had a great deal to do with it. She was ashamed of her father, an alcoholic who had often embarrassed her. No doubt she had felt a great deal of insecurity when being compared to the famous and talented children her mother taught. She also felt so overshadowed by both the school-kid stars and her older brother that she may have considered herself unlovable. This feeling of inadequacy consumed her all through her childhood, causing her to search for an escape to a better and more respectable life. She wanted to become someone out of the ordinary, a person other people would talk about and look up to. Yet, even when she had escaped the awful realization that she had failed to win her mother's approval and love, the fact that her brother was still her mother's favorite hounded her. Her lack of self-respect may even have contributed to her later treatment of me, as well as my own view of myself.

It would therefore become ironic that the things that bothered her the most about her own life, the very things that had made her feel mistreated and neglected, would become the dominant part of her own personality and lifestyle. And she even took these imperfections a few steps further than her parents had.

Alcohol, the same drug that had crippled her father and caused her to lose all respect for him, became an elixir which allowed her to hide her insecurities and feel powerful and important. At her parties, the drinks flowed freely. At the social gatherings she attended, a cocktail seemed to always find its way into her hand. When things went right, she drank, and when they went wrong, she drank too. Ultimately, she would embarrass her own children just as her father had embarrassed her, but she would never see, or at least never admit, the hold that alcohol had on her. She always believed that she could handle it. Even when she would fall down the stairs or lose her train of thought during one of her rantings, she never saw that she was out of control. Being in control, as well as maintaining the right image, were very important to her.

Because of the importance she placed on public opinion, she saved almost everything that was good in her for the public side of her life. She was a bundle of love and affection when important people were around. She knew how to give a compliment and how to make an important guest feel even more important with flattery. But all affection stopped there. The only time I ever remember her kissing or hugging me was in front of a casting director or a camera. At home, she was distant, completely unable to show physical warmth to me. It may have been caused by her illness or the fact that I looked so much like my father. With each passing day she hated him more, and because of her drinking, he loathed her too. Or the cause might have been her inability to express love. But even as a very young child, I felt as though she really didn't want me, which made me want and need her attention far more than a normal child from a normal home.

At about this time one of my nursery school teachers told

Mom that I seemed to possess a flair for acting. When Mom heard this, something clicked in her mind. She sat down and observed me for a few minutes. Later she wrote in a family album, "Lauren is beautiful. Her eyes are very deep brown and are most expressive. Her lashes are dark, and her eyebrows are certainly going to have to be plucked at an early age. Her complexion is not too fair, with rosy cheeks and just plain brown hair." I guess my hair was a disappointment to her, but still she must have seen a chance for me to become the little star she had always wanted, the little star who would put her at the very top. I didn't care why, I was just very glad to have her finally notice me.

The words she wrote on that day made me sound more like a commodity than a child. Those words also made her sound more like an agent than a Mom. But she was reacting in the manner she felt was correct. Nevertheless, the spotlight didn't shine on me for long, despite what she and my teacher had noticed; my stardom was to be deferred for a few more years. Right now, Mom was too busy with my brothers' careers, especially Billy's, which was really starting to take off.

By my fourth birthday, even with Sterling's help, Mom decided that I was not getting enough attention at home, and that it would be better *for me* to be placed in a convent. She felt the nuns would have the time to give me everything I needed. Once she found a Catholic boarding school facility, I was enrolled, and she and Billy immediately moved to New York. He won a part in the Broadway play, "Three Wishes for Jamie." Michael, my older brother, now twelve and also an odd man out, was sent to military school. Our schedule had been set up so that Michael came home only on vacations and a few weekends. I was treated with a bit more kindness; I was allowed to come home every other weekend. Of course, the only people left at home to greet us were Sterling and my father.

At the convent, I quickly and deeply missed my family. I felt as though I had been exiled to a land of nightmares. This place seemed dark and cold, and the people seemed to have little human concern. From my first day, the nuns, in an attempt to make me act more mature, would ridicule me in front of the other students. They accomplished nothing in my behavior modification, but they did greatly embarrass me by making fun of the way I sucked my thumb. In an attempt to break this "disgusting" habit, I was often put to bed with dirty socks tied around my hands or with my wrists tied to the bed post. Deep down I just knew that whatever I did, it was always going to be wrong. I was scared and lonely. Once, only a few weeks after I had arrived, I became so frightened in the middle of the night that I ran from my dorm room, down the hall, and jumped into bed with one of the nuns. At first my actions scared her, then, after pulling herself together, she lectured me and returned me to my room. This incident caused me to be watched even more closely. I began to feel more like an inmate than a student.

But it wasn't all bad. In the convent there were children to talk to and play with, and even a few teachers and nuns attempted to instill in each of us a sense of values and love. Still, because they weren't really parents, and mainly because we were ultimately only their charges, even these select few kept their distance from us kids. There was always a wall that kept them from becoming substitute parents. They could teach us lessons, but they couldn't reach out with the kind of sensitivity and care we needed. For most of us, exiled as it was to a place we didn't want to be, individual warmth and love were what we needed most and got the least. After all, most of us came from very troubled homes. Recently, even mine had begun to deteriorate.

Just before Mom had gone to New York, our home had become a battleground. I didn't really know why, but Mom and Dad always seemed to be fighting. They never hugged, *never forgave each other*, and never seemed to look at each other except during a fight. It was a strange, combative, hostile world that we called home, but it was home. The convent was a strange, combative world that wasn't home. So even as bizarre as the atmosphere in my house was, I preferred it over the place I spent most of my time. I would have given anything to escape.

Initially, every other weekend when I was allowed to go home was a joyful reunion, like having Christmas every fourteen days. With Mom gone and no one left for Dad to fight with, he and I could relax and develop a warm and friendly relationship. Now that I was able to spend undivided time with him, a positive, close bond should have developed. I should have felt secure and loved. Unbelievably, the times that my father and I were alone became some of the worst in my young life.

At first things were great. Our home was quiet and free. There were no emotional egg shells to walk on and no people to avoid. I loved being with my father. I wanted to be with him all the time. I followed him around like a puppy. And as I had done when I was much younger, I would often get up in the middle of the night and sneak into his room to sleep with him. His steady breathing, his big body, and the touch of his hand made me feel so wonderful and warm. But somewhere along the line, his hugs became more than hugs, and he began to touch me in places I had never been touched. He also began to arouse strange feelings within me, feelings that I didn't know how to deal with.

Each new episode would lead us to another step. Soon, I was touching his body and he was showing me how to give him sexual satisfaction. I was just four years old, and I was being exposed to this most adult activity, never knowing for sure that I was doing anything wrong.

I had no one to talk to about this, and his was the only hands-on affection anyone was showing me. Because I had no one to turn to and didn't know any better, the game continued. Yet, I think I must have believed that something was not right, and because of this belief, I began to dread coming home more and more. Deep down inside, I think my father dreaded it too, but that didn't keep him from continuing the game. He may have known just how wrong and sick it was, but he just couldn't stop.

As bad as my father's sexual molestation made me feel, my self-esteem sank even lower when an older family friend also began using me sexually. I had always called him "Uncle Mac." I had trusted him a great deal. I have no idea if my father knew what his friend was doing. But I do know that whenever "Uncle Mac" would come to our house, I would hide. Usually, I didn't hide well enough. And after each sexual violation ended, I looked forward more and more to going back to the convent and staying with the nuns.

I was molested for six years, from the ages of four to almost ten. During this time, I became more and more confused. I had a constant feeling of being dirty. I was always going to the bathroom and using soap and water in an attempt to get myself clean. Still, I couldn't wash away the nasty feeling that was twisting my stomach and confusing my mind. I began to hate my dad for this kind of attention, while at the same time I loved him for being the only person who cared enough to give me any attention at all. I was quickly becoming severely warped, and the line between right and wrong was becoming harder and harder to see. Everywhere I went, I felt more lost and alone. I needed help, but no one could give it to me.

Then one day I heard some very important news, news that caused my heart to leap for joy. Mother was coming home!

I couldn't wait. The two years she had spent in New York, coupled with what was going on at home, as well as my experience of the stiff and distant atmosphere at the convent, all played with my mind. With so much time to think and no time with her, I had created a vision that was much different from what she had been. I had convinced myself that she was the perfect mom, the mom who would come and take away all my problems with a hug and a kiss. I was even more inclined to believe this when she actually got home and called the convent informing them that she would be picking me up on Friday evening. She told the nuns to make sure I was ready for her arrival.

When school ended that Friday, I got my things and waited by the front door of the convent. As the minutes passed, the other children's rides came, and one by one each of them left. Within a half an hour, I was all alone, and my heart which had been pumped up all week was sinking as quickly as the sun. Finally a nun came out and told me it was time to come inside. I begged her to let me wait on the steps, but she overruled me, took me to a classroom, and told me to watch for my mother through the windows. Saying she had some other things to do, the sister excused herself, and left me alone in the large, quiet room.

The afternoon slowly drifted by, and with the sound of each passing car, my spirits would rise and fall. I paced back and forth on the old wooden floor. I would stand by the windows for a while, and then I would sit at a desk. I talked to myself, attempting to convince myself that nothing bad had happened and that the next car which came down the street would be Mother.

As it got later, I began to talk to myself more and more.

"Don't worry, Lauren, she hasn't forgotten you; she is coming to get you." Over and over again I repeated the words, but I couldn't accept them.

As the moments passed, I became more frantic, more convinced that I had been left. Fear was now playing with my senses. I began to imagine monsters lurking in the shadows. Terrified, I prayed, "Oh, God, if You really do exist, how come I feel so alone? Oh, Mommy, where are you?"

As the room grew darker, I whispered, "Oh, Mommy, I'm so scared. How come I'm the last one left? Everyone else's mother has come; why haven't you? Oh, God, don't You hear me? I want my mother. Oh, Mommy, please come and get me." And still she didn't come.

I vividly remember the ticking of the schoolroom clock. I couldn't tell time yet, but I knew that the ticking meant that time was passing. As the afternoon wore on I began to hate that clock because it made me realize how little time I had spent with my family and how little time they had spent with me. I knew I couldn't make the clock stop, no more than I could do anything that would force someone to come and get me. All I could do was wait, and at the young age of six, I wasn't good at waiting.

The classroom was eventually cloaked in complete darkness, and the various sounds of the twilight literally began to scare me to death. I heard owls hoot and the wind rushing through tree limbs; all of these noises took on the mystique and strange foreboding of a nightmare. I was convinced that something or someone was going to reach out of the blackness and grab me. I wanted to find a place to hide; yet I remained in the room, constantly looking for my mother's car. I probably should have turned on a light, but the nuns didn't let us do things like that without permission, and at that moment there was no one around to ask. Then, as I sat alone in the dark, a new realization hit me: besides my mom, everyone else had evidently forgotten about me too.

I didn't want them to, but tears began to stream down my face. The quicker I paced, the faster the tears fell. Setting my bag on the floor, I turned from the windows, and crying, collapsed in a chair.

As I sobbed, I prayed that Mom would hurry, but by now I had all but given up hope of her coming at all. The emotions I felt were even worse than the feelings of true orphans. Their parents hadn't wanted to leave them; their parents had just died. Mine were still alive, and they didn't want me. That knowledge made me feel like the guilty party. I relived my short life time and time again trying to figure out what I had done to make them hate me so. After I cried for a while, I once again got up and looked out the windows at the darkened and deserted pavement.

I had been through hours of waiting and crying by the time a car finally rolled down the street and stopped in front of the convent. All of the other children had been picked long before, so I figured that this had to be my ride. Suddenly all of my disbelief disappeared, and my faith was restored. All the misery and the pain I had been feeling were gone. I now knew I was loved, and I couldn't contain the excitement I felt knowing that Mom had finally come for me. I knew that she would hug me, kiss me, and give me some special gift she had brought all the way from New York. No doubt this was the most wonderful moment in my life. No Christmas or birthday could ever compare to the joy I felt during this instant.

But now I had another major concern. What if I didn't look good? My eyes were red and half-closed because of all my tears. How was I going to explain this? I wanted and needed Mother to think that I was pretty. I so needed her to want me that I didn't want to do anything to mess it up. I said a short prayer that she would find me presentable. Then I quickly moved away from the window.

Taking a deep breath in an attempt to calm my rushing heart, I picked up my bag and ran as hard as I could to meet Mother. I ran so hard and fast that I didn't notice the front plate glass door of the convent school was closed. Hitting the glass, I crashed through the door headfirst, cutting several large gashes in my face, and I then tumbled in a heap on the outside steps. At first I didn't even cry—I was too shocked. But in just a few seconds, I became strangely afraid. I hadn't expected the door to be closed, and I didn't yet feel the pain from my injuries. The absolute joy of knowing my mother had come for me blocked out the hurt. Then, looking up, I realized that it wasn't my mother in the car. It was someone I didn't know. It was then that I felt more pain than I had ever known before.

Lying in a circle of broken glass, with blood streaming from my face, I began to scream and sob. I still don't know which hurt worse, my face or my heart. A part of me was hoping I was so badly injured that I would die. I rationalized that if I died, maybe Mother would be sorry. Maybe she would miss me then. Yet, deep down, I doubted that she would even notice I was gone.

One of the nuns heard my screams and came running out of the school. Carefully picking me up, she took me to the infirmary and covered me with a sheet, placing a towel over my face in an attempt to slow the bleeding. As I lay there on the cot crying for my mother, wanting *her* to be holding me, wanting *her* to make the pain go away, I felt like the worst little girl in the world. In my mind that is what I had to be. What other reason would God have for doing all of this to me? As my tears mixed with my blood, I heard the nun pick up the phone, call a number, and wait for a response.

"May I speak to Mrs. Chapin, please?" It must have been at least two or three minutes before my mom got to the phone.

"Mrs. Chapin, this is Sister Mary Francis. I'm calling from the convent. Your daughter, Lauren, has been badly hurt in an accident here at school. It looks as if she needs to go to the hospital for stitches. You must pick her up right away."

There was silence as the nun listened to my mother's reply. Sounding a little exasperated, the nun then spoke again.

"I'm sorry, Mrs. Chapin, I know you're busy, but there is no one here who can take her to the hospital. It really needs to be done by a family member, and I don't think she needs to wait here very long before getting medical attention. She is cut very badly. This is really an emergency. You see, she fell through a glass door. . . ."

The nun stopped talking for a few seconds, and then she spoke again. This time her tone indicated real anger.

"Okay, Mrs. Chapin. I'll stay with Lauren now, but please send someone for her very soon. Thank you." Then she smashed the phone down on the receiver.

Through my tears I quietly asked, "Is my mommy coming to get me?"

"No! But she is going to find someone to pick you up very soon." The nun's reply was harsh, and I felt as though she was blaming me for all that had happened. My heart sank even further than it had at any time during the long afternoon. All my hopes and dreams had now been completely shattered.

Within about thirty minutes—minutes which seemed more like hours to me—Arden Hume, a neighbor's teenage daughter, arrived. Realizing the extent of my injuries, Arden rushed me to a hospital emergency room where doctors placed more than one hundred stitches in various parts of my face. But when Arden called Mom from the hospital and told her just how bad my injuries were, my mother still refused to come. When the doctors finished with me, Arden and I were left alone.

Within a few hours after my treatment, the hospital released me. As Arden drove me to our house, I was crying, frightened, and very insecure. I had blood all over my clothes, my injuries were causing me tremendous pain, and more importantly, I still couldn't believe that Mother had forgotten to pick me up, especially after she had promised that she would get me. I needed her to tell me what had happened and to reassure me that she really cared about me. As we drove up to our house, I noticed that there were cars everywhere. From the inside came the sounds of music and laughter.

Arden led me up to the house and into the front door. From there I waded through people dressed in fancy clothes, drinking, and eating finger foods. All of them seemed to be having too good a time to notice me. I finally found my Mom visiting with some people I had never seen. Hugging her, I began to cry. For a moment Mom looked very startled and concerned, then, pushing me away, she gathered her composure, called Sterling and softly said, "Take her to her room. I'll be there in a few minutes."

For a second I protested, begging for her to come with me. But she shook her head and gently added, "Sterling will take care of you, dear." Then Mom glanced at Sterling as if to say, "Take her out of here, and I'll be there soon."

Not waiting for Sterling, I ran to my room, now needing a hug and loving words worse than ever—yet I knew they would never come. Choking back more tears, I put on my jammies and went to bed. Already at six years old, a part of me disliked my mother. I wanted to be back with the people I had lived with as a toddler. I couldn't even remember their names, but I wanted to feel their arms around me, reassuring me that someone loved me again. Somehow I believed that those people had loved me, but since then I felt that I must have done something that made me unlovable. Maybe I wasn't pretty enough, or maybe it was because I still sucked on my thumb.

All I knew was that it had to be my fault and that I didn't know how to change it or how to make it better.

Then, out of nowhere, I felt someone embrace me and heard a voice whisper in my ear that everything would be all right. It was Sterling. She was once again doing the job my own mother had no time for, being a loving parent. I soon fell asleep in her big, black, soothing arms. Just before I drifted off, I heard Sterling sing an old gospel tune; the words flowed from her mouth like beautiful butterflies floating in the wind. Just listening to them made me feel warm. Some of my worries soon disappeared. At least for a few moments, I knew I was really home.

When I got up the next day, a feeling pervaded the house that I couldn't quite figure out. Perhaps it was my fertile imagination, but the mood seemed to spell hostility or anger. No matter what had created the tension, it didn't keep me from getting the loving attention I needed. My parents were kind to me. Mom even asked me how I felt. Initially she seemed very worried about the cuts, especially if they would scar me or not. But she didn't explain about the party or why she hadn't picked me up.

During the course of the day, things changed dramatically. When Mom would stop and talk to me, she began to make it very clear that she blamed me for what had happened. After all, she reminded me, I was stupid enough to go running through a glass door that I had walked through hundreds of times.

As she scolded me, bringing tears of humiliation to my eyes, I wished that she would put her arms around me and tell me she loved me. I needed a hug much more than a lecture. I wanted so badly to feel her cheek against mine and have her tell me everything was going to be all right—but it never came. By Sunday night, she acted as if nothing had happened.

I was shocked on Monday morning when I was returned to the convent. I had thought that my injuries would have at least won me a short reprieve. I was still in a great deal of pain, and I looked terrible. Despite this, Mother had me taken back.

When I got there, the nuns paraded me from class to class,

standing me on a table and showing every student what happens to bad children who run in the school building. This ridicule pushed me even deeper into an insecure state that would haunt me for years. I felt very much alone and mistreated, and I also felt great guilt. I was sure that this was my fault. Even though I tried to be tough and act like it didn't bother me, at night, when no one could see or hear me, I would cry for hours. I didn't fully understand why I cried, but I did realize that I had been rejected by my mother, and this hurt far worse than the stitches that covered much of my face.

Each night I would grab a tattered old blanket and, while sucking my thumb, would eventually cry myself into an insecure sleep, only to wake alone and with the knowledge that no one really cared enough to hold me, kiss my cuts, and make it all better. I felt very ugly and dirty.

Weeks later, after the cuts had healed and the stitches had been removed, I would still look at the red scars and remember how much I had wanted my mother and family and how they hadn't been able to work me into their social calendar. A hollow kind of pain, the same pain that I had felt that afternoon in the dark classroom at the convent, would come back again. It was during these moments that I first asked myself, "Why was I ever born?"

• Two •

JUST A FEW months after I was hurt, things improved greatly for me, but the accident and my pain had nothing to do with this improvement. With Mom and Billy working in Los Angeles again, there was no logical reason for me to be in the convent, so I was placed in a regular Catholic elementary school. For the first time in over a year, I was finally getting to spend all my nights at my own house.

Michael was home more too. And when Billy wasn't at the studio, the three of us would run and play as we had never done before. If all of this weren't enough, Sterling, the one person who seemed to love me without question, was always there too. More than at any other time in my life, I was truly happy.

Everything seemed to be going my way. I had no real reason to complain at all. Yet, for some reason, I told Mother about Dad's little sexual game. At the time, I still didn't know that what he had been doing to me was wrong. I didn't like it, and I didn't feel that it was right, but it wasn't creating a burning desire in me to talk to Mom about it. And yet, despite the fact that Dad had told me not to tell a soul what we did, I let it slip out.

I don't remember what led me to reveal the news. I know that no one quizzed me. It was probably just one of the times that I was rattling from one subject to another and accidentally hit on Dad's game. I must have just described it the way kids do things they don't understand; I'm just not sure. I don't even remember my mother's reaction. I am sure I must have been questioned, but Mom must not have shown any real emotion because that would have made a profound effect on me. Judging from the way she handled it then, I must have just assumed that the game wasn't any big deal, that she wasn't concerned about it. Later that night, however, long after Billy and I had gone to bed, she *did* react. Looking back on it now, I wonder how she was able to contain her rage for that long.

I had been asleep for quite a while when I was awakened by slamming, shouting, and cussing. I had heard my parents fight before, but I had never heard them go at it like this. The argument seemed to last forever. Between the shouts and the screams were the sounds of things being thrown across the room and crashing against the walls. I was scared. At first I covered my head with my pillow, hoping to muffle the noise. When that didn't work, I listened, attempting to understand what they were saying. When I couldn't make out their words, I jumped out of bed and ran across the room I shared with Billy and sprang into his bed. He was as frightened and confused as I was.

For a while both of us just sat there in the dark, waiting, listening, and hoping that the battle would soon end. We could tell that our folks were in their bedroom, but we couldn't hear them well enough to understand why they were mad. It didn't dawn on me that what I had told Mom about Dad's game might have been a part of it, but I did think of several other reasons. I knew that he must have hated her for the way she was always tearing him down, and I knew that he must have loathed the way she flirted with every good looking man at her various parties. Both Billy and I knew how Dad hated her drinking. So neither of us doubted that there were reasons for the fight; we just didn't know what those reasons were this time.

As Billy and I whispered our theories, another very important element in our parents' relationship was emerging, of which we were both unaware. While she was in New York, Mom had already begun to push Dad out of her life legally. She had begun the groundwork for a divorce. During her stay in the Big Apple, she had even had an affair, and, knowing Mother, she probably told on herself during the fight. So their argument could have started over any of the reasons we knew or a hundred more we didn't. All we knew was that, as we listened and as the moments passed, the battle was getting worse and worse.

Adventurous little boy that he was, Billy decided that we should sneak down the hall and peek into our parents' room. At first, I was against it. Billy may have been Mother's pet, and he rarely felt her wrath, but I knew too well how hard she would come down on both of us if we were caught. Still, always curious Billy had to know what was going on, and he refused to give in to my wishes to just leave it alone. After a few minutes of being called a sissy and suggesting that I was a yellow coward, I gave in and followed him out the door.

With my brother leading, we slowly inched our way along the short hall that led to our parents' room. The closer we got to their room, the louder their shouts became and the harder my heart pounded. I was terrified. A big part of me wanted to turn around and run as fast as I could. Still, a little part of me was too curious to turn back; it cried out to see and know the truth; it drove me on.

By the time Billy and I got to the door, the only voice I could hear was my father's. I had never heard anyone sound so angry. Hugging low to the floor, I sneaked a glance around the corner of the door.

Dad's eyes were practically glowing, sweat was dripping down his brow, and his face was contorted in such a way as to make him look crazy. Then, all at once, a strange, almost whimsical expression crossed his face. That look froze for just a second. Then, when it was gone, it was replaced by the crazed look of an infuriated man. He held his fist high above Mother for just a moment, then swiftly delivered a blow to her face. She fell out of my sight between her bed and the far wall.

There is a certain, undefined shock in seeing your father hit your mother for the first time. It immediately caused a sick, churning feeling to swell up in my stomach. The sight was brutal, one that burned an image into my mind that I will never be able to erase. But even while I felt anguish for my mother and even as a great deal of respect for my father disappeared, I strangely felt that Mom deserved it. After all, there were lots of times I had wanted to hit her too. Yet I just knew I couldn't, and it shocked me when Dad did.

The scene had confused me like nothing ever had before. I felt a need to take sides, but I couldn't. Turning from the doorway, I ran back to my room, closed the door, jumped in bed, and hid under my covers. Too scared to cry, I tried not to move a muscle for the remainder of the night, praying that no one had seen Billy and me at the door. For the next few hours, my heart pounded at such an alarming rate I thought it would burst. I silently sobbed, a torrent of tears flowing down my face just as they had so many times before at the convent. I felt scared, alone, and terribly vulnerable.

When I got up the next morning, my dad was gone, and Mother said nothing. Having a little bit of common sense, I kept quiet too. I was used to Dad being gone during the day, so the fact that he wasn't at breakfast or lunch didn't surprise me. But I was surprised to see him come home early that afternoon. He didn't say much; he just went to his and Mother's room, got his things, and left. At the time I figured he would be back. I didn't know exactly when, but I just assumed that he was not going away forever. As it turned out, however, when he closed our front door, he turned his back on my mother and never lived with us again.

For the next few months, the pain caused by the separation from my father was hard for me to bear. I knew him better than I did Mom, because he had been around while she had been gone. The transition of living without him and then finding out that my parents had gotten a divorce almost broke me. It was equally hard on my brothers. For some reason, we felt as though we carried the shame and guilt, and there was no one to tell us differently.

When I was walking down the street or playing in the yard, I now felt strange—set apart from other kids—because I was from a divorced home. In my own mind, a black mark was now written beside my name, and I wore it like a yoke around my neck. Suddenly I wasn't as good as the other kids. Everywhere I went, to school, to Cathedral Chapel, or to the playground, I thought that people were whispering, "Look, it's that girl, you know the one, she's from the divorced family." In my neighborhood in the 1950s, divorce just wasn't accepted, and the guilty feeling that it created in me would linger throughout my childhood.

In a short time, life had changed again for me. Home was now a different place, one that was not as full as it once had been. Something was missing, but we still had to go on. Michael spent most of his time away at school, and Billy, acting now more than he ever had before, was always studying lines or acting on a movie set. Mom kept very busy too, keeping up with Billy's schedule and maintaining her social obligations. The busier she stayed, the more time I spent away from my family with either Sterling or Aunt Connie (not my real aunt, but a neighbor whom Mom sometimes asked to take care of me).

Connie had kids of her own, and she was a great mother. Her home was filled with toys, food, fun, and real warmth. I loved going there because she would always find ways to entertain kids. She kept a chest of drawers filled with many of her old clothes. She had beaded gowns, hats, shawls, gloves, and old jewelry. It was like being in a costume house, and to little girls, these drawers offered a fantasy world of dress up and parties. I spent hours doing nothing more than trying on clothes, then pretending to be something or someone I wasn't. There was nothing like Aunt Connie's; it was more of a real home, filled with warmth and love, than my own.

Another family, the Lombardies, lived up the street from us. They opened their home to me anytime I visited. They had a daughter, Mary, who was my age and became my best friend. Mary and I were more alike than most sisters. People even said we looked as if we were related. We both had long dark hair and huge black eyes. She and I loved to play dress up and act out our fantasies. We would often spin records and sing in perfect harmony. Our day would usually end with my pretending I was Doris Day and Mary's pretending to be Patti Page. Singing and playing was just the beginning of fun at the Lombardies.

Eating was the real treat. Mrs. Lombardi could do things with pasta that would please even the pickiest eater. And as good as the food was, the fun of sharing it with a real family was even more special. At home I often ate alone, so sitting down at a big table, listening to Jesse Lombardi say grace, and then watching six people dig in and tell stories quite amazed me.

At every meal, Jesse would say to his wife, Juanita, "Would you please pass the peppers?" When he made this request, Mary and I would hold hands under the table and count. We knew that within fifteen seconds after getting and eating the peppers, Jesse's round chubby face and almost bald head would turn bright red while tears would run down his face. It was a painful experience he ritualistically enjoyed.

I didn't realize it then, but this very typical family was giving me a taste of what every child's life should be. They had their problems. One of their children had cerebral palsy, and they had to work hard to make ends meet. But nothing destroyed them or came between their love for one another. They were a family in much more than name only. I still believe that the Lombardies had one of the most wonderful homes in the world. From time to time, I longingly wish that I could visit that house again and attempt to recapture the brief innocence I knew as a youth.

Really, though, Aunt Connie's and the Lombardies' were not the only places on my block that offered me a chance at experiencing the joys of childhood. They were just the places I spent much of my time. Mrs. Webb, a delightful lady who lived next door to us always brought Michael, Billy, and me the most wonderful Easter baskets, filled with goodies of all kinds, topped with a special sugar egg that we could look through and see a picture.

Easter was also a special time for Grandmother Gee Gee. She would hide eggs, give us big baskets, and make sure that every element of the holiday was special in every way. Yet, it was the neighborhood, much more than anything else, that made life special for me and scores of other kids. We would go outside, get to know each other, and enjoy the simple things of life like hopscotch and playing ball. Television did not control children's every moment with its mindless cartoons like it does now, and almost everyone still had someone home during the day to bake cookies and pour a glass of milk. It is a shame that kids don't have this kind of life anymore. They miss a great deal of what is special about youth.

But even living in the "ideal" era of the fifties was not enough for me. I still missed that genuine family experience that many children miss today. Like many of them, I was alone too much. Billy and Mom were always at work, and Michael had become an almost forgotten part of our family. Mom kept him in military school, not because he was a bad boy who needed discipline, but simply because it was a way to have someone else do her job for her. Despite that fact, it turned out well for him. He was brilliant, and the challenging studies he was offered would help him prepare for a life outside of the movie business. But I missed him nonetheless.

More than anyone else in my family, I looked up to Michael, my older brother. He was always loving, patient, kind, and gentle. Whenever he would see me, he would lift me up, both physically and spiritually, always making me feel important and worthwhile. The moments I spent with him were just too few. No matter how many friends I had—and I had many—I was still lonely. What I needed was a family—people who loved me for who I was, not just for what I could do for them.

During my first and second grade years, only one thing really complicated my life and made me unhappy. This was my "Uncle Mac." Even though my Dad was gone and no longer in a position to sexually abuse me, this friend of our family was still a regular visitor at our home, and he continued to play his games. He and his wife and Mother were very close. I knew she would never believe me if I told her what was going on, and besides, I was afraid. So I just attempted to hide whenever they came over. Most of the time, unless Mom made me say hello and be nice to "Uncle Mac," I was able to avoid him.

Despite being the victim of occasional sexual abuse and being separated from my family a great deal, I was becoming fairly normal and pretty well adjusted. It looked like I might beat the odds and turn into a regular girl, having giggly friends and being nothing more spectacular than a Girl Scout. With Sterling, Aunt Connie, the Lombardies, and other positive forces influencing me, I might have turned out to be a model child, maybe even one who was God-fearing.

The nuns at my school had attempted to teach me about Jesus. For some reason, Mom felt that this was important. She even went to confession and prayed, in spite of her regular abuses of Jesus' name and, without as much as a moment of guilt, her daily violations of several commandments. Still, she tried to tell me what was wrong and what was right, but her actions spoke louder than her words. I came from a house that lived with the philosophy of "Do as I say, not as I do," which confused my understanding of how God worked and how Jesus loved. I was fearful of God, knowing that he hated sinners, or at least that is what I had learned in school, and I knew in my heart that I was a sinner. I also knew that this thing called lust was bad, and I knew that what had happened between my father and me, as well as between my Uncle Mac and me, was tied to that somehow. I thought that I must have been very bad. Somehow, in my slanted view of things, I convinced myself that Jesus could never love me because of how evil I had been in my life. Ironically, during this same period that I viewed myself as a demon, Mom was dreaming of my becoming a nun.

Whatever her plans, things changed forever when Hazel McMillian came by our house one day. While Hazel didn't represent my brothers, she was one of Hollywood's most important child agents. It was only natural that she and Mom knew each other and would visit from time to time. On one of these visits, Hazel noticed me and asked Mother why I wasn't in show business. One thing led to another, and before all the talk had ended, I had an agent, and I was a step closer to being an actress.

No one really ever asked me if acting was something I wanted to do. No one explained the time and sacrifices that were involved. It was simply decided for me. But if the truth were known, and if I had been asked, I would have answered with an enthusiastic "Yes!" I wanted to see my face in the movies! I wanted to act! I wanted to be someone just like my brothers! But more than any of these things, I wanted to become someone of whom my mother would be proud. I knew this would do it.

From the first moment that Mom introduced Hazel to me, I loved her. She was a wonderful, gray-haired lady in her fifties, who walked with a quick step and gave affection and praise easily. I knew that I wasn't going to be just her charge or product; I could feel that she truly cared about me. Just knowing this gave me a great deal of self-confidence. From Day One, we were off on the right foot.

Hazel began my career by taking me to her house, training my voice and diction, giving me acting lessons, and prompting me to respond to words, actions, and expressions in a natural but planned way. It really didn't seem to matter to her if I picked up on things quickly or did well; she would always reward my work with a smile or a kind touch. Then, after we finished our lessons, rather then immediately taking me home, she would bring out cookies and milk, and, while I ate, she would sit down at her piano and play the most beautiful music

I had ever heard. She loved to sing, and I loved being her audience. After I finished eating, I would always join her, learning not only about music but also how to share special moments and interests. She even convinced me that I was a good singer!

I had sung all my life. On Christmas and Easter, I would always sing some kind of special song at Gee Gee's family party. One of the family favorites was "How Much Is That Doggie in the Window?" and with Hazel's help, I learned it so well that I impressed my family. But much more than being a way to impress people, Hazel's gift of music turned into a great friend. Music would later become a healing balm to my soul, and it would even help lead me away from a life of no promise and into the life I needed all along. For now, however, music was just a pleasant part of my training.

After only a few acting lessons, Hazel thought that I was ready for the big time. She quickly arranged to have publicity photos taken and my biography written. The Hollywood publicity mill is a unique machine. It manufactures images, and the truth rarely gets in the way of presenting a picture the American public will purchase. My two-page biography described an idyllic home-life that Ricky and David Nelson would have envied. According to the official story, I was surrounded by dolls, my brothers, pets, and friends in my normal, middle-class home. The more sordid details were left out because they would have frightened the producers away.

With my acting lessons and my bio, I jumped into the world of show business, and as luck would have it, I entered at just the right moment. If I had begun a few years earlier, jobs would have been very hard to find. In the late forties and early fifties, independent studios were dying, and family movies, those using lots of children and teaching great moral truths while presenting ideal situations, had given way to the cold, hard edge of reality films. The end of the studio actor was nearing as more and more major stars were free-lancing. This meant there were fewer films using big budgets. A large number of child actors, those who had enlivened the cast of numerous Andy Hardy–type films, were suddenly out of work.

But by 1953, television had really begun to take off. Black and white images were flickering in almost every living room in America, and the studios were beginning to look at this new medium as less of a rival to their film products and as more of a way to make money in a new area. One of the things that television audiences seemed to crave were family shows containing the same formulas that had worked a generation before in movies. After almost being phased out just a few years earlier, child actors were now needed in larger numbers than ever before. I began looking for work the summer of 1954, so my timing couldn't have been better.

During the early fifties, radio drama had pretty much run its course, but many of its highest rated shows had jumped over to the visual medium, and their popularity had grown with this transition. "The Adventures of Ozzie and Harriet" and "The Life of Riley" are two of the best-remembered examples, but there were a host of others.

So, in 1954, Columbia went to the radio well and pulled up "Father Knows Best." The call for actors went out. Auditions were set. When Hazel found out that Columbia needed a seven- or eight-year-old girl for the show, she quickly called the producer's office and set up an interview. In her own mind she had already decided that I was perfect for the part of Kathy, the youngest of the children.

One early summer morning, after seemingly weeks of preparation, Hazel picked me up to take me to an interview at the offices of Eugene B. Rodney. As producer of "Father Knows Best," Mr. Rodney had taken complete responsibility for the final product and wanted his fingerprint on every facet of the show's formula. He was committed to making this the best, most realistic, and most honest family show on television. He wanted to do more than entertain; he wanted to touch hearts. To accomplish this, he knew he had to uncover the American ideal in each of the show's actors. So he was personally auditioning each of the over two hundred girls trying out for the part of Kathy, as well as those attempting to land the roles of the other two children. He wanted to find the right mix not only for the show's formula but also to supplement the two leads he had already cast.

Mr. Rodney was sure that Robert Young, the actor who had essayed the role on radio, would be perfect as the title character; therefore, he grabbed him first. When he signed the wonderful actress Jane Wyatt as Margaret Anderson, he was convinced that he struck pay dirt again. Yet not one child actor had sprung into his mind as perfect for playing any of the three Anderson children. He had been forced to search, preferably for actors who were completely unknown to play the roles, thereby assuring himself that the viewers would think of these actors as the characters and not the other way around. This led to my big break.

When Hazel and I arrived at Mr. Rodney's office, she signed me in and then attempted to focus my mind on the reasons we had come. The two of us went over to an alcove and began to go over all the lines of the script that the secretary had just given us. I had the ability to memorize anything very quickly, and this script was no exception. In very little time I had not only learned my part but everyone else's as well. Knowing everything there was to know about the script and with weeks of acting lessons behind me, all I had to do was sit and wait for my turn.

One by one the other little girls who were trying out for the part entered the door to Mr. Rodney's office. After just a few minutes, they each marched out. Slowly, I moved up on the list, and finally, I heard my name.

"Lauren," Hazel told me, "you will do great if you just be your own natural, little, loving self. Don't be frightened. I have every confidence that you will be perfect."

I walked away from Hazel feeling more confident than I had felt about anything in my life. Just knowing that someone had faith in me and my abilities, and just knowing someone was proud of me and wouldn't hate me and give up on me if I didn't do well enough to get the part, made me feel wonderful. Grabbing the doorknob in my right hand, I proudly strolled into the inner office, only to stop quickly when I saw this huge man standing in the middle of that big office smoking on a giant cigar. I promptly lost all my self-confidence and became scared to death.

The producer greeted me, "Hello, Lauren." When I didn't immediately respond, he rechecked a piece of paper on his desk and asked, "Lauren is your name, isn't it?"

I nodded my head. I couldn't talk, and I wanted to run.

"Well, Lauren, I'm Mr. Rodney." Then pausing for a moment to make sure that I was listening, he continued. "I guess you are here to read for me."

The office was filled with cigar smoke, and that coupled with the butterflies in my stomach, made me feel sick. Somehow, what I was feeling and the way things were going was not how I had pictured things were supposed to be. Everything about the atmosphere was wrong. This room had a desk, some file cabinets, a couple of uncomfortable office chairs, and two phones. It looked nothing like the living room of a family home, and the script we had been given was supposed to take place in that setting. My confused mind continued to worry about details until Mr. Rodney's deep voice jerked me back to reality, but what he said did nothing to make the setting or the situation feel any more comfortable.

"Lauren, you will be playing the part of Kathy in this little reading, and I will take the part of your daddy, as well as the parts of the other characters." Taking another puff on the cigar, Mr. Rodney continued, "Now why don't you stand over there against that far wall, and we'll start."

I nodded my head and walked over to the wall. As I turned around, he sat down in the chair behind the desk and began reading. When he came to my part, I just looked at him. "Is there something wrong, Lauren?" he asked. By now it must have been painfully obvious that there was; I had barely made a sound since coming into the office.

I quickly and very quietly answered, "I can't do it this way. Everything's wrong."

"What do you mean?" the now puzzled producer asked.

"Well, for starters," I began, "I shouldn't be way over here. If you're playing my daddy in this scene, I should be in your lap."

"Okay, we can do it that way if you want," the producer answered.

Now beginning to feel confident again, I walked across the room, stepped behind the desk, and got into Mr. Rodney's big lap, all the while continuing to talk. "Also, this," pointing to the cigar, "has got to go. I don't think that my daddy would smoke nasty-smelling things like this."

The producer pushed his cigar into the ash tray, then froze, seeming to wait for me to give him the next bit of direction. He guessed right; I wasn't done!

"Now, I think you will get to know me better if I do all the parts except my father's. You can do that." With that I began to recite from memory with perfect inflections, all of the script I had been given. Mr. Rodney would chime in when the part of Jim Anderson required him to speak. (On two occasions, I prompted him when he didn't speak soon enough.) But mainly he just watched and listened. As I finished my last line, an amazed look was etched on his face. I knew I had impressed him. We talked for a short while, and then as I climbed down out of his lap, he impulsively hugged me and told me that I had been very good. Smiling, I walked out of the door.

Hazel was there to greet me. "How did you do?" she asked. I shook my head, telling her that I really had no idea. Deep down, I knew that I had done well, but I didn't believe that I was as cute or talented as most of the other girls I had seen, so I didn't expect to get the part.

A few days later an excited Hazel called and informed me that I had made the top ten. I would get to do a screen test. I could tell that Mom was pleased, but I took her pleasure in stride. Though I didn't let it show, I believed that I would now begin to get my mother's attention. She would no longer dote over Billy alone. In my heart I knew that my time had come.

When the day came for the screen test, Mom was with Billy, so once more it was just Hazel and me. In all honesty, I was glad Mom couldn't come. If she had been there watching me, I know that I would have been very nervous and afraid that I would have embarrassed myself and her if I had messed up. Nevertheless, a part of me was disappointed. I wanted her to see how good I was, even though I felt that she already knew.

The actual test was far different from my initial reading. It took place in a real studio, filled with real technicians, directors, studio employees, and other actors. Each of us trying out for the part had been given a script ahead of time, and we had all learned it. I knew that on this day I would have to hit all my marks, look into the right camera and deliver the lines at the right time with the perfect inflection. There would be no second chances.

Most of the other girls trying to win the role of Kathy had an advantage over me: they had been in this situation before. They had worked with technicians and lighting people; they were comfortable with these surroundings. They knew how to take directions, and they knew the unwritten studio rules. For me, it was a new world.

At first, rather than thinking about my lines or where Hazel had told me to stand, I simply looked at all the lights, cameras, and props. My eyes wandered up to the top of the high ceilings, and then down to the miles of cable stretched across the floor. The little stage, the part actually used as the set, seemed small and insignificant compared to all the equipment. Overwhelmed by everything around me, I felt as little and insignificant as the set appeared.

I have no memories of the actual test. I don't remember the faces of the actors, and I don't remember the scene's starting or ending. I have lost that moment of my life completely. From the second they called my name until Hazel and I walked out the door to her car, my mind now draws a complete blank. Nevertheless, Hazel told me I was great, and she convinced me I would probably get the part. I told Mom the same thing when I got home. She heard me and seemed to be happy, even excited, but she was a bit under the weather, caused in large part to a blend of scotch and milk. So I didn't make too much of her reaction. Changing clothes, I avoided her for the rest of the day by playing at the Lombardies'. The experience had been nice and the studio fascinating, but I was positive that one of the other girls would get the part. This feeling didn't disappoint me or make me sad. I was ready to return to normal living.

Meanwhile, back at Columbia/Screen Gems, the cumulative film shot of the thirty actors (ten auditions for each role) trying out for the parts of Betty, Bud, and Kathy had been developed, spliced together, and delivered to Robert Young's home. On the weekend after the shooting, he sat down with his wife and daughters to view the tests. The final decision as to who would play each part was theirs.

A then seventeen-year-old Elinor Donahue was picked to play the role of Betty. Her test had been technically impressive, and she looked and acted a great deal like the Young's oldest daughter Betty.

A seasoned child actor, Billy Gray, then fourteen, pinned down the role of James Anderson, Jr. The Youngs probably had a great deal of fun picking out the boy to play this character. With no sons at their home, they had to imagine just what Bud would look and be like. Billy convinced them that he would fit into the Young household as a solid bridge between the oldest and youngest child.

As the family began to view the last ten pieces of film, Kathy Young was probably the most excited. Her part was being cast. After viewing the first of the ten tests, she and the rest of the family were convinced that they had found the child to play the part of the youngest Anderson. They wrote down the actress's name and relaxed as the other nine tests played out. If the tests had stopped at nine, that first girl would have won the role hands down, but mine ran last, and, because of it, things began to change.

My screen test complicated choosing the role. It made room for argument. Unlike the first two parts, two people had jumped off the movie screen and given the Youngs two portrayals of Kathy that they really liked. The debate didn't go on very long. Robert Young took charge, deciding that I looked too much like his own Kathy not to get the part. So it was my appearance much more than my ability that won me the role. Yet, why I got that starring role on television didn't bother me at all. I was just thrilled that it was mine.

To most of America, television was a brand-new toy. It was a novel thing, one that the people weren't quite sure what to do with or how to best use. In the public's mind, the tube's purpose was to entertain, but it wasn't to be taken too seriously. After all, it wasn't the movies, and the movies were still the real thing. Until now, Mom had viewed television in pretty much this way too. She had not considered anything but the movie business for her children because the individual jobs within that industry had paid so well. But when she realized that I was going to be issued a check every week, that this was going to be a steady income for as long as the show stayed on the air, and that forty million people were going to know my name, a light bulb went off in her head. She quickly understood the potential of television, and she knew that, by using it in much the same way she had used the movies, she could use her children and take advantage of what they could get her. This made her very proud of me.

Still, even though I was now working and doing something which pleased her, an undercurrent of bitterness flowed between us. I don't know what caused it, but it was there, and neither one of us could quite shake it. No matter what words Mother said to me, her actions spoke to me in a different manner. I never felt as if I was good enough. I continued to strive for her attention and love, but I always felt as if I fell short. Often, especially later in my life, I would try to capture this attention in some very negative ways. But for now, I just wanted to *feel* her love. For some reason, however, she simply couldn't allow herself to give me that warmth.

With my working, the routine changed at home. Unlike Billy whose work was irregular, often part-time, at other times every day for three months, I was to be at the studio at a certain time each day. When my brother was working, Mom had to find someone to transport me to my job. After several days of hardships and confusion, she finally hired Aunt Connie and her husband, Uncle Bob.

Aunt Connie was the best person in the world to begin the morning with. She was sweet, loving, tender, and a real hugger. She would spend my time off telling me stories, laughing, sharing my heartaches, and helping me with my work. She was filling a role that my own mother never filled, at least not in these ways.

Still, Mom did spend many hours with me working on my lines, helping me with voice inflection and stage movement, and just helping me to become Kathy Anderson. During these times, she was almost always sober and in a good mood. When she was like this, she had the ability to lift me into a greater awareness. She was an exhorter who could convince me that I could do anything. Sober, she was the greatest motivator in the world, but when she was drinking, this quality disappeared.

The worst part of her personality came out on weekends when Billy and I spent time with Gee Gee and my father. When we got home, Mother was generally drunk and in a foul mood. She would put us on the witness stand, demanding to know everything that everyone had said. Ultimately, it became an us-against-them war, and, for some reason, I was on the side of "them."

Mother began to call me "Daddy's little girl," pitting Billy against me. Perhaps my confessions about Dad molesting me led her to blame me for the lack of harmony in her life. The venom that spewed from her mouth created a mood that assured me that I was the guilty party. It convinced Billy too, and he would treat me as if I were a spy from the other side.

Mother demanded by her actions that I align my loyalty with either her or my father. I couldn't have both; she would not allow it. This split jerked me back and forth in such a way that I never knew whom to trust or what to say. The split was tearing me apart, and as her drinking became worse, so did her accusations. I also didn't understand why I caught it and Billy didn't. This created a rivalry that all but crushed any chance that Billy and I would have for a normal relationship. And at just about the time I had gotten over the stigma of being from a divorced family, Mother's actions brought it back into focus. For me, our home was fast becoming a miserable place, and the root of this misery was alcohol.

At the studio, however, things were vastly different. Everyone who worked with me encouraged me, helped me, had a great deal of understanding for me, and let me be a real kid. I had to memorize lines, and of course the rehearsals and filmings were work, but I really felt as if the people there cared about me more than the money they could make by selling my talent.

One perfect example of this was Bill Russell. He directed "Father Knows Best" during our initial season. He looked like a football player. He was big, over six-and-a-half feet tall. He had a barrel chest, huge hands, and a lumbering step. With his jet black hair, thick mustache, and huge nose, he could have been a very foreboding figure, but, if anything, he was a teddy bear. When he was in charge, the atmosphere of the stage was relaxed and homey. Even the very first shows we filmed had that kind of feel too. At that time, I was too young to realize his full contribution to the success of the show. I just knew I liked him.

Our weekly schedule covered five days. The first two were spent rehearsing and learning marks, cues, and lines. The last three days of the week were all spent filming. I had an extra day added to my schedule. On Saturday, I worked with Bill on a one-on-one basis. He honed my natural skills, helped me memorize my character's dialogue, and worked with me in defining how to play Kathy Anderson. He saw within me great potential and gave a great deal of his own time in order to help this potential be realized. Bill Russell was somewhat of a fatherly influence to me, as was Robert Young.

Something about Mr. Young drew me to him. He was so much of what I had wanted my real dad to be. Patient, loving, always ready with a hug, a smile, and an encouraging word, he was just like his character, Jim Anderson. Every day I could depend on his being a part of my life, and he would somehow make me feel special every time we spoke. He made everyone feel this way too.

Within two weeks of beginning work, I began to think of the people at Columbia as a real family. I suppose that deep down inside I knew that they were just a crew working together, but they seemed to be more than that to me. Jane Wyatt listened to me when I told her about something I had done at school. Billy Gray did more than pick on me; he watched out for me on the lot. Elinor, God bless her, looked upon me as the little, preadolescent pest that I was supposed to be. In other words, she treated me like a real sister. And Robert Young was always there, our constant and dependable rock.

Each day when work was over, the obvious difference in my home and my "home" on Stage 11 was becoming more clearly defined. My home, unlike the Anderson house, had no daddy coming in, saying, "Megs, I'm home." It was just Mom, Billy, and me. And each day, I was a bit more lonely. My "home" at Columbia/Screen Gems may have just been a set, but it had the feeling of family. My real home was often cold and impersonal.

On Sunday, October 3, 1954, I sat down with Billy and Mom to watch the premier episode of "Father Knows Best." For a moment I felt real pride, but only for a moment. When this passed, I suddenly became giggly and embarrassed.

"Is that really me?" I wondered, knowing it was while also feeling that it had to be someone else. "Oh no, look what I've done," I remember thinking as I appeared in another scene. In my mind, I said every actor's lines and walked every character's steps, but when it came to my own part, I would just watch. I was analyzing what I should have done to make it better, to make it sound more real. I wondered if I shouldn't have moved differently or given a different look. I really thought I looked silly.

Questions and observations rolled through my mind. "Is that how I really look? Is my smile that strange? Is that my real voice? I need to talk more clearly." Yet, all the while, my chest was swelled with pride, knowing that my mother and brother were watching and proud of me.

I didn't know then just how long "Father Knows Best" would last. I also didn't realize the deep root of bitterness that it would create would further tear me away from my family. I didn't know that, within weeks, Billy, whose credits spanned dozens of films, would feel slighted because I was the one who was recognized everywhere we went. He would later say, "I was the highest paid and hardest working, but you were the best known and that hurt me."

Ironically, I didn't want to be well known or a star. All I wanted was my mother's love and recognition and the warmth of a real family. Little did I know that my new show would take this dream even further from me. My pain, as well as my mother's, was just beginning.

• Three •

I DOUBT VERY seriously that Mom knew she was slowly trying to make me over in the image of Kathy Anderson, but from the time the show initially aired, she was doing just that. In her own eyes, she was probably just trying to make me better or maybe make me over in an image that just seemed better. Yet, even if killing my normal personality was not her goal, she was essentially doing just that.

Image, both her own and her children's, meant a great deal to her. She needed to show the world that she had, even under the strain of a divorce, produced a model family. Therefore, she began to expect of me what no director, producer, or fan could have ever expected: I was supposed to be in character twenty-four hours a day, seven days a week. No longer was I supposed to react like Lauren; I had to be Kathy—she was that perfect, little girl model. Before I ever left to go outside and play with my friends, I had to dress in very nice clothes, fix my hair, make sure my face was freshly scrubbed, and then I had to be on my best behavior. I wasn't allowed to be angry or cry or show any type of emotion that could or would be construed as a deviation from my character. I had to be a perfect little lady. For some little girls I knew, this wouldn't have been a problem, but for me it was. This Lauren was one hundred and eighty degrees opposite from the Lauren of real life.

I was a tomboy. I wanted to play rough with the boys, climb trees, chase balls, hug the dog, and go sliding through piles of leaves. Until I had gotten the part in the series, Mom hadn't cared if I did these things or not. But now I heard from her, "It doesn't look right. It is not befitting a star." In my own mind, expecting me to be any different was asking too much.

This image became a bone of contention between us. I hated so much being molded that I used it as an excuse to rebel. As soon as I left the house and was out of her sight, off would come my shoes, down would come my hair, and off I would go to the rough-and-tumble world I loved. A few hours later, when I would finally head home, I would stop, redo myself, and step back into character. Occasionally she caught me, but more often than not, I fooled her. It became a game, a game that signaled another way that we were growing further and further apart.

I can't fault her for the make-over. It was her way of trying to play the roll of a perfect mother. She couldn't reach out and hug me, and she never told me she loved me, but she did her best to provide what she believed would make me happy. I wore fantastic clothes, always made by the right manufacturer and purchased at the proper stores, received singing lessons, mime lessons from no less a teacher than Marcel Marceau, and also benefitted from dancing lessons from Marge and Gower Champion. She made sure that Billy and I always had nice toys, good books, and a purebred dog for a playmate. We also always lived in a great house. In her own mind, this was doing her best for us. She didn't see the need for any more. The fact that she didn't know how to express the warm, one-on-one loving attention and direct caring we needed, probably wasn't her fault. And if the only thing working against our relationship was the fact that she demanded I be Kathy Anderson, I'm sure that we could have worked out an understanding and survived.

Unfortunately, this would become one of the mildest of our disagreements.

The first new home we owned after I began working on "Father Knows Best" was a two-story, red barn home on Lucerne. Located in one of the best neighborhoods in Los Angeles, this house had a huge yard, a pond, big trees, four bedrooms, and enough room to entertain everyone at Columbia Studios. It was a house in which every kid would dream of growing up, one like the perfect television family would have called home. "The Barn," as I named it, was a wonderful place.

When we first moved in, I was devastated. Our house on Ridgely was the only real home I had ever known. My friends there were so special that I just knew I would never be happy again. No matter how great our new home was, I was afraid that my new neighborhood would be empty and lonely. It didn't take me too long to discover that my fears had been completely wrong.

A host of opportunities opened up to me on Lucerne. The area seemed filled with smiling and outgoing families. Happiness and warmth just flowed down the streets, and it didn't take me long to find that out. There were children my age in almost every yard, and as I explored my new territory, I began to see the wealth of possibilities it had. Still, I didn't get to take advantage of these for six months, or until "Father Knows Best" wrapped up its first year of filming, and we went on summer hiatus.

My time off began in May, and because school was still going on, I had to enroll in a public school for the very first time. I spent the last month of the year making friends and trying to be a regular kid. The latter part wasn't easy. Mom still insisted that I look and behave like Kathy, and many of the kids called me by my television name. A lot of the faculty even seemed star struck. I know that Billy, who was in fifth grade, a grade ahead of me but in the same school, noticed this treatment and was more than a little jealous. He had a right to be. He had worked longer and harder than I, and yet the kids didn't treat him as somebody special.

With no work and few responsibilities, I was a happy child. After school I would cruise into the Barn, run in the kitchen door, take a deep breath to smell the aroma of Cookie's (our new cook's) meal, drop my books on the table, charge through the dining room and into the living room. There I would run up to Mother and begin to tell her all about my day. She would then simply hold up a hand, indicating for me to wait until she had finished her phone call. More often than not, I grew tired of waiting and would run upstairs, change clothes, and go over to play with one of my new friends.

Mom had always loved the telephone, but since we had moved, it had become an extension of her ear. She almost lived on it. She and her friends, Marge, Pat, and Lois, would talk for hours. Mom almost always drank when she was on the phone, and this slowly began to have an effect on her moods. She began to have less and less patience with me, and, more importantly, she didn't seem to have any time for me. She had already given me a reason to rebel when she forced me to always play my part. Now, the phone gave me something of which to be jealous. The phone, combined with her drinking, was cutting deeply into direct times of personal contact between us.

To escape my loneliness, I would roam the neighborhood and visit with other families. The times I spent in these homes lifted my spirits while I was there. But when I would leave, usually to find Mom "under the weather" from her mix of scotch and milk, I would ask myself again and again, "What have I done to deserve this?"

Now approaching my ninth birthday, I was acutely aware that other families had fathers who lived at home. I was also aware that most of these families did a lot together. Mostly, I was aware that something was missing from our house, and that something was the affectionate kind of love that anchors a child's feet and heart on secure ground. It was ironic, but in our beautiful home filled with gorgeous furniture, I was incredibly insecure.

To try to make up for the time that I didn't get to spend with my mother during the day, I would sneak into her room at night and crawl into bed with her. There, as she lay sleeping, I would snuggle beside her, trying to let her know how much I needed her, and praying that she would reach out and hold me. But Mother wasn't into touching. Yet, all I had to do to find the displayed affection I needed was to look down at the foot of her bed. There, always in a protective posture, slept our Irish setter, Shawnee.

Shawnee was special, and in some ways she meant more to me than anyone in our home. She freely gave her love and didn't care what I looked like. She only wanted me to notice her. She was my confidante, playmate, and best friend. She was that to everyone else too.

Mother and Dad had purchased her for Michael, and I know that the two of them had once spent hours roaming the neighborhood. It may have been those treks with him that created in her a desire to explore because every time a gate was left open, off she would go.

About four months after we moved, she disappeared, and, with that disappearance, I lost the one member of my family on whom I depended for unqualified support and love. When I discovered she was gone, I was crushed. The real wonder and power of Shawnee's devotion was revealed when Mother and Billy were as devastated as I was. The loss of this magnificent animal had strangely united us.

Mother took out ads in the major L.A. papers, and each time the phone would ring, all of us would jump to answer it, hoping that it was the person who had found our pet. For two weeks our prayers were met with disappointment. Soon, even though we hoped against hope that we were wrong, each of us had to admit that the chances of ever seeing Shawnee again were slim. We finally all but quit scrambling for every phone call. One night Billy answered the phone, expecting the call to be from an agent or one of Mom's friends.

"Hello?" He then paused for a moment, before excitedly answering, "Yes, we have a dog. Her name is Shawnee. Who is this? Where are you? Hold on a second."

By now I was caught up in the excitement of a renewed dream. Maybe Shawnee could have been found, and maybe this caller really did have her. The look in my brother's eyes indicated he believed it. I began to pray, asking God to make it true.

"Mom!" Billy yelled, "Mom, you've got to come here. They've found Shawnee."

I don't ever remember seeing Mother run as fast. Grabbing the phone from Billy, she took a deep breath and then calmly stated, "Hello. I'm Mrs. Chapin, may I help you? Are you sure? What does the tag say? Uh-huh. Is she all right? Oh, poor baby. Do you want us to come get her, or will you bring her up here? Thank you so much. Let me give you directions."

I could tell from the directions that Shawnee had wandered a long way. The man was actually calling from Ventura. How our dog had gotten that far without being hit in traffic none of us would ever figure out, but when we first saw her, we could tell that the journey had been hard on her. She was thin, and her foot pads were bleeding. But one look into her big brown eyes told me that she was as happy as we were when she walked in the door. Mother was so overcome that she gave the man who found her a hundred and fifty dollars. For the next few days, all of us treated that dog as if she were a queen.

It was strange how Shawnee had brought us together. Her disappearance caused Mother to put her drinking and phone calls onto a back burner and allowed Billy to forget about his jealousy, and she had allowed me to unite with the two of them in a common goal. In a big way, if only for the time she was gone, we united into the kind of unit I had observed in other homes around the neighborhood. We were a family—but only for awhile. Soon after her return, we once again drifted apart.

A year later, however, the close feelings would return, and, once again, Shawnee would be the reason. Mother, Billy, and I had been keeping the peace the best we could, but we were still strangers sharing a home. Consequently, emotional explosions sometimes occurred. We tried to avoid these by living in our own worlds and refusing to communicate to one another. This lack of interaction had driven me back into the habit of sneaking into my mother's bed and sleeping with her. One morning, I was awakened by Shawnee's twitching at the foot of the bed.

I thought she was having a bad dream. I had often seen her chase things in her sleep. This time, she didn't just snap out of it, rearrange herself, and fall back into a quiet slumber. Sliding down to her, I petted her big head and whispered, "Don't worry, girl, it is just a dream." Rather than stop, she got worse.

Shocked, I jumped up and screamed, "Mother, wake up! Something is wrong with Shawnee!"

Quickly rubbing the sleep from her eyes, Mother helped me hold the now frightened dog on the bed. Her twitching had turned into convulsions, and both of us were scared and crying. Hearing us, Billy charged in from his room, and after seeing Shawnee, demanded to know what was going on. Neither of us knew what to tell him.

After a few minutes, Shawnee regained her senses. We helped her off the bed, and then in horror watched as her legs gave way as she fell to the floor. Billy and I petted her and cried while Mom called the vet. Before she had even completed the call, Shawnee had another attack.

We took turns sitting with her as we got ready to go; then we drove to the vet's. There, Mom joined the doctor in another room, while Billy and I waited in the lobby. Just as it had been a year before, our rivalry was put aside as we focused on the same painful fear. For a few moments, we knew that our love was all that mattered. Who was the more talented, cuter, or bigger star was not important. Our all-consuming passion was our concern over our dog's health. We both prayed for her survival.

When Mom came out, I could tell that the news wasn't good. She still had tears flowing down her face, and her eyes were swollen and red. She leaned over us and whispered the news.

"Shawnee's had two very bad heart attacks, and the doctor thinks that we should put her to sleep. But I can't do that. So, we are going to take her home, and we are going to take very good care of her." After those words, the three of us cried.

Moments such as this gave me insight into how Mother could have been different. She was definitely capable of feeling great emotion and love. If only she could have built on moments like this and used them to reach out to our concerns and needs. But as it was, she couldn't. Her own rough childhood, coupled with her dependency on alcohol, had taken her away from us. Thanks to my dog, however, I saw that she had the potential to care deeply.

For the next three days, I prayed a great deal. Shawnee had been moved into our guest room in order to keep her from having to climb any steps. In that quiet room, first Billy, then I, and then Mom took turns keeping watch. During my watch, I prayed that God would heal Shawnee, and I assured her that everything was going to be all right. She was just too young to die, and I was not going to let death take her away from me. I was bound and determined that she would be all right. She just needed a little time.

A little time is all we got. Billy was with her when she had her third attack which was even worse than the others. Mom called the vet, and he drove to our home. He gave us the news we knew was coming. As he talked, I looked at our big red setter friend as tears began to flow down my face.

Shawnee had once kept a neighborhood boy from hitting me with a baseball bat. She had pulled that bully across the yard in an effort to save me. She had been there with a soft look and a warm tongue whenever I needed a friend. I just didn't know what I was going to do without her.

"I'm sorry," the doctor lamented. "Your dog is in great pain. She has to be put to sleep. She has struggled as long and as hard as she can. If you really love her, let me take her and put her out of her misery."

I looked at her big brown eyes once more before she left, and I could still see them an hour later when the phone rang, and the caller informed us that she was dead. An emptiness overcame me, and, as I looked around the room, I knew that Billy and Mother shared the same feeling. For the next few days, each of us cried and bore our loss in our own way. But weeks later, when the two of them had gotten back into the swing of life, I still couldn't shake the gloom that seemed to hang in our house and linger in my heart. The effect of losing my pet was so great that I would call on it for years to come, whenever I needed to cry during one of our shows. We had lost the last member of my family that had had the power to unite us.

Shawnee's death seemed to affect my mother too. She was more and more drawn into periods of deep gloom, which caused her to drink and lash out more. For some reason, I was the one who almost always drew her anger and sharp words. In her eyes, Billy was perfect—he was an angel. I still don't know why it was this way. But as much as she was ruining me and my life by striking out and always reminding me how bad I was, she was destroying my brother by always telling him how good he was. Thus, Billy became not only spoiled but mean. He now knew that he ruled the roost; he knew that in Mom's eyes he could do no wrong, and he lorded this over me. He took every opportunity to abuse his power.

For instance, he knew that I was scared of the dark, so if he got the chance, he would lock me in a dark place. Once he left me locked in a hall closet for what seemed like hours. I screamed, kicked, and cried, and he and Mother just ignored me. I was terrified, completely unglued, and he still didn't answer my pleas to let me out. Finally, after he had played in another part of the house for awhile and when he had grown bored with the pleasure of listening to me cry, he released me. But both of us knew that there would be another time.

One of the things that scared me most about Billy was how violent he could be. He would haul off and hit me for no reason at all. When I would come crying to Mom, she would tell me that it hadn't hurt that much, and I needed to get tougher. The only thing that she ever told Billy was to not hit me anywhere

where people might be able to see the bruises. Hence, most of the time, he just worked over my stomach and back. And he wasn't satisfied unless he knew that he had hurt me. Billy wasn't feeling any real love from Mother either, and I think that this manifested itself in his brutal actions.

At first no one at the studio knew what was going on at my house. In public, Mom was charming. She knew how to give a compliment, how to show just the right amount of concern over her daughter, and she never missed an opportunity to give a verbal bouquet to one of the cast or crew. Because she really did look and act like the perfect mother, I didn't tell anyone what was going on at home—her drinking, her bizarre actions, Billy's violence. I doubt that anyone would have believed me anyway. Their private lives just didn't fit with their public personalities and actions.

Yet, even though I didn't complain or vent my personal frustrations on the set, the Columbia studio was a haven that offered me a chance to escape into a world where I could be myself. My situation was so ironic. At home I had to be Kathy Anderson; I had to dress like her, talk like her, act like her, and react like her. At Columbia the only time I had to be like Kathy was when we were shooting or rehearsing; the rest of the time I could be whomever I wanted. The pressure was off the moment I walked onto the set each day.

One of the reasons my job was so wonderful was that Mom was usually with Billy. He was working in the motion picture business, and when I started "Father Knows Best," he was acting a great deal. During my first years of television work, Billy was featured with Richard Egan in *Tension at Table Rock*, and he worked with Marilyn Monroe and Ethel Merman in *There's No Business Like Show Business*, and with Robert Mitchum and Shelley Winters in *Night of the Hunter*. In *The Kid From Left Field*, he was really the star. These were just a few of his scores of credits. He was a cute kid, a talented actor, and because of this he had job offers coming from every direction. Because he was on a movie set, not a "constant" set,

Mom really felt she needed to be with him. Rather than be jealous, I was grateful. I loved being on my own.

Lillian Barkely, a studio teacher, was now the person who took me to work. She was a wonderful lady who was easy to talk to. Often I would wish that my mother could have had many of Lillian's qualities. Unfortunately, even the ones she did share were being more and more overshadowed by Mom's drinking.

When Billy wasn't working and Mother would take me to work, mornings were fine. Then, when we broke for lunch, Mother and I would go to either Brewers or Naples where she would begin with a drink and then continue with one or two more throughout the meal. Many times she would even stay at the table, having yet another drink while I reported back to the set. Even at my young age, I knew that things were getting bad and that Mother was sick.

One night the three of us had gone to a wrap party for one of Billy's films. He had already gotten permission from Mom to go home from the party with one of his friends. Instead of leaving when he did, we stayed. As the evening wore on, I began to worry that Mother was going to get drunk and make a fool out of herself. So when I thought she had had enough, I attempted to step in and stop her. In one way, it was the right thing to do, but in another way, it was a big mistake.

"Mother," I interjected in front of all of her adult friends, "I don't think you need another drink."

Looking back at me, she demanded, "Do you think I'm drunk? Well, I'm not. You worry too much. Now, leave me alone. I'm the mother, not you. I'll look out for myself."

As if to prove that I was wrong, she had several more. Hours later, when it was time to leave, she could barely walk.

I was frightened when I asked her, "Are you going to drive?"

"Oh, quit worrying, Lauren. There is nothing wrong with me. Do you think I'm drunk or something?"

I wanted to yell "Yes!" at the top of my lungs, but I couldn't. I knew that it would only make her mad. Scared, I simply followed her to our car, praying that I was wrong and that she was right. It didn't take long for me to discover just the opposite.

Mother's judgment was terrible. She was swerving, braking when she didn't have to, and barely missing parked cars. The further she drove, the worse she got. I honestly thought that she was going to kill us. Screaming, I demanded that she stop, but she kept telling me not to worry, that she was in full control.

"Lauren," she said. Her voice was slurred and her words hard to understand. "You are just too emotional. You are letting your imagination run away with you."

I shocked myself by answering, "Emotional, my———! You're going to kill us both if you don't stop!"

I think that she *would* have killed us if the police hadn't spotted her and pulled her over. She couldn't believe that they had stopped her. She repeatedly stated that she wasn't drunk, and she threatened to sue them for false arrest. All the while, her blood-shot eyes were not focusing, and her words were slowly running together in a manner that showed she couldn't reason at all. I was horrified, relieved, and embarrassed. When she practically fell down while trying to walk a straight line, I knew that I wouldn't have to worry about her driving home.

The two policemen put both of us in their patrol car and took us in. They tossed Mom in the drunk tank and then came to me. I thought that surely I would be arrested.

"What are you going to do with me?" I nervously asked.

"Do you have someone you can call?" one of the officers asked.

"You mean, I'm not under arrest?"

"No. Why would we arrest you? You haven't done anything."

I called Aunt Connie, and she and Uncle Bob came for me and put me up for the night. The next morning, they took me home. They were as disgusted over Mom's actions as I was, but none of us ever got an apology. Rather than look in the mirror and see the guilty party, Mom simply blamed the officers who "were out to get her." She wasn't going to admit that she had a problem, even though it was making our home a terrible place to be.

Meanwhile, as bad as things were getting at home, I could still escape at least a good portion of the time by going to the studio. In the fifties, Columbia was a huge place. And the greatest thing about being a star at this enormous center of action was that I could go practically anywhere I wanted. If I wasn't needed in school or on the set, I was free to wander around the studio lot.

Almost every day, I would stick my head in various doors, and if I found something interesting, I would stay and watch the action. I saw more movie stars, more famous directors, and met more producers than I could ever remember. I got the chance to see big-time stars made up, as well as have the same makeup people fix me. I met idols like Shirley Temple, Dean Martin, and Jerry Lewis, as well as watched sex symbols like Kim Novak flirt with leading men and do seductive scenes. I was privy, even at my young age, to all the gossip. I knew who was going with whom, who was cheating on whom, and why certain stars simply could not find work. For my busy little ears and active little feet, this was a daily adventure that was better than a trip to Disneyland. I was so enthralled by it, that I prayed for long days of shooting, weekend work, and extra rehearsals. Never had I been so happy!

I did have to work hard, but it didn't really seem like work for me. For starters, I didn't know that I was getting paid. I never saw a check; Mom got all of those, so I just assumed that this was something I was doing while Billy was working. I figured it was like going to school, and someday I would graduate to movies. For now, work was an adventure, and I couldn't imagine being paid for experiencing an adventure, particularly when I was doing all of this with people I loved so much.

I almost idolized Robert Young. He was the centralized male authority figure that I had never really had. He had a family, loving daughters, and a wife for whom he cared a great deal. He was patient, kind, and he didn't blame me for everyone else's mistakes. No kid could have worked with a finer man than the one who starred in our show.

Jane Wyatt was special too. She was the definition of a lady. She was gracious and gentle. She never seemed to get mad. I think one of the things that I most noticed and admired about her was her ability to be always in control. She didn't use harsh words, even when situations seemed to call for them, and she always encouraged each of us and tried to give us a great deal of self-confidence—just like a real mother.

Still, even as wonderful as these two adults were—even as much as they obviously cared for each of us kids—I wasn't really that close to either one. I didn't visualize them as substitutes for my own parents. They were just nice people. But when it came to Elinor Donahue and Billy Gray, things were different. They became more like my real siblings than my own brothers were.

In retrospect, I terrorized Ellie. Even when the show began, she was on the verge of becoming an adult. It could be a tough time for any young girl, but for her it was complicated by her work. Nevertheless, she was so very normal in so many ways, much like the character she played on the show. She was dating, constantly primping, and concerned with the things that concern all older high school students. So, in my mind, she was ripe for picking on. I often followed her around, doing all the things that she did, talking to all the folks she talked to, and even imitating the way she walked. Whenever she would meet a boy on the set, I would hover around the two of them, constantly asking questions and trying to be the center of attention.

Billy, who enjoyed making Ellie miserable as much as I did, often joined the teasing and games. Watching the reruns of the show, I now realize that the televised relationship between Ellie and me was pretty much like that in real life. I was a little pest, and she was always having to put up with me. But Billy and I had a different kind of comradeship.

On the show we were constantly at each other's throats. I was a brat, and he was the teenage boy stuck with having to put up with my brattiness. When we weren't shooting, it was different. He was my pal. For both of us, the studio was an escape. It was a place to walk away from an unhappy home life and escape the pressure of trying to be something we weren't. We were so relaxed together that we couldn't help but have fun. And during those days, it was rare to see either of us at the studio without huge grins on our faces.

We would often team up with the kids from other shows that were filming around us. Certainly the fifties were a time when family shows like ours—"Hazel," "My Three Sons," and "Donna Reed"—were network mainstays. If you weren't in a happy family, then you had to be a detective or on a horse. Television seemed to be stuck on those three formats. Because of this, we had no shortage of children with whom we could identify. Like at school, recess was fun, except we had a much better playground.

As in the real world, children performers also need school, and the studio had one. We had to study the courses for the grade level that went with our age group. Yet, in all honesty, our school was hardly one that emphasized scholarship.

The classroom was a tent, pitched on a sound stage, with a few desks thrown in to help make an environment resembling a place of learning. It wasn't that no one cared if we learned anything. Our teachers tried, but the system just wasn't set up for quality education. The main problem centered around the lack of a specific schedule. Because of rehearsals or filming, we might be in class for twenty minutes or three hours, and we never knew exactly when we would be needed on the set. Nothing had a regular schedule. Hence, our learning was as scattered and uneven as our lives.

Shooting schedules were so tight, because we were shooting thirty-nine shows a year, that we never really had a week or even a day that we could just skip. In Columbia's eyes, learning our lines was far more important than learning how to spell the words on our spelling list or how to do our latest math homework. If something was going to suffer, it wasn't going to be the show. Being kids, none of us complained.

It is easy then to understand, with the fairy-tale atmosphere of the set coupled with escaping what almost every kid hates the most about growing up—school—the only really bad thing about my life was going home.

Even though she had recently been picked up and spent a night in jail, Mom hadn't cut back on her drinking. Her tolerance also seemed much lower. It was a rare day when I would walk through the living room door and not see her sitting in her chair, phone against her ear, talking to her friend while pouring down a mixed drink. When I saw her this way, I always ran quickly to my room, and then, if I was really lucky and she didn't catch me, changed into some comfortable clothes and ran down the street to my friend Sheri's house.

Sheri was a godsend, probably the best thing about my move to Lucerne. She lived in a happy home, surrounded by wonderful people. Her mother Jerri, was divorced, had three kids, and had just remarried a divorced man, Tony Cordero, who also had three children. The two of them had enough love for a hundred kids, and they saw me as just another little girl, not a television star. So I got what I wanted: normal treatment by a mom and a dad. Despite the amount of time I spent at their house, they never questioned me about why I was always eating their food or watching their television. Not once did they ask me to go home. Every day that I could, I would stay at Sheri's house until dark. Then, not really wanting to, I would sneak back home, steal in the back door, glance into the living room to see just how drunk Mom was and who she was talking to on the phone, and then run upstairs to my room. I am sure Mom must have noticed that I had been out, but if she cared, she never mentioned it. She was only put out with me if I didn't get up in time to go to the studio.

The more time I spent at Sheri's, the more I realized how much warmth my home was lacking. Tony, a head waiter at the famous Parino's Restaurant, was one of the most handsome men I had ever seen. He had Latin good looks and a killer smile. I had a huge crush on him. Meanwhile, Jerri was a school-teacher who was lavish with hugs and smiles. She had a drinking problem, but it didn't affect her like mom's did her. If anything, a drink seemed to make Jerri happier.

When I first brought Sheri home to meet Mom, Mother was anything but warm. As soon as Sheri left, she informed me that the girl was a slut, and she didn't want me to see her any more. Needless to say, we immediately got into an argument, one that ended with my screaming, "You don't know her, so why are you calling her that? You don't know anything about my friends."

I was the type of person who wanted to adopt every stray dog in the neighborhood and bring them home. Whenever I did, Mother would push them out. She did the same thing with my friends. She simply could not see any of my playmates as being good enough for me.

What I saw at Sheri's house was the warmth that I had always wanted at mine. I wanted my home to be a place where all the kids would want to gather. But, day by day, it was more of a place where even I didn't want to be.

There were many nights when I lay awake and talked to God. I didn't think that he was really listening. I could even visualize my prayers hitting the ceiling and coming back down, but I still kept talking.

"Lord, who am I? I really couldn't be from Mom, could I? I mean, the way she feels about me and my friends. Is that my real mother? And if so, why am I here? All my friends seem to know why they are here and where they are going. They love their homes. Why don't I?

"Have I been so bad that I have to struggle like this? Why can't my family be like everyone else's? Why can't I have a father who loves me and lives in my house? Why can't my mother bake cookies and play with my hair and talk with my friends? Just what have I ever done to you to make you so angry at me? Please forgive me. Please make my family love me and each other. Please make me important to my mother, and please bring my dad home again."

Sometimes these prayers would go on for hours; finally, after I had asked all the questions I knew and been convinced that the answers were not coming, I would fall asleep. When I woke up, I felt just as hopeless as when I had gone to sleep.

I walked around feeling as if no one approved of me. I knew from the reviews and the awards I was getting that people approved of Kathy Anderson, but, somehow, the things that Lauren needed were forgotten. Mom just seemed too busy to notice and take care of them.

I carried with me a cloud of guilt, convinced that I was somehow to blame for my world. I needed Mother's attention and love, and, no matter what I did, we just grew further apart. I began to notice people talking behind my back. They would see me with Mother when she was "under the weather." They would point at me and say, "Poor child." I didn't want their pity; I wanted Mother to shape up and love me. She would often remind me of all the things she had gotten me, but she couldn't see that those things didn't bring me self-respect or self-worth. Even with all I had, it wasn't enough to allow me to walk proudly, head held high, like my secure friends did.

As the months passed and as the void grew larger and larger, I became harder to bring out of my deep depressions. Even on the set, people began to wonder why I wasn't happier. Still, because no magic formula seemed to make me better, most people just left me alone. There was an exception, however.

We had met June and Russell Poland through Mom's hairdresser, Jo Wilson. June was Jo's daughter, and she had convinced Mom to go with her to visit them one summer. They lived in Oxnard, California, and they had a place on the beach. Their two children, Rusty and Jolene, were close to my age, which was eleven at this time. They didn't care that I was on television; they simply asked me to be myself and have fun.

Over the summer, we became such good friends that Mom would allow me to visit them on my own. My stays with them were wonderful. They were a real family who seemed to do everything together. These lazy, carefree days gave me a degree of worth and self-confidence, something I hadn't had away from the set in a long time. Of course, my visits would never be long enough, and I would go home to my part of Kathy Anderson.

When shooting began again for the second season, I saw very little of my friends. They were busy with school, and I was busy at work. Our worlds were once again separate. Sundays, my only real day off, became my only time to have fun. I made the most of it. It had rained on one of these wonderfully free days. Billy and I had taken off our shoes and played in the gutters that were now filled with rushing water. Mother would have killed us if she had known because my contract stated that I was not to do anything that might cause me to get hurt and miss shooting. But I didn't care; I just wanted to relax and be a kid.

I was dashing along a gutter in front of our house when I felt a sharp pain in my foot. I cried out for Billy. When he came running over, we discovered my big toe had been cut by a large piece of broken glass. Blood was pouring from the deep wound.

"Help me, Billy!" I screamed, "Mom will kill me!"

"Don't worry," he assured me as he looked at it, "I'll fix it for you. You sneak in the back door, while I run in the front. I'll meet you in the bathroom."

His plan worked beautifully, and Mother never guessed what we were up to. Still, the cut was so deep that it took Billy a long time, two tissues, and three bandages to get the bleeding stopped. The next day, with my best acting, I managed to get out of the house and off to the studio without Mother ever guessing I had been hurt. Once there, things became more complicated.

I couldn't get my foot into my shoe, and I was walking with a bad limp. I may have fooled my mother, but Herb Wallerstien, our associate producer, immediately noticed that something was wrong.

"Are you all right, Lauren?" he asked.

I assured him I was.

"Then why are you not wearing your shoe?"

"Ah—ah—I twisted my ankle."

"Oh."

Later in the day, he asked me again, "Lauren, what have you done to your foot?"

This time, through huge sobs, I told him. He took one look at it and transported me over to the studio hospital. There, the doctor had to put in six stitches.

"Oh, Herb," I wailed.

"Don't worry, Lauren," he assured me. "It's not that bad."

"No, it's not my foot, it's my mom. She will kill me."

"Don't worry," he smiled. "It will be our secret." A man of his word, he never told. Mom never had a chance to come down on me for it.

By now I was seeing very little of my dad, and, when I did, the grilling and verbal abuse I received—first from Mom and now from Billy—made the visits something to dread. I simply couldn't escape the fact that my parents hated each other, and their hate, especially Mom's, was often directed at me.

One day when she had really gotten angry at me, I ran out of our home and wandered down the street. I stopped in front of a friend's house and watched her dog for awhile. A cat spotted me and walked up to me, begging to be petted. I picked the animal up, petted him, then squeezed him, probably too tightly, because he tried to scratch me. Reacting, I grabbed his back legs, twirled him over my head, and tossed him into a pole.

All the rage that I felt for my mother and my situation now consumed my judgment and senses. Grabbing the cat again, I repeated my actions. Finally, after I had picked the animal up and thrown it down several times, it got away. As it ran off, I screamed and cried, honestly sorry for what I had done. Yet, I was left with a strange unsatisfied need to do it again. I wondered if I was going crazy.

Over a year later I lay awake one night after Mother and I had had another knock-down, drag-out fight. I thought about that poor cat. Talking out loud to God, I asked, "Is that what I did to bring all this misery down on me? Is that what I am paying for? Is that why you haven't forgiven me? Is there any way for me to make all of this up to you, and have you give me a happy life?" When I didn't receive any immediate answers, I became more and more depressed.

Unlike other times when I had had problems and bounced back, this time I stayed in a blue funk for weeks. At the studio I had now begun to notice just how beautiful Elinor Donahue was, and I wanted to be beautiful too. Compared to Ellie, however, I didn't feel the least bit pretty. Everyone called her beautiful, and nobody said anything like that about me. As a matter of fact, I was known as the short, chunky one. Just seeing the guys hang all over Elinor began to make me question if I would ever be loved by anyone at any time.

That afternoon, I went home and found Mom trying on clothes in her room. I watched her as she primped in the mirror. I envied the way she had maintained her trim waist and good figure. I wanted so badly to believe that, when I grew up, I would look like a brown-haired version of her. Finally, needing to be reassured, I asked her, "Mom, am I ever going to be beautiful?" My brown eyes were moist with tears, and there must have been a pained, but hopeful look on my face as I waited for her answer. It didn't take her long to respond.

Glancing away from the mirror, she replied, "Well, not really, darling."

She may not have meant to hurt me, but her words hit hard. I paused for a moment and then asked, "Mom, if I'm not going to beautiful, will I be pretty?"

She again looked away from her own reflection and answered, "No, not pretty either."

Shocked, I studied her for a moment and then breathlessly asked, "Then what will I be?"

Not really noting the desperation in my voice, she softly explained, "Well, honey, if you work real hard, and if you have a very good attitude, somebody will like you someday."

Her words cut me like a sharp knife. I wanted her to tell me that I would be beautiful. I wanted and needed to feel her assurance that I would be loved and that I was worth something. Instead, she all but broke what little spirit and hope I had left. I wanted to yell out that, if I ever had a little girl, I would tell her that she was beautiful, but I didn't. I didn't do anything but go to my room and cry.

For a week I avoided mirrors, but when I would look in one, all I saw was a fat little girl with a big nose—someone who was always going to be ugly. I wanted so badly to be pretty, but Mom had said that was never going to happen, so I just knew that I wouldn't be. I was ten years old and had given up ever being happy. I really felt that the best years of my life were behind me, and even those had been miserable. In my heart I knew that God hated me. After all, he couldn't have loved someone and then sent them to live in a place like this. And if God hated me, what chance did I have?

One day when I came home to find Mom drinking and Billy beginning to pick on me, I just gave up. I didn't understand why I had to live this way, and I saw no reason to continue. I knew from my friends' homes, as well as from the "Father Knows Best" script that I read each day, that family life was not supposed to be like this. Mine seemed like hell incarnate.

I ran to the bathroom, grabbed a bottle that contained about two dozen aspirins, filled a glass of water, and then poured the pills and the water down my throat. Sobbing, I ran back to my room. Looking through my closet I found a piece of small, thin rope. I made a loop in one end, and I tied the other around the rod in my closet. Dragging a chair to the closet, I set it under the rope. I got up on the chair, placed my head through the loop, took a deep breath, and kicked the chair out from under me.

For at least three seconds I hung there, feeling the noose tighten and constrict my breathing. I knew that as my feet dangled above the floor, my life was slowing oozing from me. A sense of peace began to come over me. Then the rope broke, and I came crashing to the floor. I sat in that dark closet and cried and cried and cried. Then I threw up.

After a few minutes, I walked to the corner of my room, found a blank space on my wall, and beat my head against it for at least five minutes. Finally, after I decided I wasn't even good enough to kill myself, I put a record on my record player and lit a cigarette. I sat there in my perfect room, in my perfect home, wearing one of my perfect dresses bought at the perfect store. I let my mind wander and take me away to a world where I had the perfect parents, the perfect brother, and the perfect life to go with all of my other perfect things. But even as I dreamed, I was fully aware that I would soon have to wake up and face reality. This thought almost drove me to try suicide again.

• Four •

THERE IS SOMETHING very humiliating about not even being able to commit suicide. It makes you feel as if you can never be really successful at anything. Still, as I listened to my records and came back to my senses, I didn't mind too much being alive.

I would later wonder if Mother ever found out about my suicide attempt. If she did, she never said anything. The broken closet rod and fallen clothes were probably picked up by a maid, so my futile act may have gone unnoticed. At any rate, I didn't receive the help I needed for my problem. Even though I was still convinced that I had very little worth and no real chance at happiness, I vowed to make the best of the moment. After all, Mom had pretty much convinced me that the future didn't hold much, so I had to try to enjoy the present. I felt that nothing else was left.

My friend Sheri helped me greatly in meeting this goal. I was spending more time with her than I was with my own family. Her big house with her many brothers and sisters offered me a place where I seemed to fit in. In the confines of this "normal" home, there seemed to be a family fabric which we attempted to portray on "Father Knows Best." Sheri's mom really did make cookies and help with homework. Her father (actually, her stepfather) really did live at home and play with his children, not molest them. Their home just had a glow about it, one that mine lacked.

One of the things that Sheri's family involved me in was church. While Mom had often gotten me up and sent me through the front door to walk to mass on Sunday mornings, she didn't take me. But what she didn't know was that once I rounded the corner and was out of sight, I would change course and head to my friend's house. Then I would ride with them, not to the Catholic church where Mom had wanted me to attend, but to St. James Episcopal Church. There I would eat donuts, help in the nursery, and attend the services.

A reason I had such a desire to go to St. James was Danny Curtis. He was the pastor's son, and I had a crush on him. Every time I saw him, my heart rate jumped. He was a nice, polite, warm, and friendly brat.

After church, Sheri and I would change into some of her older sister's clothes, put on lots of makeup, stuff our borrowed bras with stockings, then take a bus down to Pershing Park and try to act like older girls on the make. Most people could probably see that we were eleven and twelve. But a few guys bought our disguise and flirted back.

For us it seemed like such great fun to make eyes at sailors, sometimes even having them kiss us or hold our hands. Once, two seamen, who were barely seventeen themselves, even followed us back on the city bus to Sheri's house where we "made out" with them. To me, this was just acting, but I would later figure out that it probably signaled something much deeper—an urge that had been unknowingly unlocked when my father and Uncle Mac had molested me. This was evidenced in many places, but none more than at the studio.

People on the set seemed to think that I carried myself in a very sexual manner. I seemed to flirt more than most little girls, and I appeared to attempt to arouse instincts of which I really was ignorant. I tried to turn men on without even knowing what I was doing. Yet no one really said or did anything about it. They just seemed to let me go on my own way. Everyone passed it off as someone else's job to say or do something about my behavior. Since I was never confronted, my flirting grew more overt. Thankfully, no one picked up on it enough to hurt or use me.

During this span of time, not everything happening to me was bad. I began to realize just how important Columbia thought I was when Eugene B. Rodney (the producer of our show) personally asked me what I wanted for my twelfth birthday. Of course, when I told him I wanted to meet Elvis, he then asked me for a second choice, assuring me that he could arrange for me to get a day off and go to Disneyland. I was thrilled, especially when he told me that I could bring my old friend from Ridgley Drive, Mary Lombardi.

For a whole week I excitedly planned the rides I would take, the things I would see, and the fun I would have. It was all I could talk about. When my birthday came, Mary and I were picked up and taken to the studio. Once there, one of my teachers loaded us in a car and drove us to the Paramount lot so that we could eat lunch in their commissary. Mary and I were thrilled by this added surprise, knowing that we would get to see many stars who had never been on our lot.

At Paramount, Mary and I were escorted into a large dining room that was completely empty except for a beautiful birthday cake and numerous party decorations. For several minutes the two of us laughed and giggled, almost overwhelmed with what Mr. Rodney had set up. Then, when a side door opened, and Elvis himself walked through, we almost died.

For the next two hours, Mary, Elvis, and I ate cake, sang songs, told jokes, and talked about our work and our lives. When Elvis finally left to return to his set, we could scarcely move. I knew that I had never met a more polite, handsome, and unselfish gentleman. He was unspoiled and kind, and he had made this the most wonderful day of my life. When he left, he gave both Mary and me autographed pictures, and he even asked for my autograph. It was as close to heaven as I could ever imagine being. The six hours I later spent at Disneyland meant nothing to me. I had already been given everything I wanted. The next day at work, everybody wanted to hear my story, especially Mr. Rodney.

While I was still having a pretty good time at the studio, what I was really now enjoying were my weekend visits to my dad's home. His banking business was going very well. He, my stepmother, and her daughter—just one year my senior— had a wonderfully warm home. I loved being there. The only negative experiences I had ever had with my father had been caused by his sexual advances, and now these were no longer a problem. Nothing about his behavior seemed the least bit perverted. His home was now a haven for me, and I found myself wishing that this could be my home all the time.

As good as life with Dad had become, life with Mom was becoming unbearable. Suddenly, Billy's career, one which just a few years before had been booming, was now winding down. He had hit an awkward age. As a child actor, he was becoming too old to employ. Thus, the responsibility for paying the bills fell into my lap.

At about this time, almost five years after beginning my career as an actress, I became aware that I actually made money. When I found out that I was earning several thousand dollars a month, I was shocked. Where had it gone? Why hadn't I been allowed to spend any of it? Then I found out why.

The thought that my mom had been using all of my money for what she deemed important made me furious. I had been looking for a reason to rebel against her for some time, and this seemed to be it. But with Billy not working and the lifestyle we were used to on the downside, this was undoubtedly a lousy time to complain.

"You ungrateful little————," Mom began when I asked for some money. "Billy," she continued, calling my brother into the room, "can you believe that, after all that we have given her, all the things that our money has bought her, that she is complaining now? Oh, Lauren, you get everything you want, and then some. I just wish you were more like your brother. He doesn't cry and complain. He doesn't use his theatrical skills to overstate things."

Actually, Billy did all of those things; he just didn't buck Mom. He didn't have to. He had always been her perfect child, and he played his role to the hilt. In reality, however, if there was a perfect child in our family, it was Michael. He had been away at school since I was little, and now I rarely got a chance to feel his gentle, caring arms around me. I loved him, and I would have loved to have been like him. But Mom wanted me to be another Billy, if she wanted me as her child at all.

At that time, I couldn't see how Mom could turn her head and ignore the things Billy did. He was not only vindictive and mean to me; he was the terror of the neighborhood. There was a rage inside of him that, if unchecked, could and would develop into something very dangerous. But if Mom saw it, she ignored it at the time, or at least never acknowledged it when I was around. It was just like her drinking problem: in her own mind, his unruly behavior didn't exist.

When Billy lashed out at her a few months later, she would blame it on me. "Lauren, you little————; it is *your* fault he's angry. *You* did this to him." But when he began to strike out more at her and less at me, and when he refused to listen to anything she asked him to do, even she had to admit that he was out of control.

But she wouldn't point a finger of blame at herself. Rather than admit that she had been wrong or too easy on her son, rather than admit that she couldn't handle him, she simply called the Black Fox Military Academy and enrolled Billy for "his own good" in this school of tough training and unbendable rules. In her own clouded mind, she did this so that he could gain some self-discipline. She refused to admit that she was trying to rid herself of a problem she couldn't handle.

For me, Billy's departure meant having Mom all to myself. Sometimes this was good, and other times it was very bad. She was just not a good disciplinarian. For starters, she wouldn't punish me at the time I did something wrong. She was the type of person who, when the mood struck her, would bring up a whole list of past indiscretions and use them as a weapon. This was the fallout that often knocked me to the ground. I would do something wrong, Mom would say nothing, so I would move on, thinking it didn't matter, then months later, she would punish me for it. One of the best examples of her approach to discipline occurred when I began stealing money.

Mom had never given me an allowance. I had a closet full of nice things, and I got to go to Hollywood child-star parties, but I never received any spending money from Mom. She never saw a need for it. She told me that she would see to it that I had everything I needed. She told me I had no reason to ask for money.

The other kids at the studio had money. They could easily buy a soft drink or a candy bar. Occasionally they went shopping and purchased gifts for themselves or their friends. A certain freedom, a certain feeling of worth, went with being able to buy and choose. Yet, no matter how much I would beg, I still couldn't get any cash, not even a dime a week, from Mom.

I didn't want to be broke. I didn't want to be the only kid on the outside looking in. So I began to get into some of my teachers' and crew members' purses and take a little change from time to time. I was never too clever or too secretive about it, and it was a miracle that it went on as long as it did before someone found out and told Mom. Ironically, rather than blow up and give me a lecture, she didn't say anything. When it was happening, the subject was never brought up.

As the months went by, I did other little things that should have gotten me in trouble. I carelessly broke a fine piece of china, stayed out too late, goofed off in school, talked back to authority figures, and yet, even when she found out, Mom did nothing. Whatever had happened was seemingly forgotten about and never mentioned. So, by doing nothing, she was supporting and encouraging more misconduct. I began to believe that I could get away with anything.

One day I came home and found her in her usual posture,

talking on the phone, a cigarette and a drink in one hand and the receiver in the other. Then and there it hit me. I suddenly realized that, for the years I had been working on "Father Knows Best," she had spent more time talking on the phone than she had talking to me. Feeling neglected, I demanded to speak with her at that moment; I refused to wait. I gave her no choice. I don't remember what I had to tell her that was so important, but I do remember what she told me when she hung up the receiver.

"————you, Lauren, why are you bothering me? I'm busy and tired. What's on your mind that is so————important?"

It probably never occurred to her that I was tired too. After all, I had been working ten-hour days for years, but to her it didn't make any difference. So she lashed out at me, recalling everything I had done wrong over the last six months, also reminding me what her friends thought about me. She started with the money I had taken; then she launched into my sneaking out of the house, not doing my work, tattling on Billy, and a multitude of other things that I had forgotten and she had not felt worth mentioning until now.

Marching me up to my closet, she pointed out all of the dresses she had bought for me, told me to look at the nice room that she had provided for me, and reminded me of all the nice things she had enabled me to do. Then she told me how ungrateful I was for not living the way I should live and how I had embarrassed her by stealing and lying.

"You are a rotten, lying little————, just like that woman your father married. You don't appreciate anything I do for you. All you can do is ask for more, more, more! It's like I have never given you anything. Besides, what do you think my friends will think? Don't you care how I'm going to look in front of them?"

I didn't know how to make her realize that I didn't care a thing about her friends, the house, my clothes, or the places I had been. What I wanted was for her to share her time with me and to feel her love, but she didn't seem to want me to have any part of either. She couldn't see that everything I was doing was a feeble cry for her attention. I was acting because it might win her approval. I was stealing to get her to notice me. I was getting into trouble and staying at other people's homes until late at night to have her care enough to be worried about me. But when I did anything, good or bad, she never noticed. Later, though, long after I had forgotten doing anything bad, she brought up the wrong things and used them against me.

I didn't fully realize that I had real worth to her, a dollars-and-cents kind of worth. If I had, I might have used it against her. As it was, her lambasting, coupled with her lack of real interest in my life, had me convinced that I was unworthy of her affection. The more I believed this, the more unhappy I became.

Still, my relationship with her wasn't all bad. There were many good moments when she encouraged me to do things that were fun and exciting. Once a month, when I was twelve, she even let me go to Billy's military school for the dances. They were a highlight of my life.

On Friday before the dance, I would rush home, change clothes, and carefully dress my best for the evening. Then Mom would drive me up to the academy. There, the headmaster of the school, who was good friends with my mother, would introduce me to my date for the evening, and I would get to dance and have fun with people my own age for the rest of the night. This was an opportunity to raise my self-esteem by several notches. I felt so at home there. It seemed that bratty military boys and bratty actresses were made for each other. But, like Cinderella, the ball ended early; when it was over, I found less and less to feel good about.

Soon after Billy left for school, Mom sold our house on Lucerne. I was heartbroken. Once again, I was leaving a world that I had grown to love, being uprooted to another place I didn't know. The reason we moved was money. I was now the only one making it, and, with the cost of Billy's tuition, coupled with living expenses, money was in short supply. We ended up in an all-Jewish neighborhood on Citrus. Within a few months, Mother sold this house and leased an apartment just two blocks from Columbia Street on Lodi in Hollywood.

My new home on Lodi was next door to the Hollywood Studio Club, a place where many struggling young actresses stayed while looking for a break. I loved the opportunity of getting to meet these fresh, enthusiastic women. They had a drive and a positive attitude that gave me energy. I think they liked me because I was doing what they dreamed of doing, and it gave them hope too.

On the other side of us was Ralph Bellamy's father's home. He lived by himself, and he seemed to enjoy my company as much as any nice grandfatherly type would enjoy a young girl's trivial questions and warm giggles. He was an artist, and he often spoke of painting me, but I was simply too busy to ever sit for him, a fact that still disappoints me. Over and over again, it was work, the same thing that had given me experiences which other kids my age would have killed for, that kept me from doing the things that I wanted to do most. Year after year, work was always there to get in the way of my being a normal kid.

For five years, "Father Knows Best" ran like a clock. After struggling for a year, America had taken the Anderson Family of 607 South Maple Street to heart, and our ratings soared. In 1954, our premier season, we had run on CBS, but they had given up on us. NBC picked us up for the 1955 season, and we took off. Then, in a move that was unprecedented, CBS bought us back and returned us to their schedule in 1956. Returned to our original network, we won Emmy after Emmy. Moreover, all of us kids earned various special acting awards for children.

I won the Mars Gold Star best actress award for young females for six years running. It was one of the things that excited Mom the most about my career. She loved the spotlight that fell on me when I was given these honors. She also glowed the night I went to the Emmies.

Robert Young had won a number of Emmies for his acting, but Jane Wyatt always just missed out. In 1959, after being nominated time and time again, she was once again a finalist, but considered herself such a long shot that she was out of town on other business the night of the award show. She asked me to go in her place. Mom had dressed me in a beautiful pink silk and lace dress, and I was so excited to be going to such an important event that I could barely contain myself. My escort was Robert Young, and he and I sat through a long evening of award after award. As the night wore on, my new high heels began hurting my feet, so I took off my shoes. Now comfortable, I settled back and waited for the end.

When I heard Jane's name announced, I went into shock. At first I didn't move, and then I found myself jumping out of my seat and rushing toward the stage. Not once did I think about putting my shoes back on. Seconds after I made it to the podium, I realized that I was barefooted. Realizing my dilemma, Robert Young bounced out of his seat and strolled to the front of the stage with my shoes. The audience fell apart in laughter, and it took several minutes to get the program back to the stately atmosphere to which shows like this usually aspired. After a moment of initial embarrassment, I smiled too and a warm feeling of having a father take care of me rushed over my heart. This was a normal act, done by a normal girl, and Robert Young was the ever-gallant and caring father who rescued me. To all the world, it looked as if we really were father and daughter. No wonder our show was so successful.

Later, after I had brought a great many smiles to those gathered for the awards, I went to a backstage party and was a hit. I met Jack Benny, Harry Belafonte, Steve Allen, Jayne Meadows, and a host of others. Once again I felt like Cinderella at the ball. After visiting with Loretta Young and sharing small talk with Robert Wagner, the gala was over. It was time to go back home and rest for my next day of work. I knew that it would take more work and more success to keep moments like this coming.

Fortunately for me, "Father Knows Best" continued its popular and award-winning run. During the fall season of 1961, our ratings showed little sign of letting up. We were on top, and I just knew that we would stay there forever. The formula was perfect for a never-ending run. We were as

American as apple pie, but while the show was not having any problems keeping momentum in its ratings, behind the scenes a number of disturbing things were beginning to create a real morale problem.

Robert Young was going through severe bouts of depression. His moods, while not violent or hateful, were constantly up and down. Sometimes he had to pull himself through these times on raw courage. It was a tribute to his professionalism that he was able to hide his mood swings from the camera. When he did feel good, he still didn't enjoy what he was doing. Even healthy, he was bored with his part. He had done everything he could do with James Anderson. There seemed to be no place else to take the character.

Elinor was having her problems too. She had gotten married, was now pregnant, and was having trouble holding her marriage together. Her heart was a long way from playing a carefree college student. She was a young woman with a very complicated life; just living was a challenge. A host of things in her personal life made her playing Betty seem trivial.

Billy may have been in the worst shape. His self-respect and self-esteem had suffered terribly when he was picked up and charged with possession of a controlled substance (marijuana). The fact that the perfect television son was using grass was something that set the studio rocking. No amount of public relations releases could seem to write off this incident as a harmless little prank. Billy was therefore guilty of the unpardonable television sin: he had brought public humiliation to the studio. But I was creating waves too, therefore I shared the doghouse with Billy.

By now, I was so unhappy at home that I was constantly running away. When I ran away, usually to my dad's house, I would not bother to show up for work. Columbia would then call my mother, who would call the police, and when I was found I would be hustled to the set. I was threatened with being fired, but it did little good. The only thing I wanted was out of my mom's life, and if being fired would get me there, so be it. Hence, in no time I would run away again. Eventually the courts were called in to tie me to my home. Columbia, Screen Gems, and Eugene B. Rodney all demanded that someone get me under control. They were in a big bind; they couldn't drop my character, and no one was going to accept another actress playing my part. I knew this and tried to use it to get me away from my mother. But it didn't work. They simply demanded that Mom keep a closer eye on me. But I kept running away whenever I got the chance.

With my sometimes being gone for days, Billy's court battle, Ellie's marital woes, and Robert Young's depression, the show was never on schedule. Because of this, the studio constantly stayed on our tails; the pressure on the set was hot and heavy. On screen we may have looked like the ideal family, but on the set we resembled men and women living on the edge and looking for a place to jump.

One day, with shooting weeks behind schedule, I was asked to do a crying scene. My heart wasn't in it, and I constantly missed my mark and blew my lines. Peter Tewkesbury, our director, was feeling all of Mr. Rodney's and Screen Gems' heat, and my inability to cry at the right time was grating on his nerves like nothing ever had before. In the past, my mistakes had been acceptable, even expected, but now there was simply no time to shoot and reshoot. I had to get it right.

"————girl," he would say over and over again as we reset the shot. "You're an actress. Can't you cry when you're supposed to? Okay, let's get it right this time."

After thirty frustrating attempts at getting it right and doing nothing but getting it wrong, Peter wasn't the only one feeling frustrated. All around the stage people were shaking their heads and wondering what was wrong with me. Throwing up his hands, the director halted all action on the set and gave everyone a few minutes off. He took a seat in his chair and stared at the set, while everyone headed for the coffee machine. He looked as if the weight of the whole world were on his shoulders.

Peter was a small, wiry man in his early thirties. In today's terminology, he was preppy looking, with big glasses, a pipe, short, fine hair, and a baby face. He even wore his sweater tied around his neck. Even though he was married and had four children, I had a crush on him, and he had probably used this to his advantage from time to time to get me to deliver a line just the way he wanted. But now, as he lighted his pipe, looking very exasperated, simple motivation was not on his mind. I didn't know it then, but no amount of flirting on my part was going to save me from feeling the full force of his emotions.

While on break, Peter stared off into space, and I attempted to steal away from the set and play some cards with the prop men. Soon, Peter's booming voice calling my name caught me just as I was dealing a new hand. I immediately dropped the cards and came running, but not fast enough for him.

"You———brat, you get your———tail out here," he screamed as I rounded a corner.

Using every expletive I had ever heard, he cut me to ribbons. He humiliated me in front of all the cast and crew. He took every bit of self-confidence out of my heart, and he stuffed it down my throat. I couldn't have crawled off the set when he finished with me. I just stood there shaking, and then the sobs began. Soon, I was bawling, the tears coming not just from my eyes but from down deep in my heart. My crying was causing my breaths to come in deep gasps. I had trusted Peter, and now he had jerked me down to nothing just because I couldn't deliver on one little scene.

As he sat there and watched me cry, he suddenly grabbed me by my shoulders and happily shouted, "Now this kind of crying is what I want. You've got it, Lauren. Okay, let's get back to work."

I looked him in the eyes, stunned that he had used this cheap and vulgar method to extract what he wanted from me. Choking back my tears, a hate began to fill my heart that caused my thirteen-year-old cheeks to flush. My jaw clenched tightly; I stared Peter right in the face and shouted a stream of obscenities. Then I stormed off the set. I didn't return for three days.

Peter didn't realize just how fragile my ego was. He didn't know that my mom had been using the same techniques to control me for years. He had no way of knowing just how many times I had been jumped on and called names. He had no way of knowing the damage he had done. But he had destroyed what little self-confidence I had left.

I didn't want to go back to work at all; amazingly, even Mom backed me on this. But through court action, Screen Gems saw to it that I was back on the lot within days. Soon, I realized that the daily walk to the studio had to be a part of my life. So I quit running, but no one could make me smile.

I was a miserable little girl. I was very self-conscious, and I had a great deal of trouble getting into character. This was an even bigger problem off set, because I had been Kathy so long that now I was having problems finding her. I was even more confused about who Lauren was. I was scared and often listless. Now there was no escaping my life, not even at the studio.

One afternoon when I came home, I opened the door to our apartment only to discover that Mom was not at home, and there was nothing in the house that I wanted to eat. After saying hello to Steve Lord, a writer friend who lived across the hall from us, I left our building and walked the six blocks to the Hollywood Ranch Market. There, I bought one sack of groceries and headed home. As I started, I was happily planning to surprise Mom by cooking supper for her.

Soon, however, I became aware of a car following me after I left the store. As I walked, it kept getting closer and closer. Glancing over my shoulder, I saw a man, balding and somewhat fat, driving the vehicle. At every corner he would turn, then he would drive around the block just in time to meet me at the next corner. He didn't look like anyone that I would have to worry too much about, but the mere fact that he was following me made me very nervous. So I walked a little faster.

After a couple of blocks of this strange little cat and mouse game, he pulled the car over to the curb next to me and in a very polite voice asked, "Young lady, can you help me?"

I stopped, stared at him for a moment, and then answered with the normal reply, "I'm not allowed to talk to strangers." With that I turned and began to walk away. His voice stopped me.

"I understand that. And not talking to strangers is very good, but I'm not really that strange, and I'm lost, and I thought that maybe you could help me."

Again looking at him, I decided that he was probably harmless, and I ambled over to his car. He smiled at me and asked me if I knew where Gower Street was. As I started to explain how to get there, he opened his door and revealed to me that he was naked from the waist down. This scared me, and I froze. Then he reached for me.

Tossing the sack of groceries to the ground, I ran screaming all the way back to our building, rushing up the steps and directly to Steve's apartment door. Pounding on the door, I yelled for Steve to help me. Pulling me inside, he closed the door, but was unable to calm me down. I kept crying, "He's after me! He's after me!"

"Who?"

"A man! He's after me!"

Looking outside, Steve saw no one. Then, running across the hall, he discovered that Mom was still not home. Finally soothing me enough to get my story, he called the police. Within minutes they arrived and began questioning me.

It was horribly embarrassing to try to sit and tell two grown men what had happened and what I had seen. The more I told, the more humiliated I became. Steve was the lifesaver. He was very calm and understanding; he tried to make me realize that I hadn't done anything wrong, and there was nothing to be scared of now. After the police got all the information they needed, they left Steve and me alone. Soon, Mom arrived and heard the story. Pushing me back into our apartment, she then spoke to Steve.

"You don't believe her, do you?"

Steve indicated that he did.

"Oh, Steve, I thought you knew Lauren better than that. She probably made the whole thing up. That's what she does for attention. You know how she is; she is such a liar. I am sure that this didn't happen."

I had heard all I could take. Rushing into my room, I closed the door, turned on the television, and began to cry. My mind was crowded with all kinds of pictures, but the one that stood out the biggest and cried out the loudest was Mom's not believing me. I now believed that she never would.

Days later, long after the incident had been laid to rest, the phone rang. It was police headquarters.

"Mrs. Chapin, we need you to bring your daughter down to headquarters. There is a lineup we want her to view."

"You can't be serious," Mom retorted. "I tell you she made the whole thing up. You can't trust her word." Despite her pleas, they forced my Mom to take me to headquarters.

Emotionally, I was a wreck. The events of that terrible day, coupled with Mom's embarrassing statements, had unnerved me. But the police managed to calm me down enough to get me to view a lineup of five men.

An officer asked me to look through a peephole. He assured me that no one would be able to see me. Still, I was scared. My knees were so rubbery, and I didn't know if I could even climb up on the stool, much less look at the lineup. Finally, I worked up the courage and put my eye to the hole. I studied all five men, beginning on the left and working my way to the right. When I got to the last man, I blurted out, "That's him! That's him!"

"Are you sure?" the officer asked me.

I nodded my head.

The officer quickly turned back to Mom. "Mrs. Chapin, that man your daughter just identified was just picked up for raping a little girl only a few blocks from where your daughter saw him. I don't think she was making it up. She may be responsible for getting this creep off the streets."

Her jaw a little slack, Mom shook her head and replied, "You mean she's telling the truth!"

Not once during that evening, or for that matter, ever, did Mom apologize for attempting to make a fool out of me. She never brought up the incident again.

Shortly thereafter, when Billy would come home on weekends, he and I began to go ice skating. I loved the way it felt to glide across the ice. At the rink we would often skate with the Lennon Sisters. And all of us got along well and had a great deal of fun.

While skating, Billy met a cute girl named Mary Jane Hill. She was a skater who did pairs with a male partner, Roy Wagland. He was tall, blond, and blue eyed. As soon as I met Roy, I was in love. Within weeks, Mary Jane and Billy, and Roy and I, were going steady.

Roy offered me a chance to get out of my house and away from the pressure-packed studio. We laughed, went to movies, talked, and kissed. I was finally playing the little junior high games that most young girls play.

For the next year, Roy and I were an item. Now almost thirteen, I was doing some heavy petting. I really thought that this was what love was all about. Because of my moments with Roy, I was happy. Then, because of a couple of unrelated events, things began to come undone.

Mom and I were not getting along, which led to many harsh words between us. Billy became her enforcer when I wouldn't listen to her. On weekends when he would come home, she would tell him all sorts of bad things about me, and then "sic" him on me. He would hit me again and again, finally stopping only when he had gotten tired or I had run away.

Mom wasn't concerned about the hitting, only that Billy strike me in places that would not show or affect my work. My lower stomach took the most punishment. It was a strange, sick kind of child abuse. Because of the way it was done, it remained completely hidden.

Then, I began to miss my periods. For three months this happened, but I kept it to myself so that Mom wouldn't think

I had done something wrong. By this time, my stomach had bloated and I was in constant pain. I thought that I was pregnant. I actually believed that you could get that way from French kissing, and I had done a lot of that. I was scared to death for Mom to find out.

One Friday night, an evening in which Mom was parked on the phone, drink in her hand, talking with Marge, I was in the kitchen fixing dinner. While peeling potatoes, a severe pain hit my stomach, causing me to buckle over. Mom had just looked toward the kitchen when it happened.

"Are you all right?" she inquired.

Nodding my head, I answered, "Yeah, fine."

"Excuse me just a second, Marge," Mom said, dropping the phone. "What is wrong with you? Are you hiding something from me? I know you too well, and I know when you are doing something wrong. Look at your face. What's wrong with you?"

"I don't feel very good," I replied.

Picking the phone back up, Mom said, "Marge, let me call you back."

"Now, Lauren, what's wrong?"

"My stomach hurts, and it's really swollen."

"Have you started your period?"

"No." I was now beginning to cry.

"When was the last time?"

"Ah—about three months ago?"

She stared at me and then said, "You're pregnant, aren't you?"

I stared back at her. A part of me wanted to deny that she could have thought such a thing, but another part of me wasn't at all shocked. Shaking my head, while all the time wondering, I answered, "No, I'm not."

Shrugging her shoulders, she told me to go and rest on my bed. As I did, she poured herself another drink and called Marge. A few moments later, the pain now worse than before, I left my room and returned to Mom's side.

"Mom," I moaned, "I'm really hurting."

Staring at me, she said goodbye to Marge and called St. Vincent's Hospital. She gave her own evaluation of my problem, humiliating me with her accusations and beliefs. Pouring herself another drink, she downed it, and then announced that we were going.

"Mom, let me get Mike to drive us there. I know he's home." Mike was a homosexual who lived just down the street from us. I knew that he would help us out, and I also knew that Mom was far too drunk to take the wheel.

"No," Mom shot back. "I can do it."

"No, you can't," I replied, my pain and humiliation now mixed with a large dose of fear.

"I'm not drunk!" she yelled back, her slurred speech saying things much more accurately than her words.

"I know you aren't," I lied. "But with Mike driving, you can take care of me. You won't have to worry about finding the place."

Within minutes, I had gotten Mike, explained the situation, and he and I practically carried Mom to the car. As sick as I was, I spent the whole ride taking care of her. She was completely out of it by the time we arrived, so we left her in the car.

I explained my problem to the doctor, and after a preliminary examination, he told me that he would have to have a parent's permission to do a vaginal examination. Calling Mike in, I explained the problem, and he signed the form as my father.

The test showed that my ovaries were the size of ostrich eggs and that the swelling must have been caused by some kind of physical trauma. This would be the first of a host of female problems that would haunt me for the next several years.

I stayed in the hospital for the whole weekend, getting out just in time to go back to work on Monday. On Saturday, when Mom came to see me, she didn't mention one word about the way she had treated me or even apologize for being drunk when I needed her or for accusing me falsely.

As soon as I felt like my old self, which took about a week,

I again ran away to Dad. Mother called out the law on me. When they found me, they returned me to her. The producers at "Father Knows Best" then went with my mother to court and made sure that I legally had to stay with her until the show concluded its run, or until I became an adult. Screen Gems took this action because my dad had informed them that as long as I stayed with him, he wouldn't allow me to work. There was no way I could be replaced six years into a run, so producer Eugene B. Rodney and the company had to make sure I was controlled in a way that would best serve their needs, not my own.

After the courts settled the matter of my guardianship, my mom ordered that I never mention my father's name again. I took her at her word. Figuring I had suffered enough abuse by being rebellious, it was now time to play the game her way.

Living with her was like walking on eggshells. Most of the time, I escaped to either the Studio Club or across the street to a girlfriend's house. As long as I stayed out of Mom's way and as long as I went to work and earned my money, she pretty much left me alone. More often than not, by the time I got home at night, she was "three sheets to the wind," not caring what I did or where I had been.

The show's ratings were good as our sixth year wound down, but the set was becoming more and more miserable. Ellie, Billy, and I were in constant turmoil due to personal problems, and we were running so far behind schedule that the crew was burned out too. Nevertheless, I thought that the show would go on. No one had even mentioned that the end might be near. I just knew that every Friday we would complete an episode, and that every Monday we would begin a new one. It happened thirty-nine weeks a year. It was as sure as death and taxes, and I just knew it would never stop.

One Friday, thirty-odd weeks into our shooting schedule, I left to go home for the weekend. As I left the set, I picked up a few items, talked with a few of the crew, said goodbye to Billy, waved at Robert Young, and began my walk home. The rest of my life may have been rotten and the set may have been pressure packed, but I was still a star. At least that gave me something for which to live. And on every weekend, it gave me something for which to feel special.

As I walked across the lot on that Friday, other actors—friends like Paul Peterson who played Jeff Stone on "The Donna Reed Show"—were also getting finished for the week. Jay North, everybody's "Dennis the Menace," was picking up his things too. I waved at them when I saw them. It was just like any other day; things seemed so very normal. I remember talking to the security guards as I passed through the gates, and then I prepared myself for a weekend of staying away from Mom. Yet I knew, come Monday, I would be back at Stage 11—back with Billy, Ellie, Jane, and Robert. Even though things had been tough this year, I still felt as if these people were my real family.

On Monday, as I approached the gate to go back to work, the guard didn't wave at me. He didn't open the gate for me either. For a moment I looked at him as if he were crazy, but he just shook his head and said, "I'm sorry, Miss Chapin, they told me that your pass has been lifted. You can't come in."

"What are you talking about?" I asked.

"There's a writer's strike," he answered. "Production has shut down."

"But my school . . ."

"You can't come in, Lauren. They told me not to let you in. I'm sure that someone will call you in the near future and let you know what is going on."

As I looked through the gates—the gates which were securely locked in front on me—I suddenly felt very alone. My friends were in there, and I couldn't get to them. Behind those gates were the places where almost all of my life's most precious moments had taken place. Tears clouded my eyes as I thought about doing shows with Greer Garson, Duke Snider, and Kim Novak. I remembered flirting with Jack Jones and Paul Peterson, and pretending that they loved me too. And there were so many special moments that quickly flooded my mind.

Somewhere behind those walls was a room that Kathy Anderson had called home and a dressing room that had allowed me to find a little peace of mind. I had secret hideaways in there and special places where Billy Gray and I had talked about our lives. My life was in there, just out of view, and way out of reach.

As I turned and walked back to our apartment, I felt more and more like I was leaving my home behind me. Tears were now filling my eyes and spilling down my cheek. Suddenly, I wasn't a star; I was a nobody. Then another thought hit me. "What am I going to tell Mom? Without my working, how will we make it?"

• Five •

A FEW DAYS after I was turned away at the gate, I received a note from Screen Gems informing me that I could no longer be a student at the studio school. I was given a time when I could come by and pick up my things, and without so much as a wrap party, a final goodbye, or a parting thank you, I was tossed out. My usefulness to the studio was over, and in the big business of turning out television shows, there was no time for any sentimentality. Except for the note informing me of my status at school, nothing else was ever officially written explaining what happened. It was that cold.

Ironically, "Father Knows Best," now completely out of production, was still hot property. Even as the studio was passing the word that we had been cancelled, due in large part to Robert Young's desire to move on to other things, we were still easily winning our time slot and pulling down big audience shares. This popularity did not go unnoticed by the powers who headed one of the other networks.

Within weeks, ABC bought all rights to our reruns and, rather than film new shows, simply reran our old ones against the prime time first-run shows of the other two networks. The venture was so successful that the practice continued until 1967, almost five years after we had finished filming. Beyond a doubt, we went out on top. But the mere fact that we stayed there while most of us were on the unemployment line seemed to be the most unfair facet of the show's demise.

After some time off, Robert Young would return to television first in "Window on Main Street" and then as the star of "Marcus Welby." Elinor, now divorced from her first husband and married to producer Harry Ackerman, would immediately find work on "The Andy Griffith Show." Jane, whose career continued for four decades, didn't really need to act for the money or to prove herself, so she was free to accept occasional guest shows. Billy Gray and I were at the wrong age to do much of anything. We were too old to be cute kids and not old enough to be considered for young adult roles. The rerunning of our old show didn't help us either. It simply reminded everyone who we were in the public's eye. So Billy and I were stuck at whatever points in our lives that ABC was broadcasting on a particular week. We were never any younger or older than the show made us. We were just Bud and Kathy, typecast and positioned in a world that was directly opposite to the one in which we were living.

Because there had been no goodbyes, I felt that a huge void had been forced into my life, and for a long time I had a hard time accepting that my television family was gone. It would have been easier if we could just have gotten together and hugged or cried or something. But the whole thing was handled very poorly. "Father Knows Best" died without a funeral. Seeing the show each week on a new network just brought home even more the hurt I felt. It seemed to be so cruel.

Without any of her kids working, Mom was suddenly in a tough financial spot. She had always lived to the full extent of her income, never properly managing the money or thinking of the future. Now with just my residual money to fund us, we should have cut back our lifestyle dramatically. But we didn't. Mother either couldn't or wouldn't do so.

I was fourteen when she enrolled me in the Marion Colbert Prep School. This exclusive private high school was *the* place for all of the rich society girls and boys to learn not only educational skills but manners too. In order to attend, one's clothes, clubs, and social position were a must. Not only did Mom drop a bundle on my tuition, she put out a small fortune making sure that I was dressed for the part. I looked like a million, but I felt like two cents. I was simply not suited for life with rich snobs. I was from a totally different world.

It didn't surprise anyone that I did not do well in school. I quickly teamed up with the kids who were smoking, cutting classes, and giving the teachers all kinds of trouble. In my first semester, I bombed my courses. It was simply more fun to be a goof-off than a person who got good grades. Besides, never having been in a structured school for too long at a time, I hated it. I felt very inadequate, unprepared, and ignorant, and yet I managed to keep all of these feelings to myself. Because I didn't know the games I was supposed to play, it also took me longer to make solid, individual relationships. But, after a while, I did find several other misfits whom I came to like and who came to like me. The first of these was Jane Silberkraus.

Jane was tall, almost 5'9", and blessed with movie star good looks. She had long, dark hair, big, brown eyes, and a great figure that turned heads everywhere she went. She was the type of person who should have made me jealous, but the fact that she was almost as screwed up as I was, coupled with her outgoing, "the-world-is-ours" personality, erased my envy and replaced it with an easy loyalty. Besides, so many guys hung around Jane that I figured at least one of them might fall my way too.

Jane, as well as most of my other new friends, were from the right side of the tracks. They all had money. I looked as if I did, but it was just a front created by my nice clothes and high visibility. While their affluence was real, mine was as fabricated and illusionary as a Hollywood set: here today and gone tomorrow. This fact also contributed to my insecurity, making me try even harder to prove that I fit in and belonged. I was looking for another role to play, and with Kathy now history, the role of the spoiled, rebellious rich kid seemed suited for me.

I would meet Jane every morning before school at a café. There, after teaming up with a bunch of her buddies, we would smoke Parliament cigarettes and plan our days. We all thought that we were so sophisticated and grown-up. Judging from the looks we got from adults, we must have looked just the opposite, but we didn't care. We didn't care about much of anything. School was the least of our concerns. Often, we simply would skip our classes and catch a bus to someplace where we had friends. Jane knew some kids at Fairfax High, and we spent almost as much time at their school as we did at our own. For Jane, life was a party, and I was a more-than-willing participant. She wrote the scripts, and I played them out. I didn't seem to have a mind of my own.

Jane was the first person I had ever run with who was sexually active. I had had other friends who had talked big, but Jane lived it. Possibly, even more than her beauty, this facet of her life caused me to look up to her. I was still a virgin, something that made me feel a bit Victorian and out of step, and I longed to be a real woman. I was hoping to soon grow up the way Jane had. When I did, I knew that I would be as happy and confident as she was.

One day after school, Jane stopped me before I headed home. Cornering me in the hall, she asked, "Lauren, can you get out tonight? Do you want to catch a show with me, my sister, and her friends?"

"Sure," I agreed, all the time wondering how I would get Mom to give me the money for a ticket.

"Great," Jane replied as she walked off. Then, yelling over her shoulder, she added, "I'll come by and get you at seven o'clock."

All the way home, I planned my strategy. Secretly I hoped that Mom was simply sleeping it off, and I could just get some money from her purse and sneak out. If she wasn't, I prayed that she hadn't been drinking at all, and I could catch her in a good mood. As it worked out, neither of these two ideal scenarios presented themselves. She was drinking, but not enough to be completely out of it.

"Mom," I said, my voice giving me away from that first word. She immediately could see that I wanted something.

"What is it, Lauren?" she answered. "What do you want now?"

I knew by the tone of her voice that it wasn't going to be easy to get anything out of her, but I had already said I would go, so I had to try.

"I need some money to go to the movies with Jane and her sister."

"Oh, you do. And I suppose that you think that I'm going to give it to you."

"Well, I don't have any of my own," I answered.

"You wouldn't have anything if it weren't for me," she shot back. "Do you know that?"

From there our discussion broke down into a complete knock-down drag-out fight. These shouting matches had become more common since I had quit working. No longer taking either of us to auditions or sets, Mom had more time to think and therefore more time to dwell on what I was doing wrong. But rather than take her abuse as I had done so many times before, I would now fight back, matching her name for name. On this night, the fight really got ugly.

"You are just a little———," Mother finally screamed at me. "You always have been. You are nothing more than a slut and so are your friends."

"Well," I whispered, "What you see is what you get!" Fortunately, she didn't hear this comment; she was too busy preparing for her next assault.

"You hate me, don't you?" Her voice was now demanding and filled with venom.

"Yes!" I yelled back, "You're right. I hate you!"

"You probably think that you'd be better off without me,"

she lashed out, her words now slurred from the effects of the alcohol.

"Yeah," I admitted, "I'd be a lot better off."

"Well, I think I'll kill myself," she announced matter of factly.

I couldn't wait to answer this challenge. "Hey, that sounds like a great idea. Let me help you."

"I'm so tired of all of this," she sighed, her voice now not as loud as it had been before. "I'm tired of raising an ungrateful little———like you. I'm tired of living with a little slut who always wants to go to be with Daddy. You're 'Daddy's little girl,' and he is such a jerk. You deserve each other. You don't care anything about me or your brothers—only yourself. Well, I'm tired of dealing with a selfish little———like you. I'm going to end it all right here and now."

Staring back, my eyes locked into hers. Smiling for a moment, I answered with a challenge, "Then why don't you? What is taking you so long? If you want to end it all, do it; don't talk about it."

Charging through the bedroom, she ran into the bathroom, opened an almost full bottle of Miltowns and popped them in her mouth. Grabbing a glass, I filled it with water, shoved it in front of her face, and watched her wash the pills down.

"Satisfied?" she shouted, as tears began to cloud her eyes. "You got what you wanted now, you little———."

"No," I screamed back. "You got what you wanted."

For the next several minutes, we continued to argue. Then, when I could take no more, I stormed out of the bedroom, grabbed some money from Mom's purse, and waited downstairs for my friends. When they arrived, I turned my back on what had just happened and went to the show.

It was over an hour later, when, halfway through the movie, the seriousness of what had happened hit me. Suddenly the picture of my mother lying unconscious on the bed or in the bathroom began to sober my irrational mind. *My God*, I thought. *She's probably dead by now*. I became sick to my stomach, feeling like I was going to vomit everything inside my body in one violent burst.

As the movie played on, and as my friends laughed and giggled, I grew more silent and withdrawn. My nerves were shot. I was constantly fiddling with either my hair or my blouse. I even stopped responding to anyone's questions. All I could think of was, *I killed her; I've actually killed my own mother*. I began to shake.

Like a scene from a Hitchcock movie, this numbing thought screamed at me over and over again. I could think about nothing else. As I attempted to shift my focus, the picture of my mother, passed out, followed me, remaining onstage, front and center. For over an hour I was locked in that nightmarish vision, wondering if she were dead, too scared to get up and call, and wanting to but not wanting to go home and find out.

When the movie ended, we all drove home. Once there, I asked Jane to walk me to the door. As we walked toward it, she rattled about a multitude of different subjects, but I didn't hear anything she was saying. The closer we got to my door, the slower I walked and the harder my heart was beating. Finally, in a panic-stricken moment, I turned to my fifteen-year-old friend, and in a frantic voice begged her, "Jane, you've got to come in the apartment with me. I think my mother's dead."

She looked at me like I was crazy. I had been acting strangely all night long, but this must have taken the cake. Shaking her head, she asked me what I was talking about. Within moments I told her the whole story. Taking a deep breath, she followed me in. We were both expecting the worst, and she was trying to help me come up with an excuse so that no one would know that I was responsible.

After I unlocked the door, we stopped just inside, and I listened for some sounds that would indicate life. I heard nothing. Slowly edging through the living room with Jane right behind me, I peeked around the opened door of my mother's bedroom. There, sprawled in the place she had fallen soon after I left, lay Mother. Her mouth was open, and a thick, white foam was oozing from it. As I looked closer, I saw her chest rise up and go down. In a few seconds she repeated this motion. Looking back at my friend, I whispered, "She's alive."

Running up to Mom, I shook her hard. She didn't wake up. Pulling back my arm, I slapped both sides of her face in an effort to wake her. She still didn't respond. I knew I was in big trouble. My mind raced to Billy and what he would do to me, then to Michael and finally to the police and the newspapers. The more I thought, the more scared I became.

"————Lauren," Jane cried out from behind me. "We've got to get her some help." She was just as panicked as I was, terrified that her sister would come up and see what was going on. "Come on, Lauren, we've got to do something. Call the police, the hospital, someone!"

I could hear her words, but they weren't registering. "Yeah," my mind slowly focused, "We need help, but who? How about Marge? Thanks to Ma Bell, she and Mom have been joined at the ear for years. As much as I hate her, she might be able to help me now."

Within seconds, I had found her number and called. I rapidly explained the situation and then offered, "I'll call the paramedics and an ambulance."

"No!" Marge immediately shot back. "If you did that, it would be all over the papers by tomorrow night. Just keep trying to wake her up, and I'll get a doctor over to you."

A few minutes later, the doctor and Marge arrived. Mother was still out of it, still foaming like some mad dog. After pumping her stomach, checking her vital signs, and sitting with her for a while, the doctor informed us that she would recover, but that she was going to sleep for a long time. This news immediately set my mind at ease. Jane had left before Marge had arrived, and now that Mom was out of danger, I sent Marge home too. I was alone, and Mother was not only all right but also silent.

For the next three days, things stayed peaceful as Mom slept. For seventy-two hours I was in heaven. There was no booze, no yelling, no fights, and no talking on the phone unless

I was doing it. For three days it was wonderful. Then, she woke up. The horror was back.

Her drinking now only stopped when she was asleep, her temper was unbelievable, and she lashed out at me almost every time she saw me. Money probably had something to do with it. It had been almost a year now since I had worked. With Billy in school, there was no new income. Try as she did, she couldn't convince anyone that I was a marketable commodity in television. I was a "has been" at age thirteen, and therefore a useless source of income. All we had left were my residuals from the repeat showings of "Father Knows Best" and the little child support that Dad provided. We couldn't continue the life-style we were living on just these two paychecks. There was just no way that Mom could manage it. The thought of being poor, or at least very middle class, must have scared her worse than anything. She had figured out how to climb the mountain named success, but she just couldn't see herself coming down it.

Inside her sober mind, she probably knew that I wasn't to blame for the way things were. But when she was drunk, I was the one who caught all of her frustration and wrath. And when Billy was home, I also caught his.

I just couldn't take it anymore. I had to get out. I constantly badgered my dad for help. I would beg him to take me away from Mom's home. I wanted to be with him, and I would do anything to get there. Finally, after more than a year of begging, he called me and told me that he was ready to help. He said a judge would issue papers that would be served on my mother that evening. These papers would force Mom into a custody battle for me. He suggested that I might want to be out of the apartment when the papers were served. Never was a suggestion more on the mark than this one.

I was out for a good part of the afternoon, but I came home in the early evening. I spent the rest of the day trying to stay out of Mother's way, and I managed to accomplish that with very little trouble. All the while, my insides were eaten up with worry over when the doorbell would ring and Mother would be hit with the news of what I had done. When the papers didn't come by six, I figured that chances were good they wouldn't come that day. By ten, I felt relaxed. I just knew that I had escaped her wrath, could get up early tomorrow, and be gone before all hell would break loose.

Mother was in the front room, talking on the telephone, and completely unaware of my state of mind. Billy was home from school, in his room, lying on the bed, and watching television. In my room, I just stayed quiet, hoping to slowly escape anyone's notice for the rest of the night.

You can't imagine my surprise and shock when the doorbell rang at eleven. At first I went completely rigid, unable to move. My television was on, but I neither heard nor saw it. I found it almost impossible to breathe, and the room suddenly felt very warm. Waiting for a long moment, I stayed in bed, hoping that my darkest fears were not being realized. When I still was alone a full minute later, I relaxed enough to get out of bed and investigate. Sneaking from my room, down the hall past Billy's closed door, I eased the living-room door open just a crack. From there I could see a marshal and Mother talking. I noted a piece of paper in her hand, and I quickly turned and charged back to my room.

As I sat there and tried to focus on the television, I knew that World War III was about to break out. I expected fury and rage like I had never before seen, and I expected it soon. Even though I was praying with all my might that it would not happen, I knew that nothing or no one was going to change the next few moments. Just like a death row prisoner looking at the dawn, I tried to pretend that I could face Mother with courage and survive, but deep down I knew I couldn't. I knew that it was hopeless.

I heard the front door close, and then I could hear Mother's footsteps coming down the hall. First they stopped at Billy's room. I could hear Mom's voice as clearly as if she had been in my room.

"Billy, look at what the little———has done now. She thinks she's going to leave us. She thinks she is going to live with her dear old daddy. Well, she had better think again."

I could hear Billy's springs clank as he jumped out of his bed and followed Mother down the hall. I was staring in fright at the door when Mom threw it open, her face red with rage, her blood boiling, and every bit of hate her heart could muster about to charge from her mouth.

"Well, Lauren," she began in a sarcastic tone. "You've really done it this time. So you are bound and determined to be 'Daddy's little girl.' So you are going to go and live with Daddy. So you are going to live with your new mommy and new sister. We'll see about that, you little————!"

For years I had listened to her scream and shout. Countless times I had heard and felt her wrath. But I had never seen her face so distorted, heard her voice filled with so much hate. I wondered, as I trembled on my bed, if I would survive this assault. I knew that within moments she would order Billy to attack, and in the obvious violent mood, I thought he might kill me.

As Billy moved in on me and we began to exchange blows, I figured that I was as good as dead. He hit and hit me, striking me harder and harder, until, somehow, I managed to wriggle free. Picking myself off the floor, I took one last glance at Mom, and then charged out of my room, down the hall, and out of the house. I ran and ran until I thought my lungs would explode, and then I ran some more. I didn't stop running until I was blocks away from the apartment. Finding a phone, I called Dad.

"Daddy, this is Lauren," my frightened crying must have caught him off guard.

"What is it, honey?" he answered. "What's wrong?"

"Mom got the papers, and Billy began beating me, and I can't go home. Daddy, they'll kill me. I need you to come and get me right now."

"Where are you?" he asked.

"In a phone booth. Please hurry," I begged.

"Can you go somewhere, maybe to somebody's home? I don't want you on the streets for the whole hour it will take me to get there from Pasadena."

Thinking for a moment, I remembered a friend who lived across the street. "I could go to Mary Jane's."

"That would be great. Give me the address."

I gave him Mary Jane's address, then walked to her house. She took care of me during the long wait for my father. When he arrived, I was the happiest girl in the world. I practically exploded into his arms. I finally felt safe.

The night of terror was a Friday, and on the following Monday morning, Dad took me with him to court. The fight would begin and end on this one day. I knew that if Dad and I lost, I was signing my death warrant. I had never been so nervous.

Dad's wife, Linda, accompanied us. As we sat waiting for the proceedings to begin, I looked over at her and asked, "Do you really want me?" I wanted an honest answer, even though I assumed that, knowing what a loser I had been, how I had bombed in school, and was constantly in trouble, she would answer negatively.

Not pausing for even a split second, she replied, "Lauren, I love your father, and I will love you. If you want us, then I want you."

Just like a scene from "Father Knows Best," I cried as my stepmother's arms surrounded me. For the first time in my life, I felt as if someone really cared.

During the court testimony, I never stopped praying. I kept wondering what would happen if Mom won. I knew that I would have to run away. But where could I go? If I lost, I couldn't run to Dad again. "Dear God," I kept asking over and over again, "please let me stay with my father."

Finally, after a morning of reviewing facts and records, the judge called me into his chambers and asked me, "Whom do you want to stay with?"

I answered, "My father."

"Why?"

"Because my Mom and I don't get along," I replied. I then began to explain the years of emotional abuse that Mother and I had spewed out on each other. I went overboard in telling the judge that it wasn't all her fault, that I did things to make her hate me, and nothing I could do or say would ever change that, and I just knew I could never live with her again.

"Judge, I need a family. I need a place to go where I feel safe and secure. I want someone to really love me, and I think I can get that at my father's. I know that I could never find it with Mother."

He listened to all of my words, carefully questioned me again, and then excused me from his chambers. As I walked back into the courtroom, I glanced over at Mom and her attorney. For a second, my face turned red, sweat popped out on my brow, and a chill raced up my spine. Turning away, I quickly sat down with Dad, his wife, and stepdaughter. My heart racing, I again looked at Mom. She acted as if I wasn't even there.

As I stared at her, I didn't see any pain or anguish written on her face. I thought of a scene from an old movie, *The Champ*. In it, a custody battle was waged over a small boy. He was being pulled away from his father, and the two of them were crying and fighting to hug each other and stay together. Somehow I expected Mom to be doing this. I expected her to suddenly display all of the heartfelt emotions she had kept hidden for all my growing-up years. I somehow expected her to rush crying to me, tell the world she loved me, take me in her arms, and beg the courts to not separate us ever again. But as I watched her, none of these emotions surfaced. The judge's voice jerked me back to the courtroom, and as he spoke, I wondered what effect his words would have on Mother.

He read his statement awarding custody to my father. As he spoke the words I had longed to hear, I once more glanced at Mom. Her face showed no signs of distress or disappointment. She remained just as she had during the whole day—cool and aloof. She simply listened to the ruling, got up, and walked out. Not once did she look my way. Then I realized what had happened in that room. There had never been a real fight over me.

• •Six •

IN A STRANGE sort of way, the next six months of my life were comparable to my character's life in "Father Knows Best." I was happy, feeling as though I had a family that cared a great deal about me. I lived in a wonderful home, complete with a swimming pool. I shared a big bedroom with a new sister. By all appearances, I had it made. Even I believed that all the bad times were behind me.

For the first time in my life, at age fourteen, I had a connected family. At the heart of this new experience was my stepmother. She was attractive, energetic, warm, domestic, and a lot like the character Margaret on "Father Knows Best." She cooked, sewed, and smiled. She was fair and honest, perhaps not perfect, but a fine mother nonetheless.

My stepsister Donna was a picture-book image too. She was pretty, a straight *A* student, fashion-wise, levelheaded, and popular with both boys and girls. Donna was everything I wanted to be; I really looked up to her. I even tried to picture myself becoming like her, but deep down, I knew that I couldn't. I just didn't have the confidence or foundation to pull it off.

Nevertheless, my first few months at my father's were filled with laughter and joy. I felt real peace and security, and I also felt as if I belonged in this family. In my heart, I felt an anchor of love and trust, and I wanted to live up to the high standards I saw around me.

Because of this environment, I began to take real pride in how I looked. I worked out, swimming for hours in the pool in an attempt to hone my body into the perfect hourglass figure. I vowed to do well in school, and I even promised myself that I would make the same kind of friends and do the same kind of fun things Donna did. It may have seemed tame and square compared to my experiences with Jane, but at the time, normal happiness was worth the normal dullness that went with it. This kind of thinking indicated that I was on the right track for gaining some real maturity. But the path would prove to be far from smooth.

My first failure was at school. I just didn't get off on the right foot. I tried to play the part of Kathy Anderson, but no one believed it, not even me. I was nervous, filled with apprehension over whether I would be able to do the work and be attractive and popular enough to fit in with the right crowd. The answers to both of my questions were painfully honest from day one.

I was too unprepared to meet the challenge of my grade level. It wasn't that I was dense, just uneducated. The studio school hadn't molded me into anything but an actress. I didn't have a clue as to the normal things a high school student was supposed to already know. So even though I wasn't a dummy, I felt that I looked like one. Rather than admit that I needed help, I simply pretended that I didn't care if I failed.

My new classmates had all grown up in the Pasadena area. I was an outsider; therefore, I had to prove myself to them. Not being a good student, I couldn't wow them with smarts. Shy, out of place, and very self-conscious, I came off as the stuck-up former star, although I didn't feel that way at all.

Just when I thought I would never connect with anyone, a nice Jewish girl, Ruth Roth, finally decided to take me under her wing. Ruth was talented, a pianist and a singer, and the eldest of two children. She was also very attractive, blessed with beautiful long black hair that hit her beneath her waist, and had big brown eyes. She knew who she was and was confident enough to show it. Vibrant, charming, and popular, she took me in, making me think I had made a very important step toward being accepted. Both Ruth and I were involved in the school's drama department.

I shared my dreams with Ruth. I told her all the little things I wanted in life, and I'm sure they must have sounded very ordinary. I had no big plans of becoming famous or rich, only of being loved and happy. I already knew that fame and money didn't buy the things I needed. One thing I did need, though, was a man of my own—someone to hold me and make me feel pretty. After viewing all the available prospects, I informed Ruth that Johnny Schutz was the man for me.

Johnny was the tall, dark, handsome football star at our school. We had biology together, and I did everything I could to get him to notice me. After several weeks, we became friends. Then, a few weeks later, he asked me out. Soon, we were going steady. I now thought I had it all.

Mother would come by and see me about once a month. A court order prevented her from coming into my father's home, so she and I would usually ride around in her car or visit at her apartment. The visits were anything but friendly, and if my life had a down note during my first six months with my father, it was that I was still seeing Mom. She was the only element that marred my vision of happiness. Even though both of us tried to get along and be nice to each other, there was just too much bitterness between us.

With the influence of Ruth, Johnny, and now several other friends, as well as the security of my home, I had begun to look and act like an all-American teenager. I was striving for the right things in life, and I was even considering buckling down at school and trying to catch up. Then a ghost from the past visited me.

It was a gloriously beautiful Saturday when my stepmother and sister attempted to get me out of the house and join them for a shopping trip. I declined, not because I didn't enjoy their company, but because I had fallen in love with Arnold Palmer, and he had a golf match on television that afternoon. Excusing myself to the living room, I sat on the couch and followed all the action, hole by hole.

My father soon joined me. I caught him up on the score, and then I told him about a great medical show that would be coming on later in the afternoon. As he listened to me talk about my interests, he couldn't have known just how much his attentiveness thrilled me. He watched golf with me, and after the medical show came on, he left the room. I was really too busy to notice his leaving or his coming back. I just suddenly realized that he was beside me on the couch, his arm around me. It felt good to have him near me, and I snuggled closer to him, causing him to hug me even tighter.

It was several minutes later when I realized that he had changed from his street clothes into a silk robe. Just after I noted that change, he took my hand in his and placed it between his legs. Suddenly a flash of heat rushed into my brain. I felt dizzy and sick, and my heart was racing at a faster pace than it ever had before. Refusing to look down, I continued to stare at the TV, and while I did, he moved my hand, using me to satisfy his sexual needs.

Inside I was going crazy. I couldn't believe that this was happening to me. I wanted to run, to hide, to lash out, but I did nothing but go along with my father's actions. Moments later, this man who had rescued me from my mother, reached out and began to play with my body. I never felt so degraded. Later, after he had been satisfied, he used his handkerchief to clean us up; then he left me alone. I continued to stare at the television, refusing to believe what had just happened, refusing to even look at the spot where Dad had just been seated, refusing to even raise my hand from where he had left it on the couch.

I had never felt so dirty. Guilt rushed through my body and rooted itself in my every member. I wished I were dead, and even as the torment intensified, I tried to ignore and forget those moments. But I couldn't. Everything that was wonderful about my father was now lying in ruins. At that moment, I wouldn't have given anyone a plugged nickel for either of my parents, and I felt as if I were worth even less.

I never told my stepmother about what happened that day. I didn't know how to approach her or what I would say. Besides, she wouldn't have believed me. No one would have except my mother, and she certainly wasn't going to help me. I was trapped. Dad repeated the act again and again over the next few months. I simply prayed that the nightmare would go away, while always hoping I could avoid being alone with him. But neither happened. With each experience, a new layer of dirt covered my soul.

My relationships with other people—the same ones that I had spent months building—began to fall apart. I was changing, and Dad's actions were the cause. I couldn't handle the guilt, and I couldn't stop him and get him to see how wrong his behavior was. I tried to bury the guilt and pain deep inside me, but I couldn't do that either.

Several months later, my stepmother left to go shopping on a Saturday, leaving Donna, Dad, and me alone. Rather than suffer the shame and humiliation of having him use me again sexually, I got together with some friends and spent the day at their houses. When the three of us got home, we walked up the driveway to the back door, only to be stopped by sounds coming through a window. Looking in through a partially open curtain, we saw Donna, nude, running from the den. A few seconds later, Dad followed her.

"I don't think we should go in right now," I said to my friends. Though they didn't reply, I could tell they agreed. We drove off, never saying another thing about what we had just witnessed.

That night, as Donna and I lay in our beds, I wondered if I should say something to her. I had a million questions, but I didn't know how to put them. Still, because it had been eating at me all day, I gave it a shot in the only way I knew how.

"Donna," I slowly began, "what you and Dad are doing is wrong."

She sat up and looked back at me. "What are you talking about?"

"You know. What you and Dad were doing today—it is wrong."

Shaking her head, she denied everything, saying, "I don't know what you're talking about."

Hitting a wall I didn't have the courage to climb, I dropped the subject, but it didn't stop bothering me. For the next several weeks, the scene of Donna and Dad, as well as the ones of me and Dad, haunted me day and night.

I now can look back and realize that I spent the next several months in a state of denial. Just like my stepsister, it was easier to pretend everything was all right, that I was happy, than it was to face what was really happening. With no one to turn to, I really didn't have a choice, and, unfortunately, most sexually abused children face the same dilemma. So, rather than allow the bad times to consume me, I tried to embrace the good, but even those moments seemed to end up tainted.

For my sixteenth birthday, my dad and stepmother gave me a "Sweet Sixteen" party. I invited all of my friends from Hollywood and the old neighborhoods, as well as Ruth and Johnny and many of my friends from Pasadena High. I tried to talk Mom into coming, but she declined, even thought she did send Billy with a gift.

Billy was the only sour part of the party. Thanks to Mom's brainwashing him, he now hated Dad as much as she did, so he didn't make much of an effort to get along with the other kids. But everyone else seemed to be having a blast.

When it came time to open the presents, Billy came alive. He proudly handed me a box, and I eagerly opened it. Inside was a beautiful, gold, heart-shaped locket with the words, "Sweet Sixteen" inscribed on its face. All of my friends loved it, and Billy seemed very pleased.

The next present I opened was from my grandmother, Gee Gee. When I pulled it out, everybody just went wild. It was an open platinum heart, surrounded by diamonds. Billy's jaw dropped. Mumbling under his breath, but loudly enough for me to hear, he said, "Just like them. They try to embarrass us and outdo us every time."

I felt badly for my brother. There was no comparison between the worth of the two gifts, but that didn't mean I didn't like his and Mother's just as much. But he couldn't see that. It had been a battle to see who could get the best gift for me, and he and Mom had lost. Within minutes, he called Mom, had her pick him up, and was gone. For awhile I felt very empty. Then, when Johnny asked me to dance with him, I got back into the partying mood. I stayed that way well after the hour of midnight and long past the time everyone had gone home.

My stepmother, sister, dad, and I cleaned up, and after that job was done, everyone except Dad and I went to bed. We stayed up, listened to old records, and talked about all the fun we had had. When the music slowed down, we even danced. The mood was perfect, and I had forgotten every bad moment that had ever found its way into my life.

Suddenly Dad began to hold me in a way that was reserved for lovers, not fathers, and I became very frightened. I knew that if I didn't break free, tonight might end with us going much further than we ever had before. Pushing him away, I raced to my bedroom, locked the door, and fell into my bed. A night that should have been my happiest ended in tears.

For the next seven-and-a-half months, I managed to stay away from my father. Only a few times did he catch me alone and force me to participate in his sexual games. When he did, I simply focused my attention on something else, refusing to acknowledge what was going on. This was my only defense.

One of the things that helped me keep him away from me some was an appendicitis attack that caused me to become very ill so I had to have an appendectomy. Of course, this also served to ruin my summer. I was actually ready for school to start again in the fall.

When the new term began, I began to date a college freshman, Bill Bowen. He offered Johnny a degree of competition, even though they were best friends and neither of them knew that I was dating the other. When they found out what I was doing and confronted me, I lost both of them. It was right after the Christmas of 1961, and I just wasn't prepared to handle the breakup. They had offered me respectability and self-worth. Without them, I felt as if I had neither.

On New Year's Eve, I was lonely and blue; going to a party was the last thing on my mind. Still, not wanting to stay home, I agreed to go to a big blow-out with a few of my wilder friends. It would be a monumental way to end a very confusing year.

The party was on the wild side, and I decided to fit in the best way I knew how. I acted like everyone else, drank and pretended to be having a good time. Everyone else may have celebrated the end of a year and the beginning of a new one, but I was just getting loaded in order to ease my pain and beef-up my self-confidence. But even in the crowd, I was still lonely.

I didn't want to spend the night without a date, and the young man who caught my eye this evening was Jerry Jones. Jerry was an insecure eighteen-year-old who had spent his life in foster homes until he had been adopted at age fourteen. He had strawberry blond hair, green eyes, and even more important than his looks, a great personality and a big, blue Mercury. Sometime after midnight, Jerry spirited me into the backseat of his car, and there we began to neck. Before long, not only did I lose my inhibitions, but also my virginity. When I realized what I had done, I cried, and he held me. He told me that it was all right and that he thought I was wonderful. His words helped, but what helped even more was that he could have hit and run, but he didn't. The next day he came calling again.

For the next two months, I saw Jerry every day. I continued to see him partly out of spite, partly because I wanted to make Johnny jealous, and partly because I felt that, when I slept with him, he bought me with the act. As time passed, he taught me a great deal about my sexuality, and this was much more satisfying and gratifying than what was happening at home with Dad, so I continued to let him have his way.

By now, I had blown off school, skipping almost every day after first period. I knew when my residual check would come to the house, so I would meet the mailman, get the check, and cash it. With this money, Jerry and I would go out and have a good time, then go back to his house (his parents both worked), learn more about each other, and I would listen to him tell me that he loved me. His words made me feel good and gave me a sense of value. Still, deep down, I knew that Jerry was nothing more than an escape from my own miserable home life.

During the course of getting to know Jerry, I discovered that he actually didn't even care about the money I spent in order to buy food and fun. He was satisfied with just me. Because of this devotion, I began to tell him things that I had never told anyone else, including the things that my father had done to me. I thought that this might drive him away from me, but, surprisingly, he responded to my confession by offering to marry me and take me away from my pain. Even though I had known him less than two months, I jumped at the chance. I didn't care how little he could offer me. I knew it had to be better than what I had with either my mother or father.

I knew that Dad wouldn't allow me to get married, so Jerry and I were left with only one option: we had to run away. We took some of my money, bought two wedding rings, and then, when no one was home, packed our things. We left for Los Angeles without even leaving a note.

Once in L.A., we stopped at Sheri's house. She was already married, and she had a year-old baby named Scott. She listened to our story, thought we had every right in the world to get married, and offered to let us crash at her place. For the next few days, Jerry, Sheri, her husband David, and I all had a blast. Unfortunately, the nagging question of how to get my dad's permission hung over us like a black cloud. Finally, I simply decided to call and tell him what I needed for him to do. When he answered the phone, I almost hung up.

"Daddy?"

"Lauren, where are you?"

"Daddy, I've run away to get married."

"Like———! You'll never get my permission to do such a stupid thing. Now where are you?"

"Daddy," I began again. But deciding it was no use, said goodbye. Shrugging my shoulders, I now knew the only way out was to get Mom's permission. I called her and explained my situation and what I was doing. I tried to keep my manner and tone upbeat so that she would think I was being mature and positive. She listened for awhile, didn't get mad, and even invited us to visit her for the weekend. I agreed, praying that my problems were over.

Both of my brothers were at Mom's, and for the next three days all of them tried to talk us out of going through with our plans. Michael tried again and again to convince me that I was too young and that Jerry and I would have no way of supporting ourselves. But even he couldn't make me see what must have been painfully clear to everyone else—that this was stupid!

Finally, with the weekend nearing an end, I begged Mom to call Dad. She did, and she talked to him for quite a while, and then repeated what he had said. "She has to come back here, see me face to face, and then maybe she'll get my permission."

Jerry and I drove back to Pasadena, sat in a room with Dad and my stepmother, and listened to him rave for what seemed like hours. He was livid, and he told Jerry that he was going to have him arrested for statutory rape. I could see Jerry shaking, his own anger about to surface, and I just knew that he was going to hit Dad with all the things he knew that he had done to me. I didn't want this scene, not now anyway, so I grabbed Jerry's leg, making it clear that we just needed to be quiet and wait it out.

Finally, after Dad had repeated his threats time and time again, he gave us an ultimatum. He would give his permission for us to get married, if we did it in the next twenty-four hours. If, after that time, we weren't hitched, he was going to file the rape charge.

I jumped up and screamed, "That's not fair!"

"Take it or leave it," Dad yelled back. With no choice, we took it.

Jumping in the car, we returned to L.A.; there we found out we'd have to drive to Yuma, Arizona, in order to get married without a wait. We tried to get Sheri and David to come with us, but with the baby and David's work, they couldn't. Sheri did help me find a white dress to wear.

Jerry and I drove most of the night in order to get to Yuma. After we arrived, we spent the last few hours of darkness sleeping in the car. When we woke, we found a service station, changed clothes, and then drove to the Justice of the Peace's office.

The J.P. was an old man with gray hair. His wrinkled clothes and missing front teeth gave him an unkempt appearance. He also spit on us every time he tried to say anything. Despite the fact that I was scared to death, this old man brought a bit of humor to Jerry's and my plight. In retrospect, it was probably just the touch our marriage needed—a strange beginning to signal what was a strange future. Anyway, sometime in the very early morning of February 18, 1962, I became Mrs. Gerald Jones.

Jerry and I set up housekeeping in a tiny little apartment in L.A. It was all we could afford. I certainly didn't have any money beyond the small amount I was now getting off of the residuals from "Father Knows Best," and Jerry, with his job as a mechanic, wasn't making big dollars either. We were simply learning how to struggle and fight to get by. On the other hand, financially we were better off than most married kids our age. But from the maturity standpoint, a much different situation existed.

With Jerry working at a gas station in another part of town, he needed his car to get to his job; thus, I was usually stuck in the apartment all day long. I got bored being cooped up, and with no friends around, I began to go stir crazy. I tried to meet some people in our complex, and finally found a young woman who was just as lonely as I was. We weren't destined to become close, but she did turn me on to something new: speed. She was using it to lose weight, and she convinced me to try it. This was the start of a drug problem that would build over the next few years.

After a few weeks of loneliness, compounded by the realization that I knew nothing about being a wife, I began to have troubles with Jerry. I couldn't cook and I couldn't sew. I was a domestic flop. For some reason, possibly dating back to my father's abuse, I was now having problems making love in bed. I was becoming frigid, which placed one more burden on our marital union. About the time I figured something else bad would happen, I received some good news.

I called Jane Wyatt and caught her up on my life. When she found out that I had gotten married, she wanted to know why she hadn't been invited to the wedding. After discovering that it had been a spur-of-the-moment ceremony and that we had been given no reception, she decided that we needed some help. She set up a shower and a wedding party. For Jerry and me it would give us an opportunity to get some of the many everyday items we needed, while also announcing our union to the world.

Jane attempted to get my mother to help her with the event, but Mom refused. So Jane did it by herself. She ordered the invitations, addressed and mailed them, and then called former cast and crew members to make sure that they would be there. At the time, I thought that this was the kindest thing that anyone had ever done for me. Even now, it still ranks near the top of that list.

The party Jane tossed was gala and fun. My childhood friends, as well as many of the folks from Columbia came, and the bounty that they brought more than filled Jerry's and my small apartment. Suddenly, even thought I was still an insecure wife, and even though I knew that I didn't really love my husband, I felt strangely content. I believed that I could live with my lot. Jerry was a good guy, and not being at either of my parents' houses had removed a great deal of the pressure that had made me so confused and unhappy. When, a few days after the party, I found out that I was pregnant, I thought that heaven had come down and finally entered my world. I was now assured that my life was coming together.

Somewhere I should have stopped to realize that there was more to life than burning toast and making babies. It all seemed so simple and wonderful. And everyone said that I was so good at being a wife and that I looked so happy. I even began to believe that I had written one of those real life happily-ever-after scripts for myself. But it was my mother, or rather her attorney, who brought me down to earth.

He called and informed me that there was a suit being brought against me by my mother. She was asking the courts to award her all of my residual monies, both now and in the future. The attorney further informed me that my mother was near death's door and that, if I fought this case, it would surely kill her.

Now that I was carrying a baby, life had suddenly become very sweet to me. The bitterness and hurt had all but been forgotten. The fact that my mother, even though she was a woman with whom I had never gotten along and who had made me miserable, was now very ill and desperately in need of help awakened a new loving and forgiving spirit in me. As soon as her lawyer had finished talking to me, I called her.

"Mom," I began, "I didn't know that you were so sick. I'll be happy to help you out if I can." I never got any farther than those opening remarks. Mother began a verbal assault that lasted for at least five minutes, calling me every name in the book and informing me that I was what was killing her, not some disease. It was my cruelty and neglect that had led her to death's door. I could tell by her words and tone that she was drunk. It also hit me that she must have been very close to being broke too. She sounded desperate, and getting the courts involved seemed to echo this thought.

It was so ironic. If she had just acted as if she loved me, I would have handed over all of my residual money. I had called with that in mind. All I wanted was to hear her say that she loved me. But instead, she told me how hateful and terrible I was and said there was no hope for someone like me. Her vicious assault led me to vow to fight her with everything I had.

As we screamed at each other, she informed me that she had gotten an injunction cutting off all of my residual money until the case was settled. Yelling at the top of her lungs, she announced, "I've had to raise you, and I gave you everything. It was *me* who did all the work. *I* took you to the studio, rehearsed your lines, and took you on the publicity tours. *I* earned that money, not you."

"But Mom," I argued, "what about me? I'm the one who went to work every morning. I'm the one who was at the studio at six in the morning. I'm the one who didn't get off until six at night. It was me who was on television—not you. That's *my* money."

"Lauren, you always were selfish," she shot back. "If it wasn't for me, you wouldn't have been in show business. *I* earned that money."

Back and forth we went, round after round. By now tears of anger and pain were streaming down my face, clouding my thoughts. I shot back at her, pleading now that I realized I wouldn't be getting any more checks. "But Mom, I'm pregnant, and I have to have that money to put aside for the baby. I can't get by without it. Jerry just doesn't make enough to support all of us. You can't cut it all off. You can't take it from me."

She must have been shocked, because she didn't say anything for a moment, then after my "news" sank in, she cruelly replied: "Lauren, I pray that you *never have* children. I pray that it dies, and I pray that you never have children because all they do is stab you in the back!" Then, satisfied, she slammed the phone down.

For several moments I hung onto the line, hearing only the

mournful sound of a dial tone. For the first time I was worried about my baby.

Talking to Mom had put me back on an emotional roller coaster. For a few weeks my life had been so easy and sweet. I had been almost normal. I hadn't known real pain or hate. Now, by simply calling my mother, all the pain of my old nightmarish life came back. After I cried for what seemed like hours, I began to figure out how Jerry and I were going to make it on his salary. When I realized that we couldn't, all my anger was replaced with panic and fear. My hands were cold and my mind numb. There was no one to whom I could turn. My bridges were all burned.

For two weeks I agonized, and in those two weeks our bank account went to nothing. Suddenly we had bills and no money, and we both knew that, from here on in, it would just be getting worse. Mother simply wouldn't listen, and she seemed pleased that I was suffering and scared. In her mind, I was learning a lesson. In my mind, she was stealing my money.

One afternoon I escaped my loneliness and fears by spending the afternoon playing cards with Sheri. As I played, I began to experience cramps in my stomach. I thought that it was gas, but the longer it lasted, the more Sheri began to believe it might be something far more serious.

"Lauren," she softly said, "are you sure it's just gas?"

"Yes," I would assure her.

"I think you may be miscarrying the baby," she interjected. I could tell by the way she had spoken the words that the thought had scared her, but I couldn't believe that she would even suggest such a terrible thing.

"No," I responded. "It is just gas."

As the day went on, the cramps became worse, and by the time I got home, they had become severe. I fell on my bed, shaking, trying to hold my stomach, praying the pain would subside, but it only became more intense. I called Sheri, and she rushed over. By the time she got to me, I had the chills.

Sheri got hold of Jerry by phone, and within a half hour, he was at my side. The two of them held me, all of us crying, as

I lost the baby. I was bleeding badly, and my heart was breaking. In a room with nothing except a bed, surrounded by blank walls, I lost what I thought was my best reason for living. Mother's prayer seemed to have worked.

Three months later I got pregnant again, but I lost this one even sooner than I had the first one. Over the next two years, I would miscarry seven more times, and with each occurrence, I was more sure that Mom had caused it. After each of the miscarriages, I would go to the doctor, and he would put me on thyroid tablets and dexadrene. Rather than taking the pills at the prescribed rate, I began taking more and more each day. They gave me a surge of energy, and they numbed my mind, causing me to forget all my emotions and heartache.

During this time, we finally bought another car, a '58 Impala. Sheri and David had a '57 Chevy, and the four of us would cruise L.A. looking for drag races. I loved the speed and the excitement. I loved it so much that Sheri and I would often lose the men and go out cruising on our own. Neither of us wanted to be married, and both of us wanted another taste of freedom. Dragging good-looking men gave us a new kind of high. But for me, it wasn't enough.

Rather than stay by myself at our apartment, I began to hang around with people who seemed to be hurting just as badly as I was. These people eased their pain with alcohol, and I began to make the rounds to bars and liquor stores, looking for folks who wanted to share misery. I never had any trouble finding them.

By now so many things had caused me to lose my self-esteem that Jerry and I often ended up in big fights over my condition. Rather than shape up, I would storm out, often going on a drinking binge that would last weeks. I would usually saddle up with an alcoholic partner and use both uppers and liquor to easy my pain. There were many days when I would be walking and talking, but I wouldn't remember anything. I was dragging bottom, blacking out, and becoming further removed from the few people left who cared for me.

For nine months, this routine continued. I would go out,

beg, lie, and cheat to drink. The days and nights began to blend together as the alcohol began to numb every facet of my system. Food no longer had much of a taste, and pride was completely forgotten. I was running away from all my problems by simply trying a very slow method of suicide. At the time, it seemed painless. Always when I was in danger of slipping over the edge and doing something that would kill me, Jerry would find me and take me home. I would then dry out and run away again.

For months I kept running, and Jerry kept searching. Then one day, after I had been on a drunk for over a week, he gave up. He didn't come looking for me. And in a strange bed, with people I didn't even know, even in the dark recesses of my foggy brain, I began to realize that the last person who had any belief that I was worth saving had given up. But somehow, as I reached for another drink, even this didn't matter anymore.

• *Seven* •

FOR A WHILE I lived on the streets, surviving in any manner
I could, before finally sucking up my pride and contacting
Mom. It was not an easy thing for me to do, but I was out of
money and places to stay. I was alone, and she was all there
was left. Surprisingly, she took me in without giving me much
trouble or delivering too many lectures.

She was still drinking, but not as much. She had recently
been in the hospital for additional treatments for her T.B., and
because she had cut back on her alcohol intake, she was much
more enjoyable to be around. Still, our inborn Irish stubborn
wills and pride kept getting in the way of our working out a
long-term relationship. I wanted to live in a totally rule-free
world, and she wanted to control me with a multitude of laws
and regulations. Neither of us could find a point of compro-
mise; so we battled.

As is the case with most people who taste freedom, I had
used my time away from home to become even more sensitive
and rebellious toward any authority figures. Because of my
perception of my mother as a homebound policewoman—

laying down the law, morning, noon and night—I quickly grew tired of hanging around the house. But I couldn't go anywhere else simply because I didn't have any money. This is when I became aware of over $18,000 that was sitting in a trust fund waiting for me to become an adult. I knew that if I could get that money, I could stretch my wings in style.

Checking with an attorney, I was informed that what I needed to do was have the courts declare me an emancipated minor. He didn't seem to believe that this would be much of a problem. After all, I was seventeen, had been married, had lived on my own for about one year, and certainly didn't act my age. Within weeks, the courts ruled in my favor. I was declared an official adult and was handed the total of my trust in a number of bonds. Suddenly, I had $18,970 that was burning a hole in my pocket and creating illusions of grandeur in my head.

Looking at the bonds, I was overwhelmed. I had never seen this much money in one place. I knew that there was only one thing to do with this kind of cash—party! I called my best friend Sheri, who by now had two children, had gotten a divorce, and was living with her mother.

"Sheri, it's Lauren. I'm in downtown L.A. at the courthouse, and I'm going to take a bus over to your place. Are you going to be home for a while?"

"Yeah," she answered. "What's going on?"

"I don't want to tell you on the phone," I answered, with an obvious enthusiasm exuding through my tone of voice. "I'll tell you when I see you. By the way, while you're waiting, pack a few bags and get ready for the vacation of your life!"

Before I caught the bus, I ran across the street to a drugstore and got a map of the United States. I studied it as I rode across town to Sheri's. As the names of the cities and states fell across the page, my mind soared with the thoughts of getting to visit all of those places. I couldn't wait for my adventure to begin, and I surely wasn't going to place any limits on the trip. I wanted to travel and have fun until the cash ran out.

I got off the bus at Olympic Avenue and practically ran the

couple of blocks to Victoria Avenue and Sheri's. By the time I got there, I was breathing hard from both the expended physical effort and my excitement. Stopping in front of the large, white, two-story colonial house, I clutched my money to my chest and sighed, "This is going to really impress Sheri. She and I are going to have a blast. And we deserve it!" Then I ran to the front door.

Sheri responded to my knock within seconds.

"Come on," I stammered. "Get out here; I've got something to show you."

Like two little girls, we sat on the front porch steps. Pulling out my map, I opened it up and announced, "I've just come into a bundle of money, and I want to take you on the best vacation you've ever had. I know that you've never gone anywhere, and now is your chance. Pick out a place, and let's go!"

"You're kidding," she replied. Her face told me that she didn't believe I could deliver on my promise.

"No," I assured her, "I'm not. I've got the money. You just point your finger to a place on the map, and we'll take off. It is as simple as that."

"Let's do it together," she said.

Nodding my head, I grabbed her hand, and closing our eyes, we circled the map for just a moment, then let our fingers fall to a random spot. As soon as we hit, we opened our eyes and stared at our destination.

"Palm Springs!" Sheri screamed.

"Yeah," I smiled. "That place is full of rich people. We'll fit right in. Here we go, Sheri! We are on our way to the big time!"

"Yeah, but how are we going to get me out of here?" Sheri asked. "I've got a couple of kids, and Mom isn't just going to let me leave."

"We'll worry about that later. First let's go downtown and get a car."

"You don't even have a license," Sheri grinned.

"Yeah, well, I'll get one of those too. Come on, let's go."

After telling her mother that Sheri and I were going downtown for a little while, we caught a bus back to Hollywood. After cashing in one of the bonds, we began to look for a car dealer. As luck would have it, A. E. England Pontiac was directly in our line of vision.

Pointing to the dealership, I grinned and said, "Watch this."

For a while we just looked over the cars in the lot, then, feeling more bold, we strolled through the showroom. The expressions on the salesmen's faces showed that they were not impressed with us. With our blue jeans, sandals, and casual blouses, coupled with the fact that my size and ponytail made me look fourteen, I was sure that they thought we were a couple of kids playing hookey from school. None of them hurried over to see if they could help us.

After a short time spent just looking, a midnight blue 1963 Grand Prix caught my eye.

"Come on, Sheri," I said as I spotted the car. "I've found one I like."

When we got to it, I opened the door and looked inside. To me it looked like the fanciest piece of machinery in the world. It had a leather interior and wood-covered accessories. Everything about it shouted class. This would be the ultimate vehicle in which to cruise.

"Sheri, wake me if I'm dreaming, but this is our car!"

"Yeah," she agreed, "I can see us in this one."

Across the room, the salesmen had taken all they could. One of them broke from the pack and crossed the showroom. He walked directly up to us and said, "Excuse me, would you mind not putting your fingers all over the car?"

"Oh, excuse me," I said as I smiled sweetly, "I didn't mean to be doing anything wrong. By the way, how much does it cost, and what kind is it?"

"It is a Pontiac Grand Prix, our *top-of-the-line* model, and it is very expensive."

"I want to buy it," I grinned.

Looking at me as if he thought I was a mental case, he

impatiently replied, "A car like this costs a great deal of money. I'm afraid that you couldn't afford it."

At that point I went over to the sticker, looked at the bottom line, smiled back at the man, and said, "I'll take it." Then before he could respond, I opened my purse and took out my wallet, slowly flashing my wad of hundred dollar bills. His jaw dropped almost to the floor, and then, knowing that this was going to be the easiest sale of his life, immediately began to get his paperwork together. As he completed the papers, he asked me for my car license number.

"I don't have a license."

"You don't have one?" he questioned. From the tone of his voice, I could tell that he was shocked. Who wouldn't be! After all, I had just dropped several thousand dollars for a car, and I had no way to drive it home. It didn't make a bit of sense.

"No," I admitted, "but I'm about to get one. My friend here has one, and she will drive it until I pass my test. She will drive it off the lot for me, if that is what you want."

Nodding his head, he handed me the title, and Sheri took the keys and fired up the blue beauty. As soon as she had driven off the lot and around the corner, I stopped her.

"Okay, move over. This is *my* car, and *I'm* going to drive it."

"Sure, but you've got to go and take your test right now."

As I slid behind the wheel, I nodded in agreement. A little more than an hour later, I had the license to go with the car.

"Well, that's done," I announced as we got back in. "What do we do now?"

"To Palm Springs!" Sheri exclaimed.

"Not yet," I answered. "We're not dressed for it. First, we have to get some clothes."

Driving through Hollywood, we glanced into every shop window, but we kept moving until we arrived at Frederick's of Hollywood. We loved the flashy clothes that they had displayed in their window. Walking in, we spent the next several hours trying on everything they had. By the time we returned to the car, both of us had complete wardrobes: furs, evening dresses, pants, tops, jewelry, and underwear. With our Pontiac and our threads, we were set for some high styling. We thought we were two really hip knockouts.

Driving back to Sheri's, we cornered her mother, and didn't really ask as much as tell her that we were leaving. We didn't even tell her where we were going or how long we would be gone. With our car radio blaring "Yakety Yak, Don't Talk Back," we just drove away.

In my whole life, I had never gone anywhere, unless you count a couple of east coast promotional trips for "Father Knows Best." This trip was an adventure like no other. It was as good as going to Europe or Africa because, everywhere I looked, I was seeing things that I had never seen before. Despite so many "experiences," thanks to fast living and acting, I was really innocent in many ways. And this innocence showed in my eyes: they grew bigger and bigger as the journey continued.

Palm Springs looked like the magical world of Disney to me. There were palaces everywhere. For hours Sheri and I just drove around, looking, laughing, and sighing. We both thought we could live in this paradise forever. We never saw a time when the party would end.

At three in the morning, we finally tired of driving around and stopped at a Sambo's for a bite to eat. The restaurant was filled with smoke, and in the dim light we let our eyes wander, trying to see the crowd. We soon discovered that we were the only ones dressed in evening gowns and furs; the rest of the patrons were much more casual.

In a booth just behind us, preppy-looking kids were telling jokes and passing time. At the counter, a cowboy type— mature looking but still young—studied us for a while, then announced, "Hey, I know who you are. You're Lauren Chapin, the actress from 'Father Knows Best.' I'll bet you're a stuck-up little brat!"

I glared back at him, and then in a voice that must have confirmed his observation, answered, "Wouldn't you like to know!"

"Yeah, I would," he shot back.

"Well, you'll never find out," I replied, all the time hoping that he would try. I judged him to be around six-feet two-inches tall and weighing around 190 pounds. He had sandy brown hair, deep brown eyes, and movie-star good looks that had my heart pounding. But because we had started out on such hostile ground, I didn't think I had much of a chance to land him. As the hours passed, however, the walls between us broke down, and by dawn I knew that this man was going to be my Prince of Palm Springs.

His name was Lawrence Alexander Westby III, but everyone called him Kiko. He was from a wealthy family, and he was almost two years younger than me. His confident air and macho manner indicated that he felt very comfortable with who he was. There was no doubt in either his or my mind that he could have me anytime he wanted. For some reason, I didn't mind that he seemed in control.

After talking and flirting for hours, I noted the sun rising over the desert and inquired, "Where's the best place to stay?"

"What do you want?" he asked.

"Just a hotel with a suite. Someplace nice. I don't really care what it costs."

"Okay then," Kiko smiled, "why don't you go to the Riviera. It's just around the corner."

Thanking him, I told him he could look us up there if he wanted to. I could tell by the gleam in his eye that he would.

It was seven in the morning when Sheri and I walked into the hotel. We took a suite that had two bedrooms and a connecting room for entertaining guests. Everything in the room had been done in pink, and the windows overlooked the pool. Upon seeing it, I felt as good about it as I had my Pontiac. I knew that this was real class. For several months, this was our home base.

Over the next half year, I spent money like there was no tomorrow. I gave handouts to anyone who had a sad story. I gave away clothes and meals. I bought Sheri anything she desired, and I bought myself two more cars. The first was a white Corvette with red interior. The second was a 1963 Ford Fairlane with a fiberglass body, a 427 racing engine, and a 1600-pound clutch. It was an experimental car—one of only three in the world. It was set up to race, and soon I was speeding up and down the highway between Palm Springs and L.A., looking for people to drag.

By my third month in the desert, I was leading a double life. In Palm Springs, I was a rich playgirl, hooked on drag racing and partying. I was innocent and yet fun-loving. I was just a kid who hadn't grown up. But in L.A., I was totally different. There my friends were speed freaks, and I was using the drug to keep me awake so that I could party in both places. As the weeks rolled on, I developed a dependency on bennies.

Life was a dream for seven months. It took that long for the money to run out. When it did, Sheri left me and moved in with a guy she had been seeing. Forced out of my suite, I moved in with Kiko, worked in a dress shop, and learned to get by with one car, having sold the Corvette and the Grand Prix to get money. I was very lonely. All the people I had given money to had dropped me even more quickly than Sheri had. Just as suddenly as I had gotten rich, I had lost everything, including all my friends.

Kiko's mother finally got tired of me too. I was forced to move into a tiny apartment. Within days, I was suffering a claustrophobic fit. I felt like the walls were caving in on me, and I also felt like I needed more bennies. Depressed as I had never been before, I even began to question what use there was in going on with my life. I had become paranoid, thinking that everyone was out to get me or use me. I closed up so tightly that I didn't share my pain with anyone.

In Palm Springs, without money or a job, I couldn't fit in. So I jumped in the Ford and headed back toward Los Angeles. In a bar just south of town, I met a woman and her daughter, who, over several drinks, listened to my story. They offered me a chance to stay with them, and I took it. I was nineteen, alone, broke, a victim of several types of abuse, and I was still following other people around like a trusting little puppy.

The woman, her daughter, and I continued to build our relationship on the bottle. We didn't drink just a little; we drank a lot. We would stay drunk for weeks. In one of my drunken fits, I must have called Mom and told her where I was, because one night when I was blitzed, Jerry showed up, packed my belongings, and moved me back to L.A., but not with him. This time, he left me all by myself. Soon after that, in August 1965, we divorced.

I hated being alone. I probably hated it because I didn't like myself, and certainly there wasn't much to like. I was on my way to becoming a drunk, I had ruined a marriage, I was barren, completely unskilled, and flat broke. When I looked in the mirror, I saw an immature adolescent. I weighed about ninety pounds and had a young teenager's body that still housed the mentality of a sixteen-year-old. It was a picture I didn't want to see; I seldom confronted reality.

Rather than spend time in my apartment getting to know myself, I hit the streets, driving fast and trying to impress guys. There were a bunch of racers who hung out at a gas station just around the corner from where my mother lived, and whenever I would drive that way, I would take special pains to rev the engine to the maximum just to catch their attention. Over the weeks, I began to stop there to get gas and talk to the guys. One, Mike Richenberg, a stocky, plain-looking young man with a quick smile and gentle touch, won me over in a very special way. He became my friend. He was a rare person who didn't seem to want to use me for anything; he was satisfied just to talk.

One night he convinced me to come home with him and meet his mother and two sisters. I fell in love with all of them just as quickly as I had Mike. They were not the kind of family that the Andersons had supposedly been, but they loved each other and openly expressed concern and trust. If there was anything negative about the Richenbergs, it was the fact that they all drank heavily. While this alcohol-dominated atmosphere was probably not the place I needed to be, when they asked me to move in with them, I jumped at the chance. I wanted to be a part of a family. I needed them.

Everybody called Mike's mother "Mom," and so did I. A big, burly woman, she had a deep voice, probably caused by years of heavy smoking. Free with her hugs, Mom was the first woman who ever tried to bond with me. She even began to read me like a book within a week. She could see all my pain and emptiness; as if I had been a mistreated stray dog, she reached out to me with genuine love. She also tried to advise me.

"Lauren," she said repeatedly, "I just don't know how you've survived nineteen years with your attitude. You have absolutely no street smarts. You have no concept of common sense. Anyone could take advantage of you."

She was right. I had never been taught the right things while I was growing up. I had only been taught to follow a script. If I didn't have one, there was no telling what I would do. I had no self-discipline, and I couldn't really function when forced to make decisions. I was constantly being taken advantage of.

One of the first things "Mom" did to get me situated in the real world was help me land a job. If I was going to live with them, I was going to have to pull my own weight. Lauren Chapin, former actress, became a car hop. Ironically, I still was doing everything backwards even in this normal world. After all, this was the type of job that many actresses first got in L.A. on their way up, not their way down.

I worked the night shift, and I did a good job. I made good tips and had a solid reputation as a hard worker. But I didn't live to work, I lived to get off work. When my shift ended just after midnight, I would meet Mike and, with a bottle in hand and some "whites" in our pockets, we would get Mom, who was a waitress at a bar and sometimes its acting manager; we would grab some breakfast and head back to the apartment to sleep it off.

I was happy. I felt as if someone loved me and that I belonged somewhere. These people didn't introduce me as "Lauren, you know the girl who played Kathy on television"; they simply embraced me as me. It was wonderful being accepted and not used. What more could I want? In my mind, the drinking and pill-popping were just part of normal living. They certainly were nothing to worry about.

Yet each day, my habit got worse. It was taking a little more drugs for me to function. Mom would always get us up at eight in the morning for chores, and the only way I could help Mike's two sisters clean house was to take pills to get me going. The pills became morale builders too. Whenever I felt insecure or unable to do something, I would take them and get a sudden euphoric rush that convinced me I was indestructible. This led to my taking so many "bennies" that I was flying all day long. I had so much energy that I just didn't know what to do with it.

High on speed, I would often spend my days walking the streets, sometimes looking around at people, other times window shopping. My walks usually took me past the neighborhood barbershop. From the outside, it looked like just any other hair-cutting joint, but what made it stand out was the barber himself.

His name was Eddie Valentine, but it would be several weeks before I found that out. All I knew at this time was that he stared at me every time I passed his window. I could feel his eyes on my back as I walked by, and when I would steal a glance, I could see that he was enjoying what he was seeing.

Over the course of time, he would see me coming, stop what he was doing, and walk to his door. There, with his arms folded, one shoulder against the doorway and his legs crossed at the ankles, he would stare at me, smile, and then whistle. When he did this, I would look back, flirting with my eyes, while studying the man. I watched him, noting his smile, his mass of dark hair, and his handsome face. It was obvious by the way he dressed that he knew he was good-looking. A mesh shirt barely covered his hairy chest, and he wore the tightest pants that I had ever seen. His dark eyes shimmered with life, and his confidence made him appear much taller than his five-foot, five-and-a-half-inch height. He had to have been nearly forty, but the way he moved made him seem much younger. He just exuded sex, and he flaunted it in such a way as to make me curious and excited.

For almost a month, our little game went on with no rules and with very little interaction. He was like the cat who wanted to play with the mouse, and I was the rodent who couldn't resist seeing just how close I could get to the feline without being caught. For me it was a great way to work off the effects of speed. So every morning after finishing my chores, I would put on a pair of clean jeans, a blouse or sweater, never a bra, and a pair of sandals. Then I would stroll past the shop, enjoying his attention. Each day was even more thrilling than the day before. It was innocent, harmless fun. Then one day, Eddie changed the rules—he spoke.

"Well, here comes the Barefoot Contessa." His voice was sly, and his tone almost made me feel like a little girl.

Turning my head to the side, I shook it slightly, then stopping, shyly smiled and tried to say hello without having my voice crack. It didn't work.

Knowing he had me right where he wanted me, he grinned, ignored my nervous, squeaky greeting, and asked, "Don't you ever wear real shoes?"

Even as I shook my head in response to his question, I knew that I was out of my league. I didn't realize it then, and even if I had, I wouldn't have admitted it, but he was holding my will in the palm of his hand. Although nothing had happened, I was already his victim.

"You know, little lady," he continued as I stood there, "the way you so proudly hold your head high and the way you walk remind me of royalty."

Smiling, and feeling better about myself than I had in a long time, I turned and quickly walked off. As soon as I rounded the corner, a huge grin crossed my face; another was written across my soul. I had bought his compliment and his tone, and I knew as well as he did that I would be back. The hook had been baited, and I was ready to bite.

That night I told Mike and Mom about the meeting with

Eddie. As I stood at the sink and washed dishes, I said, "Guess what? I met the barber today, and he seems pretty nice."

Shaking her head, Mom got a serious look, then solemnly answered, "Yes, his name is Eddie Valentine, but it might as well be Satan. He is nothing but trouble, Lauren, and if I catch you with him, out you go. That guy is bad news. Stay away from him."

I couldn't believe what she had just said. I couldn't understand how and why she felt this way. I grinned and kidded her, "Oh, he can't be all that bad. I've never seen him do anything wrong."

"I mean it, Lauren," she sternly replied. "Stay away from him. Hear me well. Don't you even talk to him. He is the devil. You hear me? He is the devil!"

Being the kind of person I was, I saw Mom's words as a challenge. I now knew that I had to prove her wrong. She had actually given me an open invitation to reach out and live an adventure. With the speed I was taking, I thought I could conquer anything, and this barber didn't seem so big or so bad. I knew that I could see him, have fun, build my ego, and she and Mike would never find out. Even as she warned me, I made plans to go back to the barbershop.

I didn't walk by Eddie's place the next day, but two days later I did. I just couldn't stay away. It was like having to have just one more drink. When I passed the shop, he was waiting for me. He flirted, and then he invited me in, but I wouldn't go. I knew that once I got inside I would lose any control that I had. On the other hand, even though I was scared by it, the offer did seem appealing, and I thought about it often as I worked that evening.

For the next few days, I walked by, stopped, flirted, and talked, but I didn't go in. Finally, after a week of these little games, the barber jumped out of the shop and almost pounced on me. In a voice filled more with rage than smooth flirting, he blurted out, "You are not going to do this to me anymore. You are either going to come in the shop, or you're going to quit walking by. It has got to be one or the other. Come in or get out."

He had shocked me. I was simply not prepared for him to demand something like this. I thought that I could keep the game on a simple level. I didn't believe that he would force it to go any further. I was not ready for step two, but I couldn't walk away from it either. Pausing for a moment, I checked to see if Mom or anyone who might know her was on the streets. Then looking back into Eddie's dark eyes, I eased cautiously through the door of the barbershop. Behind me, he closed and locked the door and pulled the blinds shut. He and I were alone.

Grabbing me, he pinned me against the chair and kissed me. I pushed him away and said breathlessly, "I've got to go." He kissed me again. The look written on my face and in my eyes must have told him that I was scared to death, almost in a state of panic. I was even shaking like a leaf.

Turning from me, he walked back to the door, unlocked it, opened it, and watched as I rushed out. "You'll be back," he confidently yelled as I hurried up the street. I tried to ignore his words and deny what I felt, but deep inside I knew that he was right.

• Eight •

SEVERAL WEEKS LATER, having given in to the demon of curiosity once more, I entered the barbershop. Looking to my left was a mirrored wall and four barber chairs. On my right was a couch, a table, and another chair. At the room's rear was a folding bamboo, room divider.

"Sit down, Lauren," Eddie said as I walked in. Going over to the couch, I politely did as he requested.

Eddie walked behind the divider, then after lingering there for a few moments, returned carrying a tray. On the tray sat an ice bucket—a bottle of champagne chilling in it—a single long-stemmed red rose, and two delicate glasses. Setting the tray down on a table, he then went to the front door, closed and locked it, shut the blinds, and returned to a seat beside me.

"So, tell me, my dear, pretty Contessa, what do you do? I see you don't work in the daytime. I see that you like to go barefoot and wear tight jeans. I can clearly see that you don't wear a bra, which, by the way, looks very inviting on you. You do like that, don't you? Turning me on the way you do— watching me get excited. I mean, you have to know just how much you turn me on. You like that kind of control, don't you?"

As he spoke, my face became flushed. He was so bold and direct, and he knew my games even better than I did. This made me very nervous, even though I tried not to show it. I attempted a small laugh and replied, "Oh, come on, now. Just what do you mean?"

"You know what I mean," Eddie replied, his tone soft but assertive. "You're a very smart operator. You're always in control, and you know it."

The fact was, I was not only rarely in control, I was not even close to being in control now. But I was buying what he was selling, and I was beginning to believe that he was right; I was the one calling the shots, and he was the one falling all over me. Feeling confident, I lobbed the ball back to his side of the court.

"Well, Mr. Valentine, what about you? You stand in your door with your body displayed, looking at all the world like the big bad wolf ready to pounce at any moment. What's your game?" Smiling, I looked back into his dark eyes and waited to see if he could respond to what I thought had been a great comeback.

He did, and he continued with insightful responses every time I said anything. Yet, in the middle of all of this, he still made sure that I felt I was in control. As the afternoon wore on, we sipped champagne, and our conversation turned to things much more personal. I found out that he had come from a wealthy home and was an only child. He felt as though his parents had rejected him, and he was seeing a psychiatrist in an effort to cope with this feeling of not being wanted. As he spun his tale, I became convinced that we were much alike.

"I sure know where you are coming from," I said as he finished.

"So, you must be as lonely as I am. It's nice to meet someone who feels that way. It's nice to know I'm not alone."

I couldn't believe just how easy it was for him to talk so freely about his problems. Sipping from my glass, I complimented him: "I do wish I could be as open with my past as you are. I wish I could learn to release more of the bad."

"You can," he smiled. "I can teach you how. I can teach you a lot of things. All you have to do is let me." He then leaned over and kissed me. The kiss was long, tender, and sensuous. It made my heart jump and a lump rise in my throat. Pulling me closer, he pressed his lips more firmly against mine and worked his hand up under my sweater. I halfheartedly tried to pull away, but he held me in check, and then pushed my sweater over my shoulders.

He fondled me for a few minutes; then, when I remembered his speech about how I was in control, I pushed him away, pulled down my sweater, and walked quickly to the door. Unlocking it, I turned to him and said, "I have to go now. Thanks for the drinks." I then left. But I wasn't gone very long. The next day, I came back. Nothing new happened then or the next time. But on my third return visit, Eddie changed my life.

Once again the visit began with his closing and locking the door and pulling the blinds. But then his routine changed. As we sat there in the dark, he lit a joint and shared it with me. As I slowly got high, I felt myself losing control, and I could tell Eddie knew that I was. Kissing me, he thrilled me until, almost before I knew it, I discovered he had undressed me. Within moments, with no protest from me, we were having sex.

The room was dark, and my mind was lost in the fog created by the joint. I fell into the mood of the moment, excited that I had so captivated this mysterious man. Then Eddie woke me from my dream. He reached over and tried to turn on the light.

"No!" I forcefully said.

"Why not? I want to see you."

"No. I like it in the dark."

Eddie quickly tuned in to the fact that I didn't mind making love, but I didn't want my body to be seen. For a few moments, he pulled back from the light switch and continued loving me. When he finished, he began to tell me things I had always known but never admitted.

"You know, just like the actress you are, you are very good

with acting out sex, but you don't feel it or enjoy it. I know when someone plays a role, and that is just what you did."

Extremely embarrassed, I didn't answer, choosing to ignore his remarks and hoping he would change the subject. But he didn't.

Getting up, he took my hand and pulled me against his body. "Follow me, I've got something to show you," he said as he led me across the room. Standing me in front of the wall of mirrors, he flipped on a light. Rather than look at my reflection, I turned my head away. But he jerked my head forward, demanding that I look in the mirror.

"Look!" he almost shouted. My eyes darted to the left, but he jerked my head forward again. "Look straight ahead!"

When I did, all I could see were our naked bodies, and I could felt my face turning red, red that quickly ran through my whole body.

Eddie grabbed my hand and put it on my breasts. "Lauren, these are your breasts. God made them to be enjoyed." He then continued his tour using my hand. He explained, "God made these bodies to be enjoyed."

The more he talked, the more embarrassed I became. The seconds seemed like hours, but I couldn't move, much less run. Eddie controlled my will and my actions. I realized that his lecture would stop only when he wanted it to. Finally, he let me get dressed and go home. Never having had anyone talk to me or treat me in this way, I was extremely confused. I was both excited and frightened. I felt this man knew me better than I knew myself, a feeling that both repelled me and attracted me. As I got further away from his shop, I swore I'd never return. But something inside told me that I couldn't help myself. I knew that I would go back.

Once again, I began living two lives. In one of them, I was dating Mike and not "putting out," playing the role of the sweet little girl; in the other life, I was spending more and more time with Eddie, doing whatever he wanted me to do. As the days passed the dark side of my personality controlled me more and more.

Eddie had awakened things in me that I had never known existed, much less practiced. Besides his way of giving pleasure, he also taught me how to understand him and have him understand me. He actually convinced me that he knew what I was thinking; all I had to do was think of something, and he would know what it was. Consequently, he began to develop a way of communicating that bonded me to him. I was convinced that he was meant to help me discover my true self and find my real worth. He had me convinced that his only concern was helping me to be happy.

As my teacher, he took me through his studies of Buddhism and other strange religions. He also continued to further my sex education studies in an attempt to get me to relax and really enjoy making love to him. Yet everything he did, right to the point of convincing me that I had so much power over him, was meant to bring me more under his control. Soon he was telling me how to think. He channeled all my energies and emotions in the direction he wanted them to go, and he controlled what I believed was right and wrong. Ironically, the more he did this, the more powerful I felt, but only when I was around him. Apart from him, I felt like a lost little girl.

One afternoon, Eddie closed his shop and took me to some friends' apartment. I had no idea that his two friends were lesbians; I only knew that I had been promised a good time. Our adventure began with a marijuana high. Then one of the girls began to hit on me. I looked at Eddie to see what to do, but he just watched. The look on my face must have told him that I couldn't handle the situation because he finally grabbed me, picked me up in his arms, and carried me to a vacant bedroom. I felt as if I had been saved from a fate worse than death. I was so grateful that I couldn't let him go.

Seizing the moment, he began to make love to me. In that room, guided by my needs and emotions, he led me to my first climax. It was so powerful, I passed out. When I came to, I belonged to Eddie body and soul. He had given me what a lifetime of lovers and love had not—fulfillment. I was his!

Over the next few weeks, Eddie put phase two of his plan

into operation. Since I was now addicted to him, he suggested that I move from Mike's mother's place to an apartment that was directly above his. Although I didn't want to make this change, my will easily gave in to his wishes. When I moved, I discovered that Eddie had a wife, Ginger, and two children. At first I was humiliated and ashamed. All the time I had been seeing and sleeping with him, I hadn't realized that he was married. I couldn't believe that I had taken advantage of this pretty Mexican woman and her kids.

But Eddie soon relieved my guilt by informing me that Ginger was a call girl and that he and she had an open relationship. Ginger even told me that she didn't mind my coming to live with them. Whatever Eddie and I did was fine with her. I was in shock, but I stayed, convinced once again that this arrangement was all right.

As a call girl, Ginger brought all of her money to Eddie. If she didn't make enough during an evening of work, he would beat her. It never dawned on me that he might be planning a future like this for me. I was too much in love with him, too hung up on what he did to me and the way I felt afterward. As strange as it was, I simply wasn't streetwise enough to see what was coming. I believed in Eddie enough to let him convince me that Ginger was letting him down and that she deserved what she got. Nothing like that would ever happen to me, though, because I was special.

My one-room apartment was directly above theirs, and in no time I hated it. I was isolated from my friends and constantly lonely. Eddie forbid me to see Mike and Mom. I felt like his possession. Each day consisted of being with him, studying our bodies, making love, learning and practicing mind control, and getting high. There was nothing more to life.

Eddie was now providing for me financially. But he never gave me enough. I had no new clothes, little makeup, nothing exciting to eat or drink, and very little to do. With him controlling my purse strings, I had no choice but to beg him for money. This opened a door for him to begin Part Three of his little plan.

"You want money?" he asked. "Money is easy to get. You can get it just like you did when you were a kid—by acting."

I didn't have any idea what he was saying. I knew that the studios didn't want me, and I hardly believed that I could work on the stage. I couldn't figure out what kind of work he was describing. After waiting for me to catch up with his first remarks, he continued.

"You know, Lauren, people would pay big money to have a date with you. You could probably earn a thousand dollars a night." He again paused as he watched my eyes light up. He knew that the money had turned me on.

"Yes, little girl. I can show you how to make those big bucks, and it will be easy—real easy. You want to give it a try?"

Trusting him fully, I quizzed him again, "A thousand dollars for a date. I could do that?"

"Lauren," he assured me, "look in the mirror. Look at yourself!"

Looking back at me was a small, slender girl, someone with a 34–18–34 figure who weighed just about 100 pounds. I was hardly a bombshell; I was simply too petite and too young-looking. But as I studied myself disappointingly, he continued to persuade me.

"Honey, with the people I'll send you to, all you have to do is act like a little girl. You won't need to wear makeup. Just pull your hair down and act real young."

"A thousand dollars," I sighed, still not believing it.

"Yes. And it won't take long, and you won't have to do anything for it—just act. Whatever they ask you to do, just do it. Now, don't you want to give it a try?"

"A thousand dollars—I'll do anything for a thousand dollars."

Eddie then picked up the phone, dialed a number, and waited for someone to answer. "Hey, this is your old friend Eddie. I've got a girl over here named Terry who is just what you are looking for. She is real special. I think you would love her. Tomorrow? That will be fine."

As he went on describing me, I was already mentally spending the money I was going to make. Then Eddie woke me up from my daydream, giving me instructions for the date. "Okay, it's set. I'll pick you up at 3:30 tomorrow afternoon, and I'll take you there. You be ready."

The next day I began to get dressed right after lunch. I had forgotten about being young, so I dug out my best dress, carefully applied my makeup and false eyelashes, and fixed my hair in the latest style. I looked as good as I could, and I just hoped that it would be good enough to impress my date. After all, a thousand dollars just to go out with me was a lot of money. I thought that I had to be prettier than I had ever been before. But despite all the time I took, Eddie almost exploded when he saw me.

"What in the————!" he began. Then he ordered me to pull off my fancy dress and stockings and wash off all my makeup. Tossing a dress to me, he told me to hurry and put it on. The dress looked like it should have been worn by a five-year-old. The only thing that made it seem older was that it was my size. After I put on the dress, he turned my back toward him so he could braid my hair into pigtails. When he was done, I looked in the mirror to see a little girl looking back at me.

"You look perfect," Eddie assured me as he hurried me out to his car.

"Perfect for what?" I wondered.

A few minutes later, we arrived at an apartment building. There, I received the rest of my instructions. "Okay, sweetheart. This man you'll be seeing loves little girls. That's why you're so perfect for him. All you have to do is knock on his door; it is number 44. Go in, get his money, then do what he asks you to do. Make sure you get the money first. I'll wait out here for you.

"Now, Lauren, this is just like acting. It is just another part you are playing. It is not you going in there as yourself, but you playing this little girl. You're not doing anything other than getting paid good money for acting out a role. It will be the easiest money you will ever make. Can you play the part?"

Nodding yes, I got out of the car, found the apartment, and knocked. I still hadn't grasped what was going on or what I was supposed to say. Once inside, I was greeted by a balding, middle-aged fat man dressed in a silk robe. The first thing I did was ask him for the money. He reached into the pocket of his robe, pulled it out, and handed it to me. After I counted it, I looked back at him for directions.

The man wandered over to me and asked if he could undress me. I stood there, as stiff as a board, and said, "Whatever you want." He then began unbuttoning my dress. When he finished, he went behind me and unzipped the back. Pulling the dress over my head, he gazed at my bra and panties, then took off my top. Standing away from me, he then asked me to remove what was left. I did.

For several minutes he looked at my body from every angle, but he didn't touch me or ever remove his own robe. He just stared. Finally, he told me to put my clothes back on and leave.

Shaking and more than a little embarrassed, I quickly got dressed and said, "Thank you very much." He nodded his head in acknowledgment, and I walked out the door. I couldn't believe that was all there was to it.

When I returned to the car, I told Eddie how easy it had been. He just smiled. He knew me well enough to know just how weak my spirit was. He knew that I loved money, especially spending it. Getting a thousand dollars by taking my clothes off and pretending it was acting seemed harmless and justifiable. After all, I was special, and no one had ever told me about prostitution, that it was immoral or illegal. To me, this was nothing more than a date. I was valuable because I could help men unwind and forget about their troubles. I saw myself as a kind of psychologist. I believed that I was helping keep marriages together by letting husbands be happy in their fantasies while their wives would still have their husbands there when they needed them. Eddie convinced me that I was a humanitarian who got paid for doing good deeds.

"Come on, honey, let's get you some new clothes," Eddie

happily shouted as we drove off from the apartment complex. "Let's spend that money." And off we went.

Within weeks, I was no longer just undressing to earn my thousand dollars a night. I was having sex with people. Eddie was letting me keep a big part of the money, and I remained persuaded that I was acting and being a hands-on doctor. The fact that I was selling my body didn't enter into the equation. Besides, in my mind, it wasn't even my body; it was the body of whomever I dressed like or talked like.

My new life had further isolated me from friends and family. But because I had Eddie and a fistful of dollars, I didn't care. I was needed and accepted, and that was more than I had gotten from anyone else.

After a few weeks of turning tricks, Eddie introduced me to another experience that would make all of the others pale in comparison. He gave me my first fix of heroin. He took me to the home of an older couple from New York. This couple was into the occult. Their home was filled with candles and incense. They had altars, and they had boards like the ones I had seen Eddie use on occasion. I watched Eddie and these two closely as they chanted. Since I had been told not to talk or ask questions, I stayed in the background. When they were through, Eddie invited me to join them in the middle of the room.

Sitting on the floor was a dish, several syringes, a glass of water, spoons, cotton balls, and matches. I had no idea what they were for. Soon, the three of them began to fill their spoons with a darkish powder. Then they took matches and heated them. The smell this created almost made me sick, but I was too intrigued to turn away. I still didn't know what was going on.

When the substance was heated enough to boil, they put their spoons down, took some cotton, rolled it into a ball, and put it in the spoon. Then they drew the substance into the needles.

The woman was the first one to use her belt to tie off the top of her arm. After she began to clinch her hand for a few seconds, she took the syringe and pushed the long needle into her popped-up vein. I quickly turned my head, unable to look. But just as quickly, I turned back and watched as Eddie and the man followed the woman's lead. I could tell by the look on their faces that what they were using made them feel good, and I knew that I didn't want to be left out. Turning to Eddie, I demanded, "I want some too!"

"Yeah," Eddie whispered. "Just a minute."

After he finished shooting up, he grabbed me and led me into the bathroom. Sitting me on the toilet, he repeated the ritual, this time sticking the needle into my arm.

"Aren't you afraid?" he asked.

I still thought of myself as being completely in control. "Absolutely not," I answered.

I watched as he drew my blood, then pushed it back into my arm. He repeated this action several times before depressing the plunger all the way. I reacted almost immediately. I had never felt so high. But seconds later, I stood over the sink, spilling my guts. When the vomiting subsided, I got even higher than before. I went totally numb and became euphoric. It was the best rush I had ever experienced.

"Are you okay?" Eddie asked me a few moments later.

"Yeah, I'm fine."

We stayed on the bathroom floor for a long time before finally getting up and going back into the other room. I thought that this was the best moment of my life. But equal to that was the group sex that followed.

Soon, Eddie would fix me everyday, and in no time, I was hooked. I became so addicted to heroin that I couldn't get through even a single day without it; as a matter of fact, I was even fixing myself two more times a day.

Then, Eddie took me off the stuff—cold! I was so sick that I thought I would die. I shook and queazed; my whole body cried out in pain. It was like being in hell, while all the time knowing the answer to getting me out was just a room away. I begged Eddie for a fix. I promised him any- and everything, but he still wouldn't help me. Finally, he said he would get some stuff if I would do something for him. Without even asking what he wanted, I agreed. He then fixed me, and I escaped hell and flew back to heaven. Within a few days, however, he cashed in my promise.

Eddie's power over me was almost unlimited and definitely spiritual. I was afraid he could read my thoughts, and I believed he knew what I was doing even before I did it. He was beating me now, just to keep me under his thumb. To further humble and scare me, he would place his foot over my pelvic area and tell me, "Either get in line or I will crush it so you'll never have any children. You will be a female eunuch. You'll have nothing that anyone will ever want."

As bad as he was, he could still make me feel wonderful in bed. He was at one moment Satan; the next, an angel. He always kept me off balance and scared, causing my moods to fluctuate wildly. But no matter what he did, he managed to control me so I would do whatever he said.

I even began running a brothel for Eddie. No longer did I get any of the money from the work I was turning; he just gave me a place to live and the heroin I needed. As long as he got me the latter, I didn't even care about the money.

Ginger was working the house with me, and I was now having to turn a dozen or more tricks a night just to meet Eddie's demands. The fees for this kind of service had dropped to one hundred a pop. I was keeping up, but no matter how hard she tried, Ginger couldn't turn enough tricks to satisfy her husband. Every night he would beat her up, demanding she do more. Terrified, I watched and wondered when he would do the same to me. Trying to work even harder, I vowed to not allow myself to fall into this trap.

One night after a particularly rough beating, Eddie decided that Ginger was no longer fit for work in the house. So he sent her to work for three of his pimps in Chinatown. I knew what this meant. She would be in a cold, dirty room with a pimp outside the door. Men would wait in long lines for her to service their needs for a few dollars a pop. It was like assembly-line work. Ginger would probably see a hundred different men in one night. It was humiliation at its worst.

Deep inside I could no longer ignore what I had become or the spot I was in. I desperately wanted to get away from Eddie, but I had no money, and I needed the fixes too badly to run. So I just tried to work harder to keep him satisfied. But I knew that there would come a time when I would fail. Finally, when I came up short one night and he threatened me with exile to Chinatown, I tried to get away before he could beat me. I wanted to get to Mother's, but Eddie found me just before I got to her apartment. I couldn't have been more than a block away when he picked me up.

"You aren't going to run from *me!*" he screamed as he pulled me into his car. "I own you! You owe me, slut, and you will always owe me. I'll kill you if you ever run again." His dark eyes were now shining so brightly that he looked like Satan himself. "If you ever run again, I'll sell you to one of the Chinatown pimps."

The next night, Eddie beat me and took me to Chinatown. For six hours I worked, giving all my customers exactly what they asked. But by now my ribs were killing me from the battering Eddie had given me. I was sick, needed another fix, and was barely lucid. Then a big man, who decided I wasn't worth the five bucks he had paid, began to beat me. I was so out of it that I barely felt his fists digging into my face and ribs. He would have probably killed me if Benny, one of the pimps, hadn't pulled him off me. Bleeding in several places, I wasn't fit for anymore work that night. Benny sent me home.

When Eddie saw me, he knew that he had taught me a lesson. I now realized that I couldn't get away from him, so I stopped trying. I began to have nightmares—horrible dreams that would be so real that I would bolt upright in bed, wringing wet in a cold sweat. Unable to speak, I would then cry and shake for the rest of the night. Time after time I would fall asleep only to have the demons wake me up and take me to hell. The dreams soon stayed with me even when I was awake, leaving me a wreck.

Several months later, to give me a break and use me in a different way, Eddie took me down to Mexico to score some drugs. Since he had connections there, it didn't take us long to get a couple of balloons full of pure heroin. On our way back through the border, we were stopped. He had me swallow the balloons in an attempt to avoid being caught. I obeyed, but it didn't matter. Moments later, we were taken into custody. Someone on the Mexico side had snitched on us.

The agents strip-searched us, medically examined us, and even x-rayed us. By this time, my head was swimming and my stomach, churning. Little did I know that one of the balloons had burst and I was overdosing. As we waited for the police to finish their search, I leaned over and told Eddie I was really feeling bad. He told me to shut up and tough it out. I tried, but I passed out before the cops ever got me to a cell.

I knew that the tracks on my arms would give me away as an addict. But the police had no evidence to charge us with possession—not until, at any rate, I couldn't contain the effects of the heroin I had swallowed. When I passed out and let go of the drugs hiding inside me, the cops had all they needed to book us.

Eddie, using his rich family connections, called his attorney, asking him to get us out of jail. I would later find out that he had also tried to get the attorney to stick me with all the charges. David Horn, the lawyer Eddie had called, drove down from San Diego, met with both of us, and somehow got both of us out of jail. Still, while the charges against Eddie were dropped, the ones against me were left intact. I would have to come back to stand trial at a later date.

By now my life seemed crazy, even to me. Nothing but humiliation and fear was left for me in my relationship with Eddie, and yet, because I had lost all my esteem and had no place to go, I stayed with him. I was never normal. My life's circuits were either charged up or drained. Balance eluded me.

In retrospect, Eddie had accomplished what the producers of the television show "The Outer Limits" always claimed that they did: he had taken over complete control of my life. He controlled the horizontal, the vertical, the brightness, the focus, and the script. I didn't have the power to change the channel, the settings, or anything else. He dominated me totally.

When we had first gotten together, I experienced real joy and happiness. The sex, the lifestyle, the money, all of it together was wonderful and exhilarating. Pain was absent. But now, the times that I had fought with my mother seemed like the good ol' days. I had sunk to such a point that I wondered if I was even a human being; I felt more like an animal. I even wondered if I had lost my soul forever.

For months my existence went on like this. I would turn my tricks, give Eddie the money, get fixed, and get beaten. Whenever I was lucid enough to be aware of my feelings, I was depressed. My life simply consisted of a circle of morbid circumstances and dreadful realities. I never looked at myself in the mirror, and I tried not to think about the state of my own soul. My life was truly godless.

One day, when Eddie was in a particularly good mood, I asked him if I could see my brother and mother. By this time they had no idea where I lived or what I did. I, at least, wanted them to know that I was alive. When he handed me the phone to call them, I thought that maybe a small door of escape had opened. But my hope was shattered when, a few hours later, Billy came to see us and hit it off so well with the ever-charming Eddie that he had little time to talk with me. Billy never saw Eddie's dark side. He thought Eddie was a great guy. If only I could have gotten him alone to tell him what I knew.

Over the past year, I had gathered a lot of information on Eddie. I learned that he carried a gun. I had also figured out that the barbershop, which he still regularly opened, was a front for a drug-selling operation, as well as a prostitution ring. I also discovered that, a few years before, he had taken a job as a contract hit man for the Hell's Angels. He was as evil as any villain Hollywood had ever brought to the big screen, and yet he was still so charming that those who weren't used by him rarely imagined him to be anything but a great guy. Because

Billy was one of these, my hope of a family rescue was dashed almost the moment I had thought of it.

A few weeks after seeing Billy, I came in one night after not making enough money, and Eddie almost beat me to death. I woke up with two black eyes, several broken ribs, and bruises all around my neck. Unfit for work, he announced that I was going to go with him to Mexico again to score some drugs. I believed that the main reason I was going was so that he could kill me. At twenty dollars a pop, I was no longer giving him the return he wanted. It was less than a year-and-a-half after I had met him, I was twenty years old, and I was completely used up.

Before we left, I managed to talk Eddie into letting me at least speak to my mother. He drove me to her apartment, and he pointed a gun at me as I left the car. With a stern voice he announced, "If you say anything or don't come back in five minutes, I'll kill you and the old lady." I could tell that he meant it.

Mom was shocked when she opened the door. I was extremely thin, pale, bruised, and battered. I looked twenty years older than my age. "My God, Lauren," she gasped. "What happened to you?"

I immediately began to cry and talk like a little girl. "Oh, Mommy, I'm going down to Mexico with Eddie, and if I'm not back in three days, call the police and tell them I'm dead. Make sure they know Eddie did it. Get him put away. Promise me this, okay, Mom? I know I have not told you this much, but Mom, I really do love you. Right now, I need to leave you and keep you protected."

She tried to pull me into her apartment, but I knew that if I did go in with her, Eddie would come storming out of the car and kill us both. Pushing her away, I pleaded, "Mom, it's the truth; I'm not acting. Do it for me, okay?"

Nodding her head, she begged me to let her call the police right then, but I knew that if she did, we'd both be dead before they could respond. I finally forced a smile and turned and walked away. Then turning back, I said, "Don't worry, whatever happens, it will be okay. Just remember, I love you!"

Eddie had asked another couple, David and Mary, to go with us. David was trying to style himself after Eddie, and he was already pimping his own wife. We took two cars, and the guys brought their bikes so they could have fun riding in the desert. After we passed through Tijuana and Ensenada, we found a small hotel and checked in. We spent most of the day there, and even though nothing happened, I still feared for my life. That night, Eddie decided that he would take me up to Tijuana to score some heroin. I just knew this meant that I wouldn't be coming back.

As we walked out to the car, a crazy thought hit me. I asked him if I could drive. He consented and got in on the passenger side. Driving down the winding road that led along the coast, I began putting together a plan. A sheer cliff wall was just a few miles ahead and I decided that it would be my ticket out. I was almost sure that if we scored, Eddie would overdose me, and I would be forgotten—a footnote in the papers—but for a few moments, I was in control.

With fear driving me, I began to pray. "Dear God, forgive me because I know that murder is a sin and I know that suicide is a sin, but I'd rather die and kill Eddie than have his poison spread to any other people. Please understand why I am doing what I am about to do."

I looked over at Eddie, my mind racing, praying that he couldn't hear my thoughts. Frantic, I studied the cliff as it grew larger and larger. Pushing the accelerator to the floor, I spun off the road directly toward the mountain. Glancing over at Eddie one final time, I watched as shock suddenly registered on his face. A warm flush filled my body. I knew that he had no time to stop me now. I wanted to laugh, cry, and yell, but there was no time. As the car went flying toward the wall, I thought of all the people I had known; I remembered the recent moment I had told Mom I loved her, and most of all, I felt relief that all the misery I had experienced was just about to end. As the car smashed into the cliff's side, I felt real peace for the first time in years.

Mike, my oldest brother (9 years old), and me (at 4 months) getting off to a good start in September 1945.

My birthplace on Ridgley Drive, the "Miracle Mile," in
Los Angeles, California.

Sterling, my loving nanny, and
me around 1946.

A rare moment between me and
my brother Billy.

Me at 2 years old.

My first Communion day in 1954. Back row, left to right: a friend with Jill and Marge Ostergran. Middle row, left to right: Millie and Billy Vernon, Marguerite Chapin (my mom), Dottie Price. Front row, left to right: Pam Price, Billy Chapin, me, Patty Price.

A surprise reunion between me (9), Michael (20), and Billy (10) on the set of "Father Knows Best" around 1958.

My mother and me posing for a Screen Gems publicity shot in 1954.

My mother (on the far left) with (from left to right) Mrs. Alice Cooper (actor Gary Cooper's mother), Mrs. Ann Walters (president of Motion Picture Mothers of Hollywood), and Mrs. Marie Brown (actor Tom Brown's mother).

My television family from "Father Knows Best." From left to right: me (who played Kathy "Kitten" Anderson, the youngest daughter), Elinor Donahue (Betty, the oldest child), Robert Young (Jim, the wise father), Billy Gray (Jim, Jr., otherwise known as Bud, the middle child), and Jane Wyatt—no relation to Jane Wyman—(Margaret, the loving mother and wife).

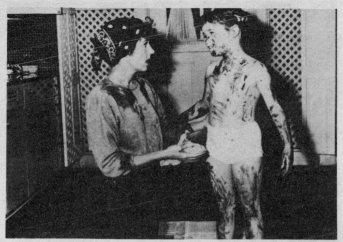

Jane Wyatt and me in a scene from "Father Knows Best."

Robert Young showing me how a movie camera works.

Robert Young was much more of a father and friend to me on and off the set than my real father was.

An encouraging letter to me from Robert Young.

Some fun time on the set with (from left to right) Herb Walerstein (Assistant Director), me, Robert Young, Jane Wyatt, and Ena, who was in charge of the show's wardrobe. The legs jumping behind mine are those of Luz, my stand-in.

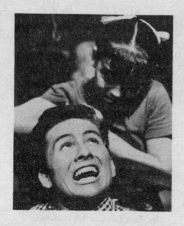

Above: Me being a real kid.

Side: Me being a brat, and Billy Gray bearing the brunt of it.

Me at fourteen between two of my favorite actors—Tony Curtis
(left) and Dean Martin (right).

Me with Art Linkletter.

WESTERN UNION
TELEGRAM

C A253

L LSD030 NL PD=TDL HOLLYWOOD CALIF 28=
LAUREN CHAPIN=

1239 LODI PL HOLLYWOOD CALIF=

AM LOOKING FORWARD TO PRESENTING YOUR MILKY WAY GOLD
STAR AWARD TO YOU PERSONALLY ON MY HOUSEPARTY
TELEVISION SHOW TUESDAY APRIL 1ST. SO THAT WE WILL
ALL LOOK GOOD REHEARSAL WILL BE PROMPTLY AT 10
O'CLOCK TUESDAY MORNING IN STUDIO 41 CBS TV CITY,
BEVERLY AND FAIRFAX. WE'LL BE ON THE AIR AT 1130=

WE ARE ALL INVITED TO AN INFORMAL LUNCHEON
ON THE LANAI TERRACE OF THE BEVERLY HILLS HOTEL
IMMEDIATELY FOLLOWING THE SHOW. CONGRATULATIONS
ON WINNING=
ART LINKLETTER=

A personal invitation to appear
on Art Linkletter's show
to accept one of my five
Milky Way Awards.

Winners of the Milky Way Award. Left to right: Lee Acre ("Rin Tin Tin"), Rusty Hammer ("Make Room for Daddy"), Billy Gray ("Father Knows Best"), Sherry Jackson ("Make Room for Daddy"), and Tommy Rettig ("Lassie").

News from Eugene B. Rodney, the producer of "Father Knows Best," concerning the coveted Look Award.

On May 7, 1959, Jack Benny won best actor in a comedy series, and I accepted Jane Wyatt's award for best actress in a comedy series.

The cast and crew of "Father Knows Best" in 1955, with the great
Dodgers' center fielder Duke Snider.

An appearance of the "Father Knows Best" cast on the show
"Good Morning America," with host David Hartman.
I'm the blonde.

Top: My wedding picture from my first marriage at age 16.

Left: When I was 21, living in the San Francisco area, and
working at the Bermuda Palms.

Right: When I lived with Eddie, to me the devil incarnate.

Me and a friend after my 120
days at CRC.

Me with my son's father, Rudy
Quiroz, in 1971.

Grandmother Gee Gee at 92,
on the day we met at the
Vinewood Center.

My son, Matt, at age 15.

My daughter, Summer, at age 10.

Soon after I was released from
L.A. General Hospital for
attempting suicide. Left to
right: Jesse Miller, me, Barney
Miller, Johnny See (Mom's
boyfriend), and "Big Pat."

Me today, by God's grace.

• Nine •

THE CAR FLIPPED three times after hitting the wall, smashing not only every window but also mangling every straight piece of metal on both the top and sides. The car was completely totaled. There was no way that anyone should have been able to survive the wreck. Neither of us was even wearing a seat belt. But it was one of those times when unasked-for miracles happen. I had been knocked out, and it took me a few minutes to come around. When I did, Eddie was standing over me with one small scratch on his face. I had been the only casualty.

"Oh, no," I thought as I came to and saw Eddie. "I'm alive! And so is he!"

As I lay in the dust, he flagged down a group of Mexican men. Talking to them for a minute, he convinced the entire group to come over and turn our car upright. Surprisingly, the tires had not been damaged. A few minutes later, Eddie even started the almost unrecognizable mesh of metal. Once the car was running, he got out, picked me up, and tossed me in the passenger side. Then he turned the car around and headed back to our motel.

151

I never doubted that Eddie knew what I had tried to do. But he didn't say a word about his suspicions until that night. Then, after a few drinks, he began to grow angry. As I lay in bed, pain racking my body from injuries that Eddie felt were too insignificant to warrant a doctor's attention, Eddie vented all of his rage on me. Over and over again he would punch me, and over and over again, I would fade in and out, never quite eluding the pain, but never feeling all of it either.

The next morning, we deserted our car and all piled into David's. As we drove back to L.A., Eddie cursed and raved, striking me over and over again in the ribs. Four of my ribs had been broken in the wreck, and his continued abuse caused even more damage to them. Finally, David's wife had all she could take.

"Eddie, quit it! You're hurting her!"

Glaring back at her, Eddie kept pounding me, while David reached across from the driver's side and struck his wife, ordering her to stay out of it. "It's none of your business, woman. Shut up!"

Somehow, I managed to survive the trip back.

That night, when I didn't seem to be getting any better, David convinced Eddie to take me to the hospital. I thought that this might be my chance to get some real help to escape. I was devastated when, after my examination and treatment, I got to my room, and Eddie was there. For the next three days and nights, he never left my side. In his hand, hidden beneath his coat, he clutched a .357 Magnum, his finger on the trigger ready to fire if I as much as looked like I was going to try to turn him in. I was like a caged rat, completely helpless and at the mercy of Eddie's whims.

When I was released three days later, Eddie took me back to our apartment and locked us in together. For the next two weeks, I was never alone. His eyes followed me everywhere, and his gun never left his belt. He was like a snake waiting for me to make a move or say the wrong word; then he would strike. I always tried to move cautiously, watching my back at all times.

I was constantly looking for a chance to cut out and run, but Eddie trusted me so little that one never opened up. After a week in exile, I was so scared and desperate that I finally decided to play it his way. I figured that if I could win back his trust he might let his guard down. First of all, I changed my personality back to that of a hero-worshiping love slave. I gave him everything he wanted, just the way that he taught me that he wanted it. Within days he was complimenting me by telling me how great I was in bed and how understanding I was when he told me about his problems. When he began to do this, I knew that I had begun to win the mind games he had always played with me. So I intensified my efforts.

I persuaded him that I loved him and no one else, and that it was the drugs that had made me crazy. I even conned him into believing that I had only been trying to kill myself, that I would never want to kill him. And now that I was better, I would never let anything pull me away from him again. Eddie knew better than anyone what drugs could do to a person's mind, so he finally bought every one of my excuses.

Within two weeks of beginning my lovey-dovey games, I had his complete trust. He was even planning our future money-making ventures. Feeling secure, he kissed me good-bye one afternoon and left.

Within seconds of his closing the door, I had called my mother and begged her to come over in her car to get me.

"Mom, you've got to get me out of here, but first call the police and ask them to give us protection! Eddie will kill you if he sees you or knows you are helping me. This guy is the devil, so please get some help!"

A few minutes later, she called me back. "They say that they can't help, Lauren. You are not Eddie's wife, and they legally can't get involved."

"But Mom," I explained, "I've been living with the guy long enough to be a common law wife, or at least something like that."

"Not in this state," she replied. Then, after pausing for a

moment, she added, "But I'll come and get you. You get your things together, and I'll get there just as soon as I can."

Working at breakneck speed, I piled all of my stuff by the front door. Looking out the window, I was praying that Mom would get here before Eddie. I knew that this might be my last chance to get away, and I didn't want to blow it. As the minutes ticked by, I prayed the same short prayer, over and over again. "Dear God, please let her get here in time. Please let me get away, and please keep Eddie away from me as long as I live."

Just when I figured that she would never arrive, I saw her drive up. Grabbing my stuff, I rushed out of the apartment and tossed my belongings into her car. Jumping in, Mom took off down the hill that led to her apartment. Just as we rounded the corner, Eddie drove up. Ducking down, we waited for him to pass by; once he did, we drove carefully but quickly to Mom's apartment, ran inside, and locked the door.

After I knew that I was safe, we looked at each other, and a warm glow filled my mom's eyes. For the first time ever, I felt as if she really would be there for me when I needed her. It was a warm feeling, a moment that seemed destined to end in a hug. Then the phone interrupted our reunion. It was Eddie. The harassment began.

Eddie hovered outside Mom's apartment for days, always waiting for me to come out. When I didn't, he yelled and screamed. Finally, he took a knife and slit all of Mother's car tires. A move like this was the one for which we had been waiting. It helped us get the police to order an injunction to keep Eddie away from us. It was our big break.

For the next week, my days became almost normal. I had almost kicked heroin before I had left Eddie, so I wasn't suffering too much withdrawal. I was eating normally and catching up on television. I was off the streets and seemingly out of trouble.

At night, however, my life was different. I was constantly haunted by dreams of Eddie chasing and beating me. Somehow, in these nightmares, I would turn the tables and catch him. I would then nail him to a cross, strip off his clothes, and then as he hung there, cut him with a razor. I would allow him to suffer until he bled to death. The dreams never changed, and they would always leave me wide awake, shaking and drenched with sweat. No matter what time I woke up, I would then force myself to stay awake, attempting to understand just why it was that I could have such sick thoughts.

Mom knew that I was having bad dreams, and she did her best to comfort me, but she couldn't really help because I wouldn't let her inside my head. I wouldn't tell her about the things that kept me awake, nor would I share with her what Eddie had put me through. I kept silent, closed-up, and thus prevented any chance of Mom's being able to calm my fears.

Even though the nightmares hung on, I began to feel safe during the daylight hours. I really thought that Eddie had forgotten about me and was looking for someone else to torment. He wasn't outside my door anymore, and he hadn't called in weeks. Then one day when Mom was out shopping, the phone rang.

"Hello," I answered.

"Lauren." I immediately recognized Eddie's smooth voice. "Honey, I'm sorry. Please forgive me."

I held the phone away from my ear, turned away, and refused to answer, but he didn't give up, and like a fool, I didn't hang up.

"Lauren, I'm so sorry; I need you. Please don't hang up. Just listen to me. I know that I've done some terrible things, not only to you, but to my family, too. But you have got to believe me when I tell you that I'm very sorry. Baby, please forgive me. I know that you don't want to talk, but just listen to me. Lauren, I can't live without you."

Holding the phone as if it were a snake, my jaw began to tighten, my temples began to pound, and my heart raced as Eddie talked. I thought that I needed to scream or run, but instead I did nothing. The fact that he was on the phone and not right in front of me made me feel safe—too safe.

"Lauren, please let me see you," he begged. "I can't live without you, and, honey, you've got to listen to me. All I want to do is drive over and see you. I just want you to come outside, and I promise I won't hurt you. I promise I won't even touch you. I've just got to see you one more time. You see, I'm going to kill myself, and before I die, I want to see you."

Even as much as I hated the man, I felt strangely compassionate at that moment. I even felt a little honored over the fact that someone cared enough about me to take his life just because he couldn't be with me. Nevertheless, he hadn't convinced me enough for me to fall headfirst into his trap. I knew just how good he was at telling lies. Swallowing hard, I said, "You're lying. You don't plan to kill yourself. You are just trying to get to me."

"I've taken a whole bottle of reds," he answered. "Please come out; I promise I won't hurt you; just come outside and see me one more time. Five minutes is all I ask. I can't live without you." On and on he rambled, and the words were almost always the same, "Baby, I've got to see you before I die. Please let me come over . . . please, baby."

I realized that if he had taken a whole bottle of reds, he would be dead in a matter of minutes. It would be almost a blessing to watch that take place, so I agreed to see him.

A few minutes later, I walked downstairs, looked around the corner, and watched him drive up. I stared unnoticed for a while, debating whether I could go through with what I had promised. Finally, I made up my mind to see him but to also kept my distance so he couldn't touch me. Gathering my courage, I walked to the end of the driveway where he had parked.

When I got to the sidewalk, he motioned me over to the curb. Feeling more frightened, I hesitated for a second, and then slowly edged over to the passenger side of the car. Eddie carefully slid across the seat and rolled down the window. It was then that I noticed a whole bag of reds on the seat and bunches more spilled out on the floor. He even had some in his hand. Staring at me for a second, he popped these in his mouth.

When he got the window all the way down, I stepped back. But as he began to speak, he looked so harmless that I again moved closer, this time just to hear him better. Suddenly, he grabbed me by the hair and stuck his .357 Magnum in my face.

"Get in!" he screamed. "Get in over there; I want you to drive. Move it!"

Scared to death, I did exactly what he asked just as quickly as I could move. I concluded that this would probably be my last drive. What hadn't occurred in Mexico would take place now. I wondered where he would stash my body and if anyone would ever find me. I was amazed at how calm my thoughts were of my own death.

As we drove around L.A., he kept reaching into his pocket and taking out more reds. I watched him eat the drugs like most folks consume popcorn. Realizing that he hadn't lied about the suicide made me feel good; at least he would be going down with me. However, even I, the girl who had done enough drugs over the last year to kill a herd of elephants, was amazed at how many Eddie was popping. The more he took, the more I believed that he might pass out before he could kill me. I tried to keep him talking so he wouldn't dwell on all the things I had done to him. Mainly, I wanted to keep him popping reds. For over two hours I drove, and during this whole time, he kept taking more pills, but he didn't pass out. Finally, just when I had given up on the pills ever taking effect, he slumped over against the passenger door. Turning the car around, I tried to think of where I could go. I eventually decided to go to my friend Linda's house. Before I pulled the car back on the street, I grabbed Eddie's gun and tossed it out the window. Searching his pockets, I took his money and pitched his wallet. I even considered dumping him but thought that might get me in more trouble than I could handle, so I just left him sleeping.

I didn't hurry to Linda's. I drove at a leisurely pace. It was almost like a Sunday drive. I looked at the trees, smiled at other motorists, and made sure that I obeyed all signals. Mainly, I just enjoyed watching Eddie begin to struggle for his breath. When I finally arrived at Linda's, I slowly walked up and knocked on her door. When she answered, I calmly told her, "Eddie has overdosed. He's in the car. Why don't we bring him in?"

Confused by my lack of emotion or panic, she followed me out to the car, and the two of us dragged Eddie inside and pitched him on the couch. Linda then ran over to the telephone and began to call the paramedics. I stopped her.

"Let's wait and see how bad he is. Maybe he will come to in a few minutes." What I was really hoping was that he would just quit breathing. I didn't want him to wake back up and hurt me anymore.

Half an hour later, when his breathing had gotten very shallow, I finally let my nervous friend call the emergency number. Within moments I was talking to the paramedics on the phone. I explained what had transpired, but I lied about how long ago it had happened.

"All right, lady, don't panic," they replied. If only they had known just how relaxed I was. "I want you to take a pin and prick him and see if he responds."

Looking over at my friend, I said, "Linda, get me a pin or a needle. They want me to prick him."

Once she found a needle, I followed the paramedics' orders and stabbed Eddie deeply into his arm. There was no reaction. Picking up the phone, I responded in the negative. Then they asked me to do it again.

Walking back over to Eddie, I pricked him, not once, but three or four times, enjoying every stab. I didn't want to stop, but eventually I returned to the phone and reported the lack of response. At this point they told me that someone would be at Linda's address in a matter of minutes and to please stay calm. As we waited for them to arrive, I continued to laugh and prick Eddie with the pin.

I was praying that it was too late, that Eddie was dead, and that all that remained was watching him breathe his last breath. Then the paramedics came and took him to the hospital, leaving Linda and me with nothing to do but look at each other. Neither of us knew what to say or do, and I knew that I couldn't explain to her how I was really feeling. Rather than try, I just excused myself and drove Eddie's car back to the apartment. When I got home, Mom was already there.

"Hi," I said as I walked in.

"Where have you been?" she inquired.

"No place, just out for a walk." My explanation seemed to satisfy her, so nothing else was ever said about my outing. A few hours later, when she was taking a bath, I called Ginger and explained what had happened. I told her that Eddie's car was parked in the street in front of my apartment and that I had left the keys in it. The next time I looked outside, his car was gone.

For a month I waited, never really sure if Eddie had survived or not. No one knew anything, and the papers didn't print a word about him. I tried to convince myself that he was dead, but deep down, I believed that he had beaten the odds and was still alive. After six weeks, however, I almost totally relaxed and decided to jump back into the everyday world.

It's a long way from a Hollywood studio to a mailroom at Carnation Milk. But that is where I found employment. In the course of a few months, I had gone from working as a prostitute to working for the company that prided itself on selling nature's purest product. Even though I didn't note it at the time, another huge irony had appeared.

I was a mail clerk, which meant it was my job to sort the letters and then deliver them to the appropriate offices and desks. Things went very smooth for a while. Then, a month after I began to work, I was informed that I had a call. Wondering what in the world my mother had on her mind that couldn't wait until I got home, I picked up the receiver.

"Hello," I said, fully expecting to hear Mom's voice.

"Lauren." I immediately recognized the caller as Eddie. When I didn't respond, he again called my name. "Lauren, why did you save me? Man, I've hurt so many people; you should have let me die."

Just like my recurring nightmare, Eddie was back haunting me again. He was like my shadow. Just about the time I had forgotten it was there, I saw it, and then I couldn't lose it. But this time, he sounded different. He seemed tired and defeated. His cockiness was gone. Only a dull, passionless voice remained.

I let his words soak in before I answered.

"I couldn't let you die, mainly because I'm not as evil as you are. I may be bad, but I'm not that bad. Now, I don't want you calling me anymore. Please leave me alone."

Suddenly I realized that, even though my words were strong, my voice was shaking and my hands were cold. A bead of sweat was also building on my forehead. I knew that if Eddie kept me on the phone for very long, all my strength and will power would ooze out of me, and I would revert to my old self. I should have hung up, but I didn't.

"Oh Lauren, I wish I had died. I've done such a disservice to you, Ginger, and the kids. I'm really sorry. Just let me come by and see you. I won't hurt you. I know that I lied to you last time, but this time I'm telling the truth. Just let me see you."

Feeling myself growing weaker, I sighed, "I can't let you see me. I have things to do."

Eddie didn't give up, though, and over the course of the next fifteen minutes, he worked to persuade me to see him one last time. I reluctantly agreed, hoping that it would close this chapter in my life.

When Eddie came by, I talked to him in his car, and he seemed calm and controlled. I wanted to believe that he had found religion as he told me he had, but a little voice inside me kept warning me to watch out. Underneath his puppy-dog exterior, I still felt there lurked a snake. Nonetheless, he was convincing. He was so kind, apologetic, and tender that he began to win me over. He even cried while begging for my forgiveness. Then he suggested that I call Mom.

"Tell her you're going out to dinner with a friend. Don't tell her with whom, just tell her it's a friend from work. I just want to spend a little time with you, talking and sharing a meal. Please allow me this. I really love you. You know, out of all the people I have been with, I loved you the most. You were the most understanding, and I just want to try to make up a little for all the ways that I've hurt you."

Shaking my head, I felt myself losing control. But I managed to maintain my distance. "I can't; Mom wouldn't appreciate my lying to her." A few minutes later, however, my defenses collapsed. I found myself calling Mom and telling her another lie.

"Mom, I'm going to stay down here for a while—got to work late. I'll catch something to eat, and then I'll be home around nine. Don't worry. Goodbye."

After Eddie promised to get me home early, I got into his car. Minutes later we were on the freeway headed out of town toward Malibu. Ringing my hands as the time and the miles passed, I began to wonder where he was taking me and what he was going to do.

"Where are we going?" I asked.

"I thought we'd go out to the beach and have dinner there. Don't worry about the distance; we'll have a great time."

"Eddie," I protested, "that's too far. By the time we drive all that way and then eat, I'll be late getting home. I told Mom that I would be back by nine. It is already seven. We can't make it that far in time. Let's turn around and eat somewhere in town."

Glaring at me, he didn't say anything, but I knew his answer. I also knew that everything he had told me had been another pack of lies. Now I was trapped, but this time I wasn't going down without a fight.

"————you," I screamed. "I don't want to go to the beach. I want to go to L.A. Turn around and take me home."

All the way to Malibu we argued, him calling me name after name, and me returning the insults just as quickly. When we got to the beach and I thought his rage had peaked, he hit me just as hard as he could, knocking me against the door and causing the door's handle to dig deeply into my back. For a split second, I laid back, filled with pain and shock. But then, rather than take it like I had in the past, I screamed at the top of my lungs, "No way,————. Not this time you don't!" I struck back, hitting his face just as hard as I could with both of my fists. The move caught him by surprise and cause him to fly into an even hotter rage. Jumping out of the car, he ran around to my side and jerked me out, tearing my blouse in the process. Tossing me on the ground, he began to kick me. Rolling over, I caught his shoe, pushed his foot away, and jumped up and began running across a restaurant parking lot. Eddie was following me step for step. Pushing through the front door, I ran screaming through the dining room, frightening both patrons and employees, and then climbed over the bar and hid behind it. Looking up at the bartender, I began to beg. "Whatever you do, don't tell him I'm here. Please! This guy is not my husband, and if he finds me, he is going to kill me."

A few moments later, Eddie began searching the place. No one gave me away, and when he got to the bar, the bartender stood up for me.

"Listen buddy, I haven't seen her, and if I were you, I'd move out of here in a hurry. If you don't, you're going to be in big trouble." He then picked up the phone as if to call the police. Eddie rushed out the back.

When I gathered the courage to stand up, my fear had turned to humiliation. My stockings were torn, my blouse almost obscene, and I had no money or identification. I had looked and acted like a madwoman—a human possessed by demons—and there was no way for me to explain my actions. I didn't have any idea how I was going to get home or what I was going to tell Mom. Trying to get myself together the best I could, I thanked the bartender and eased out the back door. Walking down the highway, I stuck out my thumb and hoped I could hitch a ride.

Sporting a torn blouse, I didn't have to wait too long. As soon as I got in the car, the guy offered me a joint, and as I smoked it, I began to relax. My ride took me all the way to Mom's apartment, but as we drove up, I spied Eddie's car parked around the corner. Urging the man not to stop, I gave him instructions on how to get to Linda's. As soon as I got inside her house, Eddie called. Linda lied about my whereabouts, giving my safety for the night. It was the last time I heard from Eddie for three years. When we did meet again, I was stronger and finally able to close the door on that chapter of my life.

I began working during the day and going out at night. Bars were my favorite places to go dancing, allowing me to release some tension I had built up trying to function in a normal world. At a night spot called Jamaica West, I met Jack Hale. We immediately hit it off, and within weeks were as close as brother and sister.

Every night we played, laughed, fell in love with other people, and used drugs together. One night we even bonded ourselves together by cutting our fingers and mixing our blood in an Indian ritual. Jack and I never really dated, nor did we have a physical relationship; we were just close friends and rarely apart. There were many nights I would even spend the night with him.

I stayed with Jack for several months, and then moved on, this time to the valley area of L.A. There, in another bar, I met my next lover.

I had noticed him when I came in. As I drank, I sized him up. I estimated him to be about six feet tall. I was immediately attracted to his green eyes, and I concluded that he must work outside due to his muscular build and deep tan. I was particularly intrigued by his goatee. Still, I didn't think that he would notice me. So I decided to walk over and introduce myself.

"Hi," I began.

"Hi, yourself," he answered.

"My name is Lauren. What's yours?"

"Jerry."

"Isn't that strange," I said, putting forward my best charm. "My first husband's name was Jerry."

Over the course of the next few hours, he bought me several drinks, and I gave him a sugarcoated view of my life. I left out a few little things, like prostitution and drug addiction, but I did tell him about being an actress. By the time the night was over, he had grown as infatuated with me as I was with him. Three days later, I packed my bags, moved out of my mother's house, and in with him.

Jerry was a building contractor by trade, but he also sold drugs. He wasn't trading in the heroin market, but he was dealing LSD, grass, and speed. He could supply my needs, and this made him extremely valuable. He was so valuable to me that, within two months of meeting him, I married him.

The wedding took place in Las Vegas, and the highlight of the whole affair was Billy (my brother), Jerry, and me getting so high on acid before the ceremony that none of us could really focus on anything while vows were exchanged. At a reception which Mom and some of her friends set up, the three of us were all so loaded that we couldn't stop laughing. It didn't take a social worker to see that something other than love was at the center of our relationship.

Back home in Jerry's apartment, I quickly found myself with more time and less to do. I wasn't working, but because of his jobs, Jerry was gone a great deal, leaving me alone to watch television. I was bored, and this made me dangerous. Within a month of getting married, I began looking for new kicks that offered some excitement. I didn't have to go far. I found them in our apartment complex. In the laundry room, I ran into a young girl named Lois. Something about her hit me as being different; she had a spirit that reminded me of my own. We were almost like lost sisters.

Lois and I became close in a hurry, but our initial visits were limited to the pool or my apartment. Because she never invited me to her place, I felt as if she was hiding something from me. When my curiosity got the best of me, I invited myself up to her place. As we sipped coffee and traded small talk, I decided to make a bold move to see if my suspicions were correct.

"Got any dope?" I asked.

"What do you mean?" Lois answered, sounding as if she really was confused.

Rolling up the sleeve of my blouse, I showed her my needle tracks, then smiled and asked again, "Got any dope?"

Now grinning, Lois responded, "And I thought you were Miss Priss—you know, the square one. You sure didn't seem like someone who used. I can't believe it!"

Smiling back, I said, "Well, I thought the same thing about you for awhile, but something told me that we had a lot in common. Now that it's out in the open, have you got any stuff?"

"Yeah!"

That first fix led to Lois's and my using heroin at least twice and sometimes three times a day. Jerry didn't know, and I always kept myself together enough to hide what I was doing. But while the secrecy was no problem, finding money was. My habit was costing me fifty a day, and I didn't have that kind of cash. So Lois and I turned to shoplifting to pay for our stuff. We'd lift some goods we could fence, then turn around and use the money we made to buy more dope. This cycle went on for weeks.

One day Lois excitedly told me about a shooting gallery in Hollywood that had some China White. I had heard about the stuff; it was almost pure, and it delivered a trip that was incredibly euphoric. I couldn't wait to try it. A few hours later, money in hand, my friend and I arrived at the dealer's house. As we walked in, Lois warned me, "This stuff is powerful and gets people all the time. Don't you overdose, you hear?"

"Yeah," I laughed, "you don't worry about me, sister. But if I ever do, just roll me out in the gutter." Never once did it dawn on me that I could overdose or die. I just knew that the drug would make me fly, and flying high was all I wanted to do. I'd worry about landing on the way down.

I was thrilled when we walked in the door. I had never been in a big-time dealer's place. I felt like I was really hitting the top. A slender, attractive Indian woman greeted us. Looking first at me, then at Lois, she pointed back at me and asked, "Who's that?"

Lois answered, "Jacquie, this is my friend, Lauren."

Jacquie took a step toward me, noting my girlish appearance, bell-bottom jeans, and dyed red hair, and then said to

Lois, "I don't think so. She is too innocent for this kind of place. Get her out of here."

"Wait a minute," Lois argued. "Lauren is a user. Man, I use with her all the time. I know her. She's not a cop or anything. She's cool."

"Are you sure?"

"Yeah, you know me. You know I wouldn't lie to you. She's okay."

Giving in, Jacquie led us into a room that was filled with people in various stages of fixing and getting high. It took us time just to work our way through the crowd to find a place to sit and set up. When we did, Jacquie brought us our China White. I repeated the ritual that Eddie had taught me. By the time I injected, Lois and Jacquie had already fixed. I used the same needle they had and stuck it deep in my vein.

Jacquie's head had already hit her chest and she was rubbing her nose, moaning, "Wow, this is so good!"

Lois was also well on her way and talking about how great the stuff was. I couldn't wait to see what it did to me. Pumping my blood in and out, I was vaguely aware of Jacquie's warning, "———, I hope you don't blow it for me." Then, pushing the plunger down, I released all the stuff into my body. Within seconds, the world began to fade away. I was losing all sense of everything. Somewhere, way in the background, I heard Lois screaming, "———, she's OD'd."

The next thing I knew, I was experiencing terrible chills. As I began to become aware of my surroundings, I discovered that I was nude, lying in a bathtub full of ice water. My vision was messed up, and everything I saw appeared in shades of gray and white. Nothing looked real, and a strange, echoing ringing filled my ears.

Trying to focus on my body, I discovered that I was covered with bruises. As I breathed, my lungs ached, and my breath was coming in short, painful bursts. I thought that I might be dreaming, and I prayed that the world that now surrounded me was not real.

The ringing in my ears grew louder, and it was joined by a

pounding sound, kind of like a drumbeat, only uneven. Trying to locate the source of the noise, I pulled myself out of the tub and stumbled through the bathroom and a living area and to the front door. Opening it, I discovered Jerry on the other side.

My husband took one look at me, then drew back his fist and hit me in the chin as hard as he could. I flew across the room and landed on my rear. Picking me up, he screamed, "———, where have you been?"

I soon discovered that I had been unconscious for three days, and during that time, he had searched everywhere for me. Somehow, Lois had managed to get me back to her place and hide me, until I either came to or died. She had also managed to keep Jerry from finding me—that is, until now. Jerry hated heroin addicts worse than he hated anything. When he finally figured out that it was heroin that had left me in this condition, he flew into a rage. Wrapping me in a sheet, he carried me home, and then wondered what to do with me.

I was very sick. Pneumonia had set in and was tearing me up. I couldn't hold down food, had no energy, and seemingly had no will to live. I was detoxing drugs, and I was all but helpless. I just lay in bed and moaned. I wanted to die.

Several days later, when I showed no improvement, Jerry let Mom and her long-standing boyfriend, Johnny See, come by and visit me. I was in bed when Mom came over. One look at me convinced her that she couldn't leave me with Jerry. She easily talked him into letting her take me home.

Sometime later, after I began to get well, Mom and I learned that Jerry still had a wife that he had married years before. Seizing this opportunity, I filed for and received an annulment. With another bad marriage behind me and an overdose that almost cost me my life, I knew that I had yet another chance to straighten out my life. As I began to regain my strength, I promised myself that this time I would make the most of my opportunities to improve and go right. But once again, I would break my own promise.

• Ten •

EVEN AS MOTHER was nursing me back to health and I was
preparing to turn my life around, a bit of old news came back
to haunt me. The indictment over the drug incident at the
border almost a year earlier was now ready to come to trial.
Eddie's lawyer, David, had called me and informed me that we
had a tough case to fight. He also admitted that Eddie had told
him to stick me with as much as he could. David had then
dropped Eddie, and was now working as hard as he could to get
me a fair shake. While he couldn't get the charges dropped, he
did get me probation.

With that behind me, I returned to Mom's and rested. I
weighed ninety pounds and moved like someone at least twice
my age. For six weeks Mom did all she could, pumping me full
of food, vitamins, and medicine. Slowly I began to return to a
state that at least allowed me to look presentable in public.

My appearance had initially so shocked Mom that she had
forced herself to cut back on her drinking in order to be at her
best while working with me. With her doses of liquid hostility
now consumed in smaller quantities, she and I got along pretty

well. Also, because she probably feared that I might go back to walking the streets, she kept filling me full of positive reinforcement, trying to get me to believe that I could make it in the regular world. She kept repeating, "You can do anything you set your mind to do; all you have to do is get in there and fight." Several times a day, she spouted statements that reflected not as much a belief in my abilities as a fear of what I had become and what I might go back to. If she had only done this ten years before, I might have avoided many, if not all, of the obstacles and pitfalls I had faced. But her help was too little too late.

I'm sure that by this time she knew that I was a hard-core drug addict, but in her mind an addict was someone who got high on heroin or LSD; prescription stuff didn't count. All she was concerned about were the street drugs. Her motives were great, but her ignorance of just how bad and far-reaching my problem was kept her from really helping me completely kick it. Besides her personal supply of prescription drugs, she had a closet full of uppers and downers that various doctors had prescribed for her. Without her knowing, I abused them as badly as I had the drugs I had gotten from dealers.

When not nursing me, Mother was working on my future. I had given up on that. I had too many strikes against me. I was an addict, not well educated (I didn't even have a high school diploma), and not very attractive at this stage in my life. I believed that I was fit for nothing. But Mom didn't let little things like that get in her way. She had a friend at the California Department of Education, and the two of them put together, not only a great-looking high school transcript, but a number of college hours too. They bundled up copies of all these forgeries and sent out letters to all the major airlines. Somehow, Mother had decided that I was going to be an airline stewardess. When she told me, I laughed.

I knew that "Laurie" Chapin was simply not cut out to be a flight attendant. I lacked the proper education (I didn't know what Mom had done in this area), height, and knowledge of a foreign language. I simply didn't measure up in any way, shape, or form. You can imagine my shock when Pacific Airlines called and asked me to interview the following week.

For the next few days, life was just like it had been when I used to go to auditions for acting jobs. Mom was constantly quizzing me, making sure that I would give all of the right answers and smile at just the right moments. I had never been coached this hard before, but I still had my doubts whether it was worth it. I thought that I was preprogrammed to crash and burn.

On the day of the interview, Mom and I drove the LAX Airport and found the proper room. While we waited, a deep urge to get high hit me. I needed a fix, and I didn't know if I could live without one. As I sat there, a sick feeling started floating through my body, the room began to spin, and my stomach began to churn. I probably looked like someone who was airsick. I knew that this would make a great impression on a group of people looking for someone to work at 30,000 feet.

By the time the interview took place, I was so sick that I had problems simply focusing on the people who were talking to me. The whole process took fifteen minutes, and when it was over, I really thought I bombed. But all the way home, Mother was convinced that I had impressed them. After a couple of days without anyone calling, I wrote off the experience as just another bit of wasted time. Then, on a Friday, a registered letter arrived, asking if I could fly to San Francisco for a second interview. Three days later I was there.

I felt much better going into this interview. Thanks to Mom's drugs, my system was perfectly balanced, and I was flying steady and high. After I visited with the executives, I knew I had turned the trick. Within hours, Pacific Airlines was setting me up for a six-week extensive training course so I could earn my wings. Back home in L.A., I packed my bags, hit Mom's drug supplies to get enough to make it through the time I would be away at school, and began to feel good about myself.

I flew through the school. No one, not even my roommates, suspected my drug habit, and I faked my way in so many different areas, thanks largely to my acting ability, that I graduated near the top of my class. As I approached my twenty-first birthday, everything seemed to be going well. I thought I had it together. So did Mom, but there was still a rather large, invisible monkey on my back.

For the next year, I lived in San Francisco with a number of other "stews," did a great job on the planes, partied a lot, and still managed to keep my highs a secret. If I had a problem, it was with money. Even though I was doing well financially, I was spending a big portion of my income on drugs; thus, I was usually broke.

But I didn't allow my financial condition to get in my way until Christmas rolled around. With no money to buy Mom a present, I did something stupid. Walking into a department store, I shoplifted a coat for Mother's gift. I wasn't caught, but one of the other "stews" saw me and turned me in to Pacific Airlines. I was promptly fired. Once again, I had no job, no future, and a big black mark on my job record. I called Mom.

By this time she was wearing the coat, and I managed to convince her that I had really bought it, and that the other girl had lied because she didn't like me. I used all my acting skills again to appear as a victim of circumstance. I also informed her that I was going to look in the San Francisco area for work. I promised that I would call soon.

Within a few days, I had landed a job as a waitress at Whitney Litchfield's Bermuda Palms restaurant and bar. Working in the bar, I began to meet people who could supply me with drugs. For me, it was a perfect scene. I had found just the crowd I needed to get high whenever I wanted. A few weeks later, I really scored when I waited on a dealer named Mike.

Mike was more than a little perverted. He got his kicks by overfixing people on pure heroin and speed so that they would almost die. He loved to watch as a person's breathing grew irregular and their eyes rolled back in their head. The closer the fixed person got to death, the more he enjoyed it. This was the price he charged for drugs.

For months I all but died for my fixes and really didn't care. I needed drugs so badly that going to the gateway of death seemed like a very small price to pay for them. Then, just at a point where life had very little meaning for me, I met Philip.

He was tall and good looking, and I had met him at Litchfield's while waiting on his table. From the moment he said hello, I was head over heels in love. He was impressed too, and asked me out. That chance meeting and first date began a great relationship. For the three-month period we dated, I managed to hide my hard drug addiction from him. He really believed that I was the all-American girl. Eventually, he invited me home to meet his parents.

I had never been so nervous, not even during my first audition or on my first trick. I was scared to death. I loved this man, and he was a good, caring, straight, respectable human being. I didn't want to blow it in front of his parents. So, with all of these wonderful and pure thoughts going through my head and with this chance of a lifetime, I should have been straighter than I had ever been. But a junkie's mind doesn't work the way a normal person's does.

The night of dinner with Philip's folks, Mike came over with a bag of crystal. I could tell by the smile on his face that he was up to no good, and yet, I listened as he talked.

"This stuff is hot! You've got to try some, Laurie. You're going to love it." He kept insisting that this was the best dope ever.

"Mike, I can't," I explained. My words were saying one thing, but my body and soul were saying something else. "I'm meeting Philip's folks tonight, and I've got to stay straight. I don't want to screw it up."

"Yeah, that's understandable," he answered, his voice now soft, not demanding. "But you don't want to miss what I've got for you. I'll tell you what I'll do. I'll give you just a touch—a little touch—and then we can have the rest at another time. Come on, Laurie, a little isn't going to hurt you. You're a big girl. You're used to this. It will make tonight even better. You'll be more relaxed."

As he tied off my arm, a booming voice inside my brain was telling me how stupid I was. It was yelling at me to look at all the things that drugs had cost me, and even as scenes of turning tricks, getting beat up, landing in jail cells, and losing jobs and friends flashed through my head, I ignored them. My desires and my eyes focused on something better. At this moment, all that really mattered was finding the perfect high.

"Mike, you ———" I started to scream as I noted the huge amount he was shooting into my arm. But it was too late. My mind quickly fogged over, my body floated away, and suddenly I was out of the real world.

In the background, I was aware of Mike laughing. His laugh rolled across the room like thunder, and yet it sounded as if it were a million miles away. Everything in the room looked like it was being reflected in a warped mirror. Getting up, I staggered to a table. My balance was so bad that I felt like I was walking through an earthquake. Finding Mike's form, I tried to force my lips to make words, but all that came out was nonsense. Pulling my arm back, I tried to strike him, but I couldn't finish my swing. I fell down, my mouth began to fill with foam, and the foam ran down my cheeks and onto my neck. I must have looked like a mad dog. Glancing back up, I saw Mike leave, still laughing, still enjoying my folly. Reaching out to grab a coffee table, using it as a crutch to get me back on my feet, I watched in horror as my hand passed right through it. I thought, *I'm disappearing. I'm a ghost.* Dropping back to the floor, I watched the ceiling spin as my heart raced even faster, beating so hard that I thought it was going to rip a hole in my chest. For hours this manic trip continued. Then the room slowly began to steady, and my vision began to return.

Staggering to my feet, I stared at my reflection in the mirror. My eyes were glassy, the pupils dilated, and my skin blushed. Stumbling to my room, I tried to clean up and get ready for Philip. A half hour later when my doorbell rang, I was still wired. When I answered the door, I could tell from his expression that I didn't look the way he had expected.

Smiling, I explained, "I'm not feeling too well this evening." My words were slurred, and I had great difficulty even putting this simple phrase together. It took me three tries to finish it. Still, rather than call the whole thing off, he grabbed my arm and walked me to his car.

That night at Philip's parents' home, I barely said anything, and when I did, it made very little sense. I also didn't eat or drink anything. I'm sure that the family thought I had come in on the last spaceship from Mars, and if they had thought this, they would have been very close to the truth. But somehow, I managed to make it through the night with Philip's parents thinking I was very shy, a little under the weather, and possibly very weird. They didn't pick up on the fact that I was on drugs.

If ever a situation should have awakened me enough to get help and get straight, this one should have. But it didn't. The next time Mike offered me a fix, I accepted. And if he hadn't offered, I would have begged. My need for drugs was much greater than my need for love. For almost nine more months, nothing changed. Philip would make life worth living, and Mike would almost kill me.

In the middle of August, Mom called and asked me to fly home for her birthday. It had been almost a year since I had seen her, and I decided that being with her for a short weekend wouldn't be so bad. Since I had no money, I had to ask her to pay for my ticket. She agreed to send me enough to get me home. She assured me that she would buy me the return ticket when it was time to leave.

I hit up Mike for enough drugs for the weekend, and on Friday, August 16, 1966, I caught a flight back to L.A. Mother met me at the airport. By the time we got home, we were at each other's throats. Because of my drug habit, I was real crabby. The dope I had taken before getting off the plane didn't help produce a logical frame of mind. Moreover, Mom found fault in everything I said, and vice versa. Every one of Mom's remarks hit me wrong. The bickering and name-calling continued all the way to Mom's place and through the rest of the night. It was just like it had been during my teenage years.

Saturday was just like Friday. The bickering made me so crazy and mad that I took all of my drugs in the course of twelve hours. As the drugs moved through my system, I could handle Mom, but when I came down, I crashed hard. I was without money or a fix and had another whole day to go before Mom would buy me a ticket to take me back to my drug connections.

By the time Sunday rolled around, my craving for a fix was driving me wild. I hadn't been able to sleep at all. I was seeing things, and sweat was popping out of every pore in my body. It was as bad as anything I had ever experienced. Then, when Mom announced she wasn't going to fork over the money for a trip back to Frisco, I blew up. We shouted at each other all day and most of the next. When I could take no more, I stormed out of the house.

I hadn't been in L.A. for a year, and my connections for a fix were gone. Wandering the streets, irrational, and starving for drugs, I must have looked like an escapee from a mental institution. My pace was rapid as I raced across street after street, down block after block, looking for a way to get money for a fix. Then, on Hollywood Boulevard, I stopped. The door to a recording studio was open, and no one was in the front room.

Dashing in, I began to open the desk and file drawers looking for money. In the top of one of the drawers was a checkbook. Ripping out the top two checks, I closed the drawer and ran back out into the streets. I knew that a branch of the Bank of America was only a few blocks away, so I quickly ran to their building, walked to the service desk, used a pen, and carefully filled out both checks to myself for three hundred dollars, signing the name of the executive listed at the bottom of the blank signature line as the signee. On the top left corner, I put the word *payroll*. In my hurry, I misspelled it. I dashed to a teller before noting my mistake.

After she took and glanced over the checks, she explained that she didn't have enough money in her drawer to cash them. Asking me to wait, she said she would return after getting some more money from the vault. I thought nothing of it. I was thinking of little except the drugs and the plane ticket I could purchase with my bonanza. Suddenly, someone grabbed me from behind. Turning my head, I saw that the person was a cop. I then felt the click of handcuffs over first one wrist and then the other. Pushing me over to the side of the bank's lobby, he read me my rights.

I was now once again on stage front and center. I was the star in a brand-new show. Scores of employees and customers watched as I was taken from the building, out the main doors, and placed in the backseat of a squad car. As the door shut, the reality of the situation hit me full force. I had been busted for my need of a single day's worth of drugs. They had cost me again, and this time in a potentially bigger way than ever before.

• Eleven •

WHEN WE GOT to the police station, I was put into a holding cell where I got to keep my personal belongings. Knowing that if the tracks on my arm were noticed, I'd get busted as a user, I took some tweezers from my purse and scratched up the inside of both my forearms. There wasn't an inch of arm that wasn't covered with blood or big red scratches. Even with all that, I failed to cover up all my tracks.

Using my one phone call, I contacted Mother and she bailed me out. Then, running as soon as she turned her back, I escaped into the world of hard-core heroin addicts. If it was a drug and it could be snorted, swallowed, or shot up, I'd use it. I took so much stuff so fast and so often that I lost three months of my life. They were not even a misty memory; they just weren't there. I have no idea where I stayed, what I did, who I was with, or if I even ate. I was simply high—always high.

One day, stoned out of my mind, I was picked up and again thrown in the county jail. I thought I had experienced the worst of everything, but the county jail made everything else I had been through seem like easy street. With no fixes, no friends, no one to call, I was in deep trouble.

Crashing hard, I was almost unaware of the procedure I went through to check in. But I woke up when I was tossed in a holding cell with a murderer and an anti-social thief. The guard looked at me, now shaking, dripping with sweat, glassy-eyed, and scared witless, and pointed to a three-eighths-inch foam mattress lying on the floor beneath the two bunk beds. "That's yours, sweetheart. Sleep well!" Then she laughed.

Over the next few days, I tried to run from my female "roomies," run from the food, run from the guards, and run from my own image. I also needed a fix in the worst way, and I cowered at the prospect of being unable to fill my need in any way at all. But I'm a survivor. So I learned as much as I could about jail life, doing my best to stay alive and alert day by day.

It didn't take me long to realize that in this world of steel bars, I looked like a prima donna. I also discovered all kinds of cliques in jail. The lesbians had their group, the Mexicans theirs, the whites theirs, and the blacks theirs. If you didn't attach yourself to a group, you were at the mercy of everyone. Judging the strongest group to be the blacks, I joined them.

Over the next week, still coming down hard from my drug addiction, I latched on to these black cons like they were my Lord's protectors. I followed them everywhere, and, in a fight situation, I stood with them. When one of them got very ill, I was the first to jump on the guard who wouldn't send her to see a doctor. When the guard ignored me, I got ugly.

"—— you!" I screamed. Then, after filling the air with every obscenity I knew, I pushed my face against hers and threatened her. Suddenly, I found myself knocked to the ground. Two more matrons showed up. The first guard, her voice filled with rage, pointed at me and said to everyone around her, "She's going to lockup. Get her out of here!"

Jerking me up, they marched me through several doors to an elevator. When the elevator reached the basement, I was led off, dragged past corridor after corridor of dark, unlighted rows of cells, and then tossed into one of them. Uncuffing me, the guards then stripped me to my undergarments, took my clothes, and left me in a dark, six-by-six concrete cell. The only thing in the cell besides me was a hole for a toilet and a thin foam sleeping pad. Except for the huge, thick, iron bars on the cell door, everything else was black. I was in solitary confinement.

Behind my cell was another one that was a part of another long corridor of solitary units. In the next row, the county kept the psychotic and the retarded prisoners. These were women who had slit their own babies' throats, killed their parents, husbands, or neighbors, and were so sick that they would never stand trial for what they had done. These were people full of pain, and the only way they knew to unload that pain was to scream and cry. That was all they did, all night and all day long. Their moans echoed off of every wall and corner of the floor. Covering my head with my pad didn't shut them out of my mind. Combined with my cold-turkey withdrawal, this environment began to take what little sanity I had left.

I was given just two meals a day, and the gruel I was served hardly classified as real food, but I knew that I had to eat it in order to maintain my strength so that I could last. I did somehow survive my seven-day sentence. When it was over, I was released to the main prison population only to get in trouble within minutes and find myself back in the hole. One maddening week turned into two, and two into three, and so on. Finally, after sixty-two days, the guards let me out. I was a complete basket case.

The entire time I had been in, now almost three months, I hadn't even thought about my charges. I had been too busy just surviving. But when I finally read them, I determined that a good lawyer might be able to get me out of jail. An inmate who was a trustee offered to help me. She got me some paper and a pen, and she smuggled a letter to David, the attorney who had gotten me off with probation on an earlier possession charge. Within a few days, he came to L.A. and bailed me out. I couldn't thank him enough. For hours I bowed and humbled myself to him, even promising to get my life together. Yet, as soon as he was gone and I was on the street, I connected with some of my junkie friends and got the high I had craved for the last three months.

Finding the apartment that one of my old shooting partners, Jack Hale, shared with two of his friends, I managed to get myself invited to stay, and then proceeded to lock myself in a closet in an attempt to hide from the world. By this time, I had developed into a complete paranoid schizophrenic. In that closet, filled with old clothes and blackness, I rocked myself to sleep. At three in the morning, I woke up, sneaked out of the house, and walked the streets of L.A. I was so messed up that I would hide in the bushes and behind walls whenever I would see a car. I was scared that the whole world was after me.

Just about dawn, I found the address of a woman I had met in jail. Her name was Cookie, and she had told me to look her up when I got out. I don't know if she was expecting me this early, but she welcomed me and let me stay.

For the next few days Cookie, her husband, and I used every drug we could buy, steal, or beg. These constant highs keep me from being frightened or remembering what I had lost. The only problem was that, from time to time, I came down.

One afternoon when my head was clear and I was longing for something more than just existing and getting high, thoughts of Philip came into my mind. I began to cry, thinking of how close I had come to having a normal, healthy love and life with him. My heart aching and not knowing what else to do, I called Mom.

"Where in the world have you been, Lauren?" were the first words out of her mouth. I didn't bother to explain; I just wanted to know if she had any calls for me. I was also hoping for some money or pity. What I got instead was the news that a letter had come addressed to me in care of my mother. It was from Philip. It was short and sweet. He said goodbye.

The news that Philip had given up on me didn't surprise me. But knowing he had really walked away from me hurt deeply. He was the only straight thing left in my life, and now he was gone. In my mind, I had lost every reason to live.

A few hours later, after Cookie, her husband, and I had fixed, we went to a rock 'n roll club on Hollywood Boulevard and began drinking heavily. I was almost rigid. The world and my thoughts were moving in slow motion. As midnight welcomed a new day and the gang partied on, I was crashing hard. I got up and went back to Cookie's place. For hours I sat alone, remembering not only the good times I had had with Philip but the terrible months I had just been through. The longer I thought, the more pain I felt.

My mind reached back and replayed scenes of my troubled past. Then, a thick cloud of depression settled over me. Convinced that I was incapable of giving or receiving love, I felt terribly empty. I couldn't believe what a mess my life had become. I had ruined my marriages, lost all my self-respect, lost my family, almost lost my mind—and it was all due to drugs. Then there was Philip. He could have led me out of my mess, only drugs cost me him too. As I looked in the mirror, I remembered how much he had loved my long hair. Taking a pair of scissors, I whacked it all off, leaving myself a skinhead. I cried and screamed.

Tears were now rushing down my face; I was desperate and completely out of touch with God and the world. Looking back in the mirror, I decided to end it all. I tried to find some pills, but for the first time since I had moved in, I found none. Wandering into the kitchen, I searched the drawers for something to stab myself, but everything was too dull. Finally, I roamed out the door of the apartment and across to a neighbor's. Pounding on their front door, and yelling I woke them up.

"I need a good butcher knife," I informed the girl who answered my knock.

"Do you know what time it is?" she sleepily asked.

"Yeah, but I have to cut up a chicken. We're having company, and I need to cook it." I knew that she thought I was crazy, but she was too tired to allow me to bother her anymore. Leaving the door, she returned with an old meat cleaver. I thanked her and assured her that I would return it. Shaking her head, she just shut the door in my face.

I didn't bother to go back to the apartment. Instead, I wandered around until I sat on the curb under a street lamp. It was at least 2:30 A.M., and there was no activity on the street at all. I was alone with my thoughts, except for a newfound pet—a golden retriever that had attached herself to me.

As I laid the cleaver in my lap, I began to talk to God, explaining every bad break I had ever received in life. I wanted, even needed, to justify what I was about to do. For at least an hour, I pleaded my case, and then, when I had rationalized enough, I took the cleaver in my right hand. The steel blade caught the light, and for a moment I saw my own reflection. I stared with a distracted interest at the image of myself reflected on the cold blade. My eyes were hollow and lifeless, my expression almost blank. I looked dead. I noted an involuntary tear running slowly down my cheek.

Inside me, a voice cried out, "If thy hand offend thee, Lord, cut it off." I don't know why, but of all the Bible verses I had learned at the convent, this one now came back to me. Over and over it rebounded inside my head. I began to look at my left hand, and then at my arm. Shaking my head, I cried out, "If it weren't for this hand, I wouldn't have done drugs. This hand made me this way. If I could just get rid of it, the pain would go away. Then the voice came back, telling me, "Do it now. Cut off thy hand! Do it!"

I laid my left arm on the curb. I then moved it forward so that my hand dangled over the edge, my wrist right at the point where the concrete angled down. Taking careful aim, I raised the cleaver, and then with all the power I had left, I drove the cleaver down into my wrist.

I heard the cleaver strike the bone, a few fragments flying out and mixing with the blood that quickly shot out and covered my clothes. But as I looked down, I casually noted that my hand was still attached, and my bone had not been completely broken. I wondered if I had done enough to kill myself. I decided I hadn't.

Raising the cleaver again, I once more struck my wrist. This time my hand hit the curb, and even though it was not severed, I knew that I had accomplished what I had to do.

Forcing myself up, I began to walk down the street, with dog in tow, feeling nothing but the coolness of the night air. I walked past a television store where a row of new televisions played out images of an independent station's late-night offering. "Father Knows Best" was running and Kathy was charming the few late-night viewers who were tuned in, but I didn't recognize the little girl as myself. A block or so further down the street, a large bank of fog rolled across my mind, then my world went blank. My body now limp from the injury, I fell to the sidewalk in a heap.

• Twelve •

"WELCOME TO THE living," a man's voice quietly said. Opening my eyes, his white coat began to come into focus. "The police found you wandering the streets with your dog. They followed a trail of blood from a street corner to where you were. They picked you up and brought you here—L.A. General. That was a couple of days ago. For a while we didn't know if we were going to save you. But you're a pretty strong girl."

As the doctor continued to speak, I became aware of the intense pain coming from my left arm. Glancing over, I could see that it had been bandaged, encased in an open cast that was hanging from a hanger over my bed. My hand was swollen to at least three times its normal size. It looked like a part from an elephant.

"You know," the doctor said even as I stared in amazement at the results of my work. "You're lucky to be alive. Would you care to talk about it?"

I shook my head, the doctor nodded as if he understood, and then waited for a few minutes to see if I would change my mind. When I didn't, he tenderly encouraged me to rest and left the room.

For the next three days, I talked little. The doctors and nurses gently tried again and again to figure out what had happened to me—to get me to open up. I wouldn't. Repeatedly they told me how lucky I was to be alive and how fortunate I had been not to lose my hand. Each of them would react with concern and care whenever I would moan in pain from my injury, which, despite heavy medication, literally throbbed day and night.

At the end of five days, my first doctor examined me again and then informed me that I would be well enough to leave soon. It was a sobering thought, since I had no place to go. With the doctor's permission, I worked my way across my room—pulling my traction bar and an IV stand loaded with two different solutions—across the corridor, and over to the pay phone. Now in intense pain, I rested for a moment, even thought about backing out, then called my brother Michael.

"Michael," I pleaded, "you've got to come and help me. I'm scared. I tried to cut off my left arm, and I don't know why." Tears began to flow down my cheeks.

Michael was the only one in my family who was a responsible person. He didn't do drugs, wasn't an alcoholic, and had a level head. More importantly, his heart was full of love and compassion. The few times I had seen him in the last few years, he had always pulled me aside and tried to get me to open up and tell him what was hurting me so. He had always tried to help.

Slowly, I explained all of what I could remember about the night I had tried to kill myself. I then poured my heart out to him, confessing all my problems and disillusionments. Finally, after unloading everything I had bottled up inside myself, I begged him to help me. But I was unprepared for his answer.

"No, Lauren, I'm not going to help you this time. Yes, you need help, but not from me. I think it is time for you to bail yourself out of trouble. It is time for you to get your own help. This is one that you have to do on your own."

Crying harder now, completely disillusioned, and feeling totally abandoned, I hung up the phone. I knew that if Michael wouldn't help me, no one would. I was beaten.

Later that day, when the doctor who had first spoken with me came by to see how I was doing, I admitted that I needed some in-depth psychological and medical help. He brought me papers to sign that would transfer me to the psychiatric ward.

I didn't really know what to expect, and in a move that was probably meant to keep me from going into a state of complete shock, a nurse shot me full of thorazine as soon as I entered the locked ward. The shot made me both rigid and limp at the same time. I couldn't move at all. As I looked around, strange, mumbling people were everywhere. Some of them were walking in circles, others were laughing, and still more were crying. *These people are crazy,* I kept thinking. Never did it dawn on me that I was too. I had an arm encased in an open cast dangling from a pole to prove that I was a member of this same fraternity.

After several days of immobility, a nurse came into my room, and with a happy, singsong voice said, "It's time to get up."

Still drugged out of my mind, I answered, "Dream on, I can't move!"

"Oh, yes, we can. Now, come on." I hated the woman's happy voice, but I admired her determination.

For the next hour she dragged me around the floor. I was nothing more than a limp rag, but she kept pulling and pushing. Finally, as she put me back in my chair, she wondered out loud, "Maybe we should have your dosage cut." I totally agreed with her. I wanted to have some control over my movements.

Over the next few days, the doctors returned me to some kind of normal frame of mind, and I began to walk around this strange world in which I had requested to be placed. It didn't take me long to discover that the people who were my roommates were much more worse off than I had ever imagined. Some of them told me about killing people. Others just talked about being people who were long dead. Many didn't talk at all, at least not in a way that anyone could understand.

Just when I began to believe that I was never going to see anyone with whom I could relate, I ran into a nice young lady who was calm, seemed well adjusted, and looked as out of place on Floor Thirteen as I did. We talked about our problems for over an hour. There was no doubt in my mind that this woman was as normal as any I had ever met. Later, she looked me up again and asked me for a cigarette. *A buddy who smokes*, I thought. *This kid is all right*.

As we smoked, we talked some more, remembering better times and finer surroundings. I finished my cigarette first, crushing it in an ashtray. I watched as she continued to smoke hers, enjoying every bit of it before taking a final drag. Then she pulled up her sleeve and smashed the burning butt into her bare arm. My eyes quickly travelled from her arm to her face, which reflected nothing, not even a hint of pain or emotion. Glancing back down to her arm, I noticed a long line of identical burns and scars.

Grabbing a nurse, I announced, "She's burning herself. Please help her. She's trying to hurt herself. You've got to help her."

I had never seen anything like this. I had never witnessed a person methodically burn herself and show no signs of pain. It made my stomach churn. It also brought out my maternal instinct. I wanted to help this girl, hold her, and tell her that she didn't need to hurt herself, that everything was going to be okay. But I couldn't, and I knew that it would be a long time before she would be all right.

After the nurse came, medicated her, and took her away, I was told that if I wanted to be friends with the girl, I could never give her matches, cigarettes, mirrors, or anything else she could use to inflict pain. Shocked, I nodded and walked away.

As I wandered down the hall, I passed a room with another very normal-looking young woman. I stopped and observed her brush her hair for several minutes. She seemed to be carefully studying each stroke in her hand mirror, and when satisfied, she would repeat the stroke again. Entering her room, I went over, sat beside her, introduced myself, and then asked if I could look in her mirror.

"Sure." She smiled and handed it to me.

Looking at myself for the first time in days, I was surprised at what I saw. The person reflected back at me looked crazy. I vaguely remember having cut off my hair, but I was surprised when I discovered that it wasn't just short—it was cropped to the skull. Any closer and I would have looked like Yul Brynner. As tears ran down my face, I wondered, *What happened to me? How did I get this way? I look like a little boy.* I cried myself to sleep the next several nights, deeply depressed that I had entered a world so foreign to me, and even more depressed that I was now a person whom I didn't know.

Day after day the doctors worked with me to try to find out why I was so confused. They ultimately told me that I was a severe manic depressive who was trying to live up to the perfect image of Kathy Anderson. Therefore, in my own mind, Laurie—as I now introduced myself—was everything I wasn't supposed to be but was, and Kathy everything I should be but couldn't. I was constantly setting myself up to fail. But even though they decided that this was my problem, they didn't tell me how to change my condition.

For a long, dreadful month, I survived in this horrible place. Mom came to see me several times, but I didn't really respond to her visits. Michael also visited, but he didn't have much of an impact on me either. I was simply marking time, hopelessly depressed and disillusioned. I had no faith, no goals, and no reason to live.

The staff knew I wasn't well and was still a danger to myself, but they could keep me only thirty days. As a volunteer commitment, that was my time limit. As I walked out, I am sure that most of them expected that I would either die or be back within the month.

I went back to Mom's for a few days. I knew that I couldn't stay alone; I couldn't even dress myself, and I needed a nurse. Mother was a good one. I hoped that I could heal in a hurry because I wanted to go back to San Francisco. But something important was holding me in the L.A. area: my court appearance for attempted forgery. After consulting with my attorney, I decided to cop a plea and admit to the judge that I was an addict who had stolen the checks to get a fix. I thought that, since I hadn't been in trouble like this before, I would get a probated sentence. I was stunned when, instead, the judge sentenced me to seven years in the California Rehabilitation Center, known as CRC, in Norco. As he read the sentence, and before the shock had even settled into my face, I was taken into custody. My plan had backfired, and my freedom was now completely gone.

Initially the state placed me in a hospital ward for almost three weeks. During this time, I was isolated from the main patient population, had daily visits with psychologists, and was heavily medicated. They watched me like a hawk, believing that I would try to kill myself again.

Mom wrote me constantly, but rather than cheer me up or bring a bright spot to a dark day, her letters added to my depression. In her words, she was trying to show me that she loved me, but I was left wondering why she was expressing all of this concern and love now that it was too late. It left me filled with confusion. It was obvious that Mom wanted to build a bridge between us, to try to find some common ground, but the memory of her pushing me aside for alcohol and her friends was too fresh in my mind. I couldn't forget and start again, not with CRC facing me. Inside, I was still blaming her for most of my heartaches.

When, after twenty-one days, the state's doctor judged me physically fit, I was packed off to Norco, California. I was frightened as I boarded a bus with a group of other women sentenced to do hard time. The journey took a couple of hours.

The time gave me one last chance to reflect and to look at the free world—to realize just what I was giving up because of a drug habit. Even with these scenes flashing before my eyes, I refused to blame myself.

Looking around the bus, I noticed an old acquaintance from my street days. Frankie Staco had been a dancer in a club I had frequented. She and I spent a few minutes sharing our troubles, and then decided that when we had both paid our debts to the state, we would get together. I was deeply disappointed that she had been sentenced to Chino, a maximum security women's prison, because I would have felt much more secure with her being with me at Norco. I knew that I needed a friend.

When we arrived at my unit, I got off the bus only to find the lesbian inmates standing off to one side looking over the new admissions. They were actually planning their next conquest. My skin crawled, knowing that they would soon be hitting on each of us in person. As we were marched inside, their eyes never left us.

Over the next hour, each of us was stripped of all our clothes and jewelry, searched, medically examined, prodded, sprayed with insecticide, and given our uniforms. In the course of just a few minutes, I had gone from being a person to being a number: N1148. I didn't feel very much like a human being. Here it was, less than a month before Christmas, and, in most people's minds, I had just earned the title of an animal. I was scared and hurting.

As far as my "prison" went, this one was nice. The inmates shared rooms with two-to-four beds each. We had a psychotherapy room where we had daily two-hour sessions, we got to watch television when we weren't working, and we had the opportunity to use outside recreational areas. Still, the fences around CRC were always there, reminding us who we were.

Just beyond our compound was a men's prison. This area was more tightly guarded, but you could see the men in the distance, working and playing—surviving just like us. I later discovered that many of the women inmates had husbands and boyfriends close enough to wave to but too far away to touch or talk to. This made their stay even more awful.

A day before Christmas, when I didn't have a friend or a hope in the world, another bus arrived with a new batch of inmates. In this group was a young friend of mine from San Francisco, a girl named Leslie. Seeing her and receiving her friendship again made things a bit more bearable as the new year rolled in.

My arm was still in bad shape and giving me all kinds of trouble. I had lost all feeling in my thumb and first two fingers, so I had to depend on my roommates to help me do things, including getting dressed. The doctors gave me a rubber ball to squeeze, but I didn't use it much because of the pain it caused. I noticed that my fingers seemed to be constantly infected, but it took me awhile to figure out that I had been burning them every time I smoked. I just couldn't believe how messed up I was.

Mom sent me all my old clothes and some gifts for Christmas. Rather than making me happy, this bit of kindness actually made me feel more rejected. I seemed to think that this act meant she was wiping me out of her life. Almost everything that happened was leaving me depressed.

Mom visited me for a short time, but her visits caused me such pain that counselors suggested that she stop. Billy, David Horn, and a Catholic priest named Brother Stanley were the only people who were allowed to come somewhat regularly.

Brother Stanley may have been my strongest ally. He had gotten to know me at the L.A. County Jail, and, even though I had not been very nice to him, he had not given up on me. He had even come to my trial and supported me there. He seemed to be a guardian angel, a man who was assigned to remind me that, even in the "prison" I was living, there was a way out.

During my days in county jail, talking with a priest got you out of your cell for awhile. It was a breath of freedom. So when this five-foot, four-inch, 170-pound Friar Tuck visited, I used him to enter a different world. I didn't want to admit it, but I liked him. I may have cussed, and I may have tried to say every ungodly thing I could in an attempt to shock him, but I still didn't want him to give up on me. As the weeks went by, as I became more accustomed to his big brown eyes, his quick dimpled smile, and his short white hair, the more I looked forward to our discussions. I was surprised and elated when he began to make monthly trips to Norco to see me. I also began to listen to him a bit more than I had before. Now, more than a ticket to a different location for a time, he was a friend, and I didn't have too many of those left.

My first month at CRC didn't go that badly. It could have been better if I had chosen to make it better, but, all things considered, it was an easy ride compared to L.A. County Jail. Then, on January 1, 1967, a rebellion broke out in the men's prison. I didn't know anything had happened until I came face to face with a male inmate in my hall. He had a hatchet in his hand and a stocking pulled over his face. When I saw him, he instinctively raised the weapon, causing me to turn and run to my room. But out of fear, my roommates had locked the door. I couldn't get in.

"Help me!" I screamed as I pounded on the door. "Let me in! Please let me in!"

"No way, honkie," one of them shouted back. "You stay out there. We don't know who's with you."

"——, there's no one with me, let me in!"

"Go away, we're not unlocking this door for nobody!"

Quickly turning, I noted that the man who had been chasing me was now running down another corridor, so I dashed back to the television room. I now saw several different men, all in a hurry, and all seemingly looking for a place to hide. One of them grabbed me, begging, "Please, you've got to help me. You've got to hide me somewhere."

I calmed him down, led him back to the middle of a meeting room, and talked to him for several minutes. This poor guy was more frightened than I was. He was afraid that one of the other rioting prisoners would kill him or get him in enough trouble that his sentence would be stretched for a longer time. All he wanted was to get back to his unit without being spotted. I showed him a hallway that led to a point not far from the men's prison. I wished him well, and he left. The remainder of the day, I sat in the center of the meeting room, just waiting for things to return to normal. And even when they seemed to, they really hadn't.

A guard had been shot and an inmate killed, and some of the men had raped some of the women. Others had just escaped to points unknown. Much property had been destroyed. It was not a pretty scene, and all of us paid for it. For the next few months, the prison and the women's unit were shut down tightly. Nothing moved unless orders came from the top dogs. It was late spring before we had the freedom we had when I had first come to Norco.

As spring turned to summer, I became more and more of a loner. I wouldn't talk at all in the group sessions. I wrote letters to old friends, including one to a boy in the mental unit to whom I poured out my heart, but I didn't let anyone on the unit get inside me. I was still hostile.

Mom's boyfriend died about this time. I knew that Johnny's passing would cause her great pain. I wrote to her and offered my deepest sympathies. I knew that she must have felt almost as alone as I did. Soon she had a mild stroke, and I began to blame myself for her condition, thinking that my life had caused her to lose her health. I now began to carry more and more guilt about situations far out of my control, and I isolated myself even more.

But not everything I was doing was negative. I had taken enough courses to earn a high school diploma, I did my regular work well enough to get a good job in the medical unit as a psychiatric secretary, and I began to attend Alcoholics Anonymous meetings with some of the other women from our unit. Even though I wasn't opening up to anyone, I did want to improve myself. Most of the staff viewed my actions as positive signs. Nonetheless, they wanted me to look inside myself too—to work on my self-understanding and character, not just on my behavior.

Dee Hayden, a staff member on my unit, never gave up

encouraging me. In fact, our friendship lasted far beyond my incarceration. Kay and Andy Kara, outsiders who ran the A.A. meetings, began to make inroads too. I had to admit that I even liked them. They encouraged me to get my act together so I would be considered for parole. They promised me that they would do all they could to help me.

Two times I followed their advice and went before the parole board, only to be refused release both times. Despite my job, my degree, and my A.A. attendance record, the numerous marks against me for verbally lashing out at authority figures and other people ruined my chances. Each time I was refused, I would pretend that it didn't really matter—that I was too tough to care. But inside, I would come completely unglued. It devastated me. I wanted so badly to be free again.

Sixteen months into my sentence, I was twenty-three and finally accepted for parole. I had thirty days to wait while my papers went to the area I was to live—that is, San Francisco. Once accepted by the city, the papers were returned to me, and I was released. Free at last!

A bus took me to San Francisco the day I was released, and I went straight to Litchfields, hoping to land my old job. Whitty was wonderful. He hired me right away. But the job didn't last long. I just wasn't ready for all the freedom that was now mine.

Like most people who have spent time away from the real world, be it in prison, in a war, stationed overseas, or whatever, I was completely out of touch. Almost two years had gone by since I had been on my own. I was disoriented, unable to make my own decisions, and felt as if I was carrying a neon sign that told everyone where I had been and what I had done. My freedom was far from liberating—it was deeply depressing. I wasn't ready for it.

I called my old A.A. group leaders Kay and Andy Kara. Andy drove up and stayed with me in the motel room I had rented. For one week he tried to help me adjust. But I adjusted little, cried a lot, and spent a good part of my time still disoriented and scared. The worst part of the week was that

Andy and I ended up in bed together. I had been out of prison for less than a week and was already being used, and I had to admit that I was using people too.

Sex was nothing more than another way for me to escape and build some false self-esteem. For Andy it was easy, and he rationalized it by assuming that I needed love. After a week of talk and sex, he convinced me to come back to his home in North Hollywood. I thought that once I got there, the affair would end. I was completely wrong. Not only did it continue, but Kay encouraged it, telling me that it was all right with her. So, I was caught in a relationship with two strange people, and I had no place to go. I was once again at a dead end.

I hated my life, and the only thing I looked forward to was the weekend Narcotics Anonymous meetings that were being held at the Karas'. This allowed me to meet a new group of people and escape my own dismal existence for a few moments. At one of these meetings, I met a man ten years my senior, Danny Amado. He was Mexican, good looking, romantic, and had just been released from CRC also. Within a couple of weeks of dating and romance, Danny had convinced me that we shared more than I ever had with anyone else, and he asked me to move in with him.

Being with Danny was great fun. He was sensitive and loving, always calling me "Cozy Fox." We would laugh and love for hours. As a bonus, he had access to drugs. He was a dealer. For the next two years, I lived with him.

I secured daytime employment at Pearl's Drapery Service as a secretary. I was good at my job, and my bosses liked me. But while I wasn't at work, I was slipping back into old drug habits. Danny and I used drugs every other day. We would clean out our bodies once a month in time for the urinalysis test required by our parole, and then we would celebrate our deception by using some more. We were convinced that we had the system licked. However, the authorities watched our every move, hoping to catch us doing something that would nail us to the wall.

One day, almost a year and a half after we had been on the

streets, they informed us that we could no longer live together. We either had to get married or separate. We were convinced that we couldn't function without each other. So on a trip to Mexico to score drugs, we were married. I was twenty-four and in another doomed-to-fail marriage.

As always happens with small-time dealers, the heat began to get to Danny as the police came closer and closer to shutting him down. No one would have ever guessed the pressure he was under by talking to him or watching his actions. Everything looked normal because he was almost as good at acting as I was. But when we were alone, he would break down and tell me that he thought our days were numbered. He knew that we were going to get caught. I tried to look at the bright side and ignore all of his gloom and doom predictions. To me, life was too easy to be worrying now. I was even getting along fairly well with my own family. Moreover, Billy and Mom had met and visited with Danny, and they liked him. So I came to believe that nothing could go wrong. Danny, however, talked more and more about taking a fall.

I must have loved that man a great deal, because over the course of a few weeks, he convinced me to take a rap for him. He actually got me to go to the parole board, confess to possession, turn myself in, and take a 120-day sentence. I thought that four months wouldn't be bad, and it wasn't. But when I got out and the heat was still on Danny, I realized that my time had all been for nothing. I also began to see that Danny was using me.

For the next few months, Danny and I spent increasingly more time looking over our shoulders. In our minds, a cop was behind every tree and hidden in every bush. Every deal was a setup. Even though no one was busting us, we just knew it would happen, and soon. But our sense of doom didn't keep us from doing what we had always done. Our fear of being caught was not nearly as great as our fear of having to get off drugs.

When he was by himself one day, Danny got busted and spent the next four months in jail. At my job, my coworkers and bosses wanted to see me get it together. They believed that

I could, now that I was away from Danny. They even went so far as to threaten me, telling me that, as long as I stayed clear of my husband, they would do all they could to help me; but if I saw him when he got out, they would do everything they could to make sure that both of us were caught with drugs.

In my sick mind, drugs were far more powerful than words or threats. Words just rolled off my back, but a fix worked on my head. I knew that when Danny was released, I would go back to him.

With Danny in prison, Mom and I were once again not getting along at all. She also needed money, and she knew that I was not going to be a trustworthy source of income.

Mom's health had slipped considerably over the past few years. She looked older than she was. And as time slipped by, she had turned to more alcohol and drugs to ease her pain—not just the pain of age and poor health, but the deeper pain of loneliness and hate.

One day I called her to ask her for my jewelry. I was broke and needed money badly, and my jewelry was the only possession I could think of that would temporarily buy me out of poverty. I exploded when she told me that she had sold my jewelry and that the money she had received for the sale was already gone, used to pay herself back for what she had spent on me while I was in CRC. She yelled at me when I asked her how she could sell things that didn't belong to her: "You owe it to me! I gave you everything, and all you gave me back was shame and embarrassment. What do you think my friends think of you?"

"Frankly, my dear," I replied, "I don't give a ———what they think."

After we had both exhausted our venom, we both slammed our phones down. That was the last time I would ever talk to her.

Feeling low, I decided to go and drown my pain at a bar. While I was drinking, I met a young drug addict who was suffering just as much as I was. After a few drinks, I went back home with him to his small trailer. We spent the night talking before we finally passed out.

When we woke up, we decided to score some dope. Pooling our resources, we got some China White from his brother, then returned to the trailer. The stuff was heaven. After using, we both nodded out. When I came to, my new friend looked peculiar. I poked him, trying to rouse him, but he didn't respond. Puzzled, I touched him. He felt strangely cold. Checking for a pulse, I found none. I thought, *This guy is dead!*

Using what I knew about mouth-to-mouth resuscitation and CPR, I frantically worked on him. I prayed and cursed, and then prayed some more, but he wouldn't breathe. I was still suffering from the effects of the heroin; my vision, as well as my mind, was not clearly focused. When, after a few minutes, he didn't come around, I called the police and gave them a tip about a possible overdose. I didn't leave my name. I thought I would be safe, completely out of the range of the law, but a neighbor saw me leave the trailer. It didn't take long for the police to track me down. They arrested me for murder.

I couldn't believe it. I frantically told them the real story, how I had nothing to do with the guy's death, but they wouldn't listen. Calling Gloria Davidson, my parole officer, I tried once more to explain what had happened. She heard me out and went to work in my behalf. I spent three horrible days in the county jail, while she attempted to get me cleared. It was like going back to hell, a place that I knew I had visited numerous times over the past few years.

When Gloria finally convinced the legal officials that I was a victim of circumstances, I was released. As I walked out, Gloria met me and offered to drive me over to Billy's. "You can stay there, Lauren," she said. "That is, until you get yourself back together. Then you're free to go home."

I nodded my head, caring little about where I went or what happened as long as I was free from jail. As I got into my parole officer's car, I believed the worst had to be over.

Gloria had not always been easy to talk to, but today was an exception. As we drove, she began to quiz me regarding my feelings about my mother. It didn't take long for me to open up. I told her everything. I told her how I hated Mom for all the things she had done to me, and how her friends had influenced her—how she cared more for them than for me. Over the course of the hour drive, not a single good word came from my mouth. I just blasted away, hitting Gloria with round after round of hatred toward my mother. When we arrived at Billy's and his wife's house, I was still raging. Gloria then explained to me that Mom had been very sick. I smiled and exited the car. As I walked into the house, Sue greeted me with tears in her eyes.

"How's Mom?" I asked, oblivious to the emotion and pain written on my sister-in-law's face.

"I'm not supposed to tell you until Billy gets home," she answered.

"Tell me what?" I demanded. After spending three days in the county jail, I was in no mood to be given the runaround.

"Lauren," she replied, now really sobbing, "your mother died last night."

"She what? No, not her too."

Not understanding my reaction, Sue just stared at me. She hadn't known about my three days in lockup or about my friend's overdose. Only Gloria and I knew about that. There is no way she could have known the shock I was suddenly feeling—not mourning or heartache, only shock.

The official ruling on Mom's death was natural causes, even though her body contained large amounts of alcohol and drugs. Billy, Michael, and I knew that the cause had really been suicide. She tried to die. It was her only way to be free. She was penniless and hopeless. Finally, one night while lying in bed watching television, with a drink on the nightstand and a lighted cigarette in her hand, she had escaped for good.

There was a big crowd at her funeral. Most of Mom's friends were there, a host of old business associates, and, of course, us three kids. Just as we were about to walk into the church, Dad appeared. As I looked at him, I realized that at one time he must have really loved this woman. He sat through the whole service, performed in the Catholic church where he and Mom had first gone to services together, without showing any real emotion. At the end, he shook Billy's, Michael's, and my hands, and left, never saying a word. Obviously, the love that had been there was now completely gone.

I had been the picture of strength in the service, but as I walked past the open coffin, I lost control. I began to cry uncontrollably. I felt both sadness and anger. And as the minutes passed, the anger inside me overcame my grief. I was mad at Mother for dying and not making up with me first. I thought she had died just to make me feel bad. I knew that she wanted me to feel guilty, and I did. I hated her for it. As I stood over her grave, even before the first scoop of dirt had been tossed in, I vowed, "I will never come to visit you. I will never come here again. I'll be —— if I will."

At the gathering after the funeral, Billy and I got as high as we could. We partied. When Michael came by to mourn with us for a few minutes, the distress that he felt over our conduct was obvious in his eyes. He couldn't believe how sick his brother and sister were. I didn't care. I felt like singing the song from the *Wizard of Oz*, the one with the line, "Ding dong, the witch is dead," but Michael wouldn't have understood, so I didn't.

Over the next few days, after I had come down from my high and thought about what had happened, I still felt rage inside. I wanted to be reconciled to her but couldn't. I cried. For weeks I would lie awake at night and on impulse dial Mom's number, only to get a disconnect message. Then I would get angry all over again. I wanted—even needed—so badly to talk to her. But she wasn't there to listen. I felt rejected again.

For the next several months, I was on an emotional roller coaster. Every time I began feeling good, I would think about Mom, and all the anger and guilt would come back. During the day, I acted and looked normal, but at night I was going to the black section of L.A. and scoring cocaine and heroin. I would stay up at night fixing speedballs over and over again, for months.

Gloria knew that I was torturing myself. She tried to work with me, not test me or turn me in. After four months, she finally knew she had to make me wake up to what I was doing to myself, so she told me, "Honey, I'm not busting you. But you need to face your problems and work on solving them. I want to help you, and I will be here for you if you need me."

I didn't listen to Gloria. Instead of cleaning up my act, I got even worse. I scored and got high more than I ever had before. I would often go into seizures while I was getting myself high. I would walk around in a daze; turning to no one for real help or friendship.

One morning I got up after shooting up some bad coke. I was experiencing severe seizures, and I figured the only way to feel better was to get a fix of heroin. I walked to a dealer's house that was only a few blocks away, bought some heroin, and as I tried to get home, passed out on the street. Some one called an ambulance. If I could have spoken, I would have asked them *not* to. With my record, coupled with the fact that I was obviously using and possessing, I was a sitting duck for another bust. But I was so out of it, that I didn't even realize what was going on, much less that I had just bought a ticket back to jail.

• Thirteen •

I HAD BEEN caught red-handed, and I knew that this time there was no way out. No lawyer, no matter how good he was, was going to convince a judge that I was a victim. I had walked on the wrong side of the street too long to even hope for a miracle. I knew that I could only pray that whoever ruled on my case would take pity on me.

The judge's name was Murphy, and I told him pretty much the straight truth. By this time, so much had happened so rapidly that even I had problems remembering all the facts. After I completed my ramblings, I made a very simple request: "Judge, I know what I am. I know that I have many problems, but I don't think that a prison term is going to solve any of them. I am a hopeless heroin addict, and I pray that you will allow me to go to a methadone treatment program. As I see it, that is my only hope."

Judge Murphy looked at me for a few seconds, then once again studied my record. Pausing to think, he then addressed me: "Miss Chapin, I think you are suffering from the lowest self-esteem I have even seen. You have absolutely no faith in yourself. You have written yourself off. Well, I haven't. I have a lot more faith in you than that. I'm therefore going to sentence you to ninety days at the Camarillo State Hospital. They have a great drug treatment program. If you fail there, I'll have them bring you back before me, and we'll consider methadone."

Gloria Davidson picked me up at the county jail and drove me to the hospital. All the way she encouraged me to get my life together. I ignored her. I resented her having the gall to tell me what to do with my life. I was feeling the effects of drug withdrawal, and my system wasn't allowing me to look at anything with a very open mind. I needed a fix, and I wasn't going to get one. Even though she had been so kind to me over the past few months, I reacted with hostile words and angry tones.

As we drove through the gates of the hospital, I felt like a caged rat. My hostile attitude continued to expand inside me. I couldn't wait to lash out. I wanted to be left alone. I didn't want anyone changing me.

Once in the hospital, I was placed in a locked unit. All around me were men and women of all ages dressed in weird costumes. I wondered what planet I was visiting. Some of the people were wearing big painted signs that said things like, "Beware, I'll kill my brother," or "I'll lie about anything," while others were carrying little notebooks, looking up every few minutes and screaming, "I am a baby. I need someone to teach me right from wrong." Some were even wearing baby bonnets and sucking on bottles. It was the most bizarre place I had ever seen.

As strange as this place was, it didn't take the attendants long to initiate me into its pace and programs. I was forced to get up early, have group and individual think-tank sessions, and do loads of busywork. But most of the day they left my mind free to consider where I was and how I had gotten there. More than once, sometimes without my being cognizant of what I was doing, I had tried to commit suicide by overdosing, and I hadn't made it. I had been just outside death's door on so many occasions. During those moments I had decided that hell must be a place where you want to die but can't. For me, that is what the world had become. Unlike others who had terminal diseases and prayed for a cure, I desired a cure for life. For me, it was the living that was like hell. Getting through to someone with this viewpoint is more than difficult. I was an all but impossible case.

Often I would cry for hours, screaming out, "God, why don't you let me die? Do you hate me so much that you take pleasure in my pain?" But the pain would still be there when I had finished my pleas.

As I worked and thought, I began to remember the things that Gloria had said to me just a few days before. "Lauren, you are going to have to make a decision. You are going to have to love yourself and stop hating yourself for things for which you are not responsible. If you can never have children, accept it. Accept and put behind you your relationship with your mother and father. Put the past in the past, and work for a better future. Reject all your doubts, and get on with your life. Look for yourself. If you don't, you are going to die."

Her words made a lot of sense to part of me. I knew she was right, but I didn't feel I had what it took to turn the whole mess around. The task looked too big and seemed too hard. So rather than admit she was right and put the responsibility on my own shoulders, I just ignored my better judgment and rebelled against any- and everyone who tried to show me a way out. I even gladly told people I was happy with the way things were. From Day One, many of those in charge also viewed me as a hopeless situation. But a few men and women, who had once been as far gone as I was, thought I might climb out.

The hospital probably would have been a place where I could have survived and prospered had it not been for one man. Jack Hale ran into me just a few days after I had been admitted. At first it felt so good to see him. Here was someone who was going to have just as bad an attitude as I had. Here was my "brother," my soul mate, someone who was as confirmed a drug user as I was. He and I could act our way through this program and never break a sweat.

"Little sister!" he yelled when he first saw me. As he came toward me, a thousand memories flooded my mind. He and I had called each other white witches and had even become blood brothers. We had gotten high more times than I can remember, and we had shared everything other than sex. Heaven only knows how many days I had spent in his company. I certainly didn't remember. Those days had all become just faded blurs. But, with another hard-core addict from the old days, here, I knew that surviving would be no problem. I now had support.

"It's good to see you, little sister," Jack began as he threw his arms around me. "I'm so glad you're here. This program is just what you need."

I couldn't believe what Jack had just said. Was he faking, or was he one of them? The more he talked I discovered that he wasn't just another patient or prisoner; he was the director of the drug rehab program on the floor just under mine. He was up on my wing recruiting more students. The guy had sold out to the other side. He might as well have been a narc!

Now I knew that I was in real trouble. Jack knew me as well as anyone could. He knew all my lies, all my games; he knew everything. I had no secrets from him, and he was now working for the enemy. With Jack feeding them information on how to get to me, I found myself no longer able to hide behind my mask. He was stripping it away, all the while encouraging me to come to his longer program downstairs. He was relentless!

Within a week of seeing Jack, I was in the program up to my gills and looking for a way out. There wasn't one. All the doors were locked, the windows nailed down, and the staff positioned where escape wasn't possible. On top of that, we could receive no mail, nor could we make or take any phone calls. They even forced us to carry pencils and a notebook everywhere we went.

At first I didn't understand the purpose of the notebooks, but when people began to write things down as they looked at me, I figured it out. Everybody in the place was a snitch. On top of that, if you saw someone doing something wrong and didn't write it down, you got in trouble. It was the first place I had ever been where snitches were heroes. This broke every code of honor that a drug addict or a con ever learned. But this was only the beginning.

Once you did something wrong, they placed a rope around your neck and attached a sign to it. The sign was a small billboard that announced to the world just what you had done wrong. One lady I saw on my first day in the program had at least seven signs, one right under another. The first one clearly announced, "I am a mother lover." I soon was wearing signs that stated, "My smile is false. I'm really hurting."

Many people were emotionally crushed by their signs. They would do anything to get rid of them. I would see them crying, begging, wallowing, and pleading. I prided myself on not being that way. I was a "mud-holder." I didn't care what I was called or what I had to do; no one was going to break me. My mother couldn't, and these people were amateurs compared to her. Still, when I would do something against the hospital's rules, like talk back to authority figures or refuse to talk about my past, I was forced to stand still with my face against the wall for an hour as punishment. I began to hate every moment of my day and wonder if I could survive this treatment for three months. Ten years in prison started to look good. I was frantic for a way out.

One day I walked up to Jack and demanded to know how I could get out of this crazy world. After listening to my sad stories of how my being here was all a mistake, Jack simply smiled and said, "Little sister, there are two ways out. You can come downstairs into my program, or you can leave in a pine box."

"What the———are your trying to sell me?" I retorted. I had tried to show him that I was dying, and all he was giving me was the runaround.

"Lauren, aren't you tired? It has been such a long road for

you. You should be tired. If you leave here today and go back on the streets, you are going to die. It will happen in either a gutter or a strange bed, and you will probably be found lying in your own puke. Are you ready for that?"

I didn't answer him. I tried to act as if I had ignored him altogether. I simply walked off. What Jack was saying was probably right, but I didn't want to hear it. Rather than admit I was hurting and needed help, I persuaded myself that Jack had wimped out and that I didn't need that kind of friend. I wanted someone who was tough, someone who wouldn't give up. He had sold out. In an addict's mind, there is no one worse. I never wanted to see him again.

The problem with being in a jail-like atmosphere is that you can't walk for very long without bumping into the same faces over and over again. At least once a day, Jack would find me, and when he did, all he could talk about was his year-long program downstairs. Even when I refused to listen, refused to admit I had a problem, told him I didn't want to change, he didn't stop selling his program. I grew very tired of him, but try as I might, I couldn't avoid him.

Another hassle I faced was my own program. Every day I would do more things wrong, break more of their silly rules; thus, each day became worse than the previous one. With both the patients and the staff watching me, I felt as if my mother were haunting me through a hundred different people. I was being punished more often than anyone else. Worse yet, I was so hostile and rebellious that even the other patients hated me. I didn't have anyone to whom I could turn to support my side of things. And then there was Jack. I hated seeing him, but little did I realize that I hated him because he kept holding a mirror up to my face, and I didn't like what I saw in it. I just wouldn't face the truth.

One night, somewhere around two in the morning, unable to sleep, I got up, left my dorm wing, and went to the center meeting area. There, sitting in the office, was a young Mexican man. I opened the door and stepped in.

"Hi, what's your name?" I began.

"Rudy," he smiled.

"So," I quizzed, "what's your job? Are you paid staff or one of the snitches?"

"Paid staff?" he laughed. "No. No snitch either. I'm in the program, just trying to keep my nose clean. I don't have a long time, and I really need to complete it. Otherwise, I'll get sent to prison. Can you dig it?"

"Yeah," I answered. "Me too. I was picked up on another possession—stupid me—and was sent here for a ninety-day opt. Do you like it here?"

"It's okay," he replied. "By the way, what's a nice girl like you doing picking up a possession rap? Don't you know better?"

I almost laughed when he called me a nice girl. I believed that I could show him what a real nice girl was, although I certainly wasn't one. Rather than let him in on my secret, I just resumed our conversation.

"You married?"

"No, my old lady split. I've got two boys, though. How about you?"

"It's kind of crazy. I had an old man, and we were married down in Mexico but never filed it up here, so legally we're not really married. No kids either; can't have any." I didn't mean for it to, but my last statement, meant to sound so casual, suddenly hit me in my heart. I began to cry. Moved with compassion, Rudy came over and put his arms around me. It had been a long time since anyone had held me, and when he did, I allowed the fortress-like walls that concealed my real life to fall down. I told him everything. We talked for at least two hours; it was just before dawn when I decided to go back to my room.

"Thanks, Rudy," I smiled. "You've been great to talk to. I hope that I can see you again."

"Yeah," he replied. "I hope so too. Now, you'd better go before you get into trouble. Have a good day!"

As I wandered down the hall to my room, I already felt that Rudy and I would become lovers. Little did I know that my love for him would last over seventeen years and that he would touch my heart so deeply that, no matter what I did, no matter how far we were apart, the bond between us would remain strong.

Over the next few nights, I visited Rudy again and again. It wasn't too long before we had added the act of lovemaking to our times together.

My relationship with Rudy made me even more hostile than I had been before. It gave me a feeling of superiority. I was getting away with breaking the rules, and all those little people with notebooks were missing it. Naturally, this attitude set me even further apart from the other residents. Even the staff, using their most effective device, couldn't bend my stubborn will. But they persisted.

During the evenings, I was called in front of the staff interrogation squad to go over the list of bad things I had done during the day. While every one of the residents went through this, I was the one who never broke down. There, with a single white spotlight shining right at me, with questions and accusations flying from every direction, I would smile and admit nothing. Inside I was raging, but on the outside I was cool. Finally, one night, someone on the panel (we never did see them or find out who made up this group) asked me a heavy question.

"Okay, Chapin, we heard that you have had sex with Rudy Quiroz. What do you have to say about that?"

Smiling, I answered, "No way."

The same person repeated the question. I replied the same way. For fifteen minutes, I was yelled and screamed at, constantly being asked to admit to what I had done, but I wouldn't break down. I wouldn't even quit smiling. But even though I hadn't been broken, the next night Rudy was not on duty. He had been reassigned, and I wasn't going to get to see him anymore. Someone had snitched, and I knew that I had had it stuck to me again. This made me even more hostile.

Over the next few days, with Rudy downstairs, me above, and no way for us to get together, I began to take Jack Hale's invitations more seriously. I needed Rudy, and I needed his attention. I wondered if maybe I could do better downstairs with him. It wasn't the drug program or kicking my past life that enticed me; it was Rudy. So in a move that probably even surprised Jack, I asked to join his group. I told the attendants that I wanted to lick my vicious drug habit. Actually, I wanted to do something entirely different.

The first step in the process of getting into the downstairs program was going before a board to be interviewed. The key to making an impression on this group was total honesty. With a notebook full of comments written by the other residents, the panel knew my history and knew what I had done. I couldn't deceive them. But I still tried. I did well through the first part of the questioning, and then, just when I thought the interview was going my way, something I had done was shoved back in my face.

"Lauren, have you and Rudy had sex?"

My "favorite" question was coming back to haunt me again. Even worse, Rudy was in the room watching me being questioned. I knew that if I told the truth, he would be disciplined: he would have his head shaved; he would have his outside passes taken away; he would be stripped of his level of responsibility; he would be in deep trouble and watched like a hawk for months. On the other hand, if I lied, I wouldn't get to be with him and be in the program. I would lose either way. So I didn't answer.

I was then excused from the room, and Jack's ex-wife was ordered in. She was also a candidate for the program, and she was apparently interrogated as I had been. In the process of these questions, she told the panel about Rudy and me.

When they finished with her, they called me back in, and there, before Jack Hale, Rudy, and four other senior class men, I waited to be grilled. Instead, they just laughed for awhile, talking in whispers. I knew that I had been busted.

After waiting for several minutes, the question about sex was put to me once again. Off to one side, Rudy was nodding at me to go ahead and tell the truth, but I knew that inside he was hoping I would lie. I really didn't know what to do. As I tried to work it out, I remembered a question that Jack had asked me on numerous occasions, "Lauren, do you want to live?"

I hadn't ever really thought much about that. Obviously, from all the times I had overdosed and the other times I had willingly tried to take my own life, the evidence said that I didn't. But recently, despite my belligerent attitude and cruel words, I had grown to like living a little. Did I really want to live? Or did I just want to escape this program and flee to a drug-filled world that was more like death than life? I thought about my old world, its pain, and its hurt. I thought about running from Eddie, knowing that he would never have controlled me if it hadn't been for my addiction. I thought about my night in Chinatown, the night Eddie beat me with his gun and then urinated all over me. I even thought about my mother's death and how guilty it made me feel, and I wondered what would happen if drugs hadn't been such an integral part of my life. Thinking back to a night in San Francisco, I realized that I might have even known real love, but I traded it all in for a high. Maybe if drugs weren't the center of it, then maybe life did offer something. It was then that I silently told myself, *Yes, I want to live*. A tear filled my eye. I had admitted something important: I thought that I was worth saving.

Then I remembered something else Jack had repeatedly told me. "If you want to live, you need to get away from the drugs that are killing you. *You need this program*. Here, you can get your life back. If you want to live, you must come to grips with your destructive side and take control by being honest with yourself for the very first time in your life."

It was then that I realized that I had to answer the panel's question. I didn't have to tell the truth for them but for me. Sex and protecting Rudy were not as important as getting right with myself. I wanted to know myself, even like myself, and I sensed that this program might just help me do that.

Deep in my mind, I was saying no, denying these desires, just as I had denied having a habit I couldn't control. Everyone at the hospital was sick except me. But if I played by their rules, did things their way, let them inside my personal life, then I thought that I would be admitting to being sick too. I didn't want to do that. I was okay. It was Jack and the rest of these fools who were screwed up. What difference did it make what I did or what rules I lived by? It was my life, wasn't it?

A war raged in my mind. The old Lauren didn't want to submit. I had never really had rules. Mother had never really cared what I did as long as I made money. I could go where I wanted and do what I wanted as long as I didn't bother her. I had had no premarked paths to follow. I could make my own.

Then a new Lauren began to argue. It was this Lauren that pointed out that I had done a poor job blazing my own paths. I had always gotten myself into trouble. My only days of real happiness were spent at the studio, and there I had rules to follow. Maybe Jack's program would have a script that called for a happy ending, just like my old shows used to. After all, he certainly was different now. The only way to find out if he had sold out was to try what he was now hooked on. I was an actress; surely I could fake my way through this mess even if I didn't like it. And besides, if I could just get through the year, maybe I would get a clean bill from the courts and escape my record. Maybe I could fake them all out, or maybe I could learn something too.

Looking back at Jack, I clearly answered, "Yes, I had sex with Rudy."

Jack proudly smiled and the others took notes. Rudy just sat there, a horrible look etched across his face. As I stared at him, a horrible knot twisted in my stomach. I knew that I had made the right decision, but I wondered what I had done to Rudy. Suddenly, all the demons that I had wanted to escape by getting into the program ran after me. They tried to get me to change my mind—to take the easy way out. They forced me to think about what I was doing to Rudy and not what I was doing for myself. They also begged me to change my mind, to let them once again take control, to hide behind all of the false images that they could create.

For the first time, I resisted taking the easy way. I knew that Rudy could handle whatever they did to him, and I could now begin to get the help that might change my life and set me free. Besides, no matter what we both were about to experience, Rudy and I would be together.

• Fourteen •

I WAS READY to kick my habit. I was ready to become just another normal person. I was ready to leave behind all the nightmares that had been a part of my life. I was ready to take a good look at myself. But I surely wasn't ready for what the downstairs, long-term drug program was going to ask of me.

As soon as I moved down, they took away all my clothes, makeup, and jewelry. I was issued a prison wardrobe, told to wash my face and keep it clean, and was given a baby bonnet to keep on my head at all times. Finally, I was handed a pencil and notepad and told to snitch on anyone who broke any rule, no matter how minor.

One of the first rules I learned was that I wasn't allowed to initiate a conversation with anyone other than another person wearing a baby bonnet. If I did, not only was I ignored, but someone recorded my infraction. I was considered an infant, and everything that could be done was done to make sure that I knew that I was nothing more than a baby.

My day was planned for me. I got up at five in the morning and went to the track with other infants for one hour of hard physical exercise. At six we came back to our rooms and made up our beds; then at seven we ate breakfast and began our day of work. The chores assigned were not so much necessary work as they were just program elements to humble us and keep us busy. If one of us badly messed up, receiving a host of write-ups, then that person had to clean the bathrooms with a toothbrush or stand up with his or her nose touching a wall. I did both of these things a lot.

After supper, all of us gathered in a large meeting room and stood for hours, if necessary, with our noses and our toes touching the wall in front of us. We could move only when a staff member called our name, and we couldn't talk. When we were allowed to leave, we were taken into a room, lighted only with a bright light shining directly onto us, and questioned. The first part of the interrogation consisted of ratting on yourself. You could make it through the session pretty easily if you were completely honest. But if you lied or omitted something, the panel knew because they had everybody else's notes. One way or the other, everything each of us did was accounted for, and we paid the price.

For fifteen minutes the people behind the light grilled each of us. Then, after they had torn us down as far as they could, making us feel like dirt, they spent five minutes praising and rebuilding us. This routine continued every day except Sunday—the day we were allowed to go to church.

The services were conducted by various churches. But it wasn't until after the service that my real religious training began. My Catholic priest, Brother Stanley, would drive up from L.A. just to meet with me. When I had been sent to the hospital, I had expected him to forget me, but he didn't. Every week he would come to visit. Because of his devotion and the fact that he was the only visitor I ever had, I looked forward to seeing him. For some reason, he was a man who hadn't given up on me. I also found him refreshing. I enjoyed the hour or so I spent with him each Sunday, and even though I didn't believe what he did, I started thinking of this man as a father—the father I had never had.

As much as I looked forward to Sunday afternoons, I hated Sunday nights. I knew that, when I woke up the next day, it would mean the beginning of another week of humiliation and hard work. Sometimes, I was so keyed up about going through the next day that I found it difficult to relax and sleep. Sleeplessness made what I was going through even worse.

Then there were times when sleep just wasn't allowed. Some nights we'd be awakened at midnight, tossed out of bed, and put into a group session for intensive self-analysis. We were broken down, built up, then allowed to go back to our room just minutes before we had to get up and start our routine again. Once there, we found that someone had come in and messed everything up. We were ordered to make sense out of the chaos. This kept us from going back to bed, and it made me angry. I hated being abused like this. It was like boot camp, only worse, because all of us needed something we couldn't get—a fix. But slowly, each of us at our own rate grew up. After a couple of months of intense work, I had matured enough to be allowed to take off my baby bonnet and graduate to the "teen stage."

There were four stages in the program, and with each stage came fewer rules and a little more responsibility. I couldn't wait to move up. Another person at the same point in the program and just as eager to leave it behind was Phil Stein. Phil was the first man, including Jack Hale, who really knew how to push my buttons. He could tell when I was acting and when I was really being me. He therefore knew that I spent most of my time acting, but he was so caring, so loving, so warm and tender, that I really didn't care that he could see through me. Like Brother Stanley, I just appreciated the fact that he was my friend without wanting anything in return. He gave me a small feeling of worth.

Phil and I talked a great deal. Even though he should have, he didn't write me up when I broke a rule. The rule I was now breaking the most often was sneaking away with Rudy every time we could find a place to hide, which was usually in the elevator. We had gotten so good at covering our tracks that, outside of Phil, no one else knew about our ongoing relationship.

By this time I was feeling pretty cocky. I had over a third of the year-long program behind me, and Rudy and I were deeply involved, and Brother Stanley and Phil were there to make me feel loved even more. I was surviving, but I wasn't really taking hold of the problem that had put me in the program in the first place. I wasn't unloading all of the guilt I felt from being considered unworthy of love as a child or an adult. I wasn't admitting my own pain to anyone. I was just pretending to be tough, hiding behind a wall of false strength. I was acting, playing a part that could fool most of the world, but I could no longer fool myself.

Every month there was a forty-eight-hour lock-in called a "love-in," in which all of the negative junk that was constantly hurled at us was left behind so we could all get together and talk about good things. In a word, it was a two-day hug session, and most of the time, I loved it.

Joe Scales, a three-hundred-and-fifty-pound, six-foot four-inch teddy bear, ran these sessions. Joe was the perfect man for the job. He had a Santa build and a Jesus heart. He called us his kids, and we all called him Papa Joe. Together we would cry, laugh, hug, and heal. For almost everyone who became a part of these groups, a tremendous emotional healing began to take place. Most people started to realize that they had been searching for love while fixing on dope. Through Joe they started looking in the right place for a "fix": their own hearts.

I enjoyed the sessions from the beginning. It was a great relief to get away from the killer routine I was living most days. It was nice to relax.

The sessions would begin with our entering a large room devoid of furniture except for pillows and mattresses on the floor. Each of us had to follow the rules: no sex, no pairing off, no sleep, and two full days of no hostility!

As we sat in a circle, Joe would begin: "Okay, who wants to go first?"

As he looked around, everyone would fidget, saying nothing

until Joe finally announced, "Okay, I'll just pick someone myself. Karen, come on over here."

Karen would then cross the room, sit between Joe's legs, her back against his stomach, and he would embrace her. Then he'd say, "Karen, I love you." Turning her face toward his, he would then earnestly repeat this statement, his tone and look indicating his sincerity. When he was convinced that she believed him, he then said to all of us, "Now, each of you tell Karen how you feel about her. I want to hear no negatives, only good and loving remarks." For many of us, this time was very hard. Some of us didn't have much practice at being nice, but we still had to follow the rules or return to the unit.

Karen was the first of many people I watched go through this love drill. I observed, almost in a detached way, as a boy on my right began: "Karen, I think you're nice."

Waiting a second for something more, Joe then demanded, "Give us more than just that."

Thinking for a moment, the boy then added, "Ah . . . I think you are pretty, too!"

Still, this wasn't enough for Joe, and the boy knew it. Joe then asked, "Why do you think she is nice and pretty?"

Struggling to come up with another sentence about Karen, the boy responded. "She is nice because she's never done anything to me, and she is pretty because she keeps herself looking good." I couldn't help but laugh at his answer, and a lot of others did too. Smiling at the boy, Joe then went on to the next person. He did this until he had gotten all the way around the room. Meanwhile, Karen had to sit and hear all of the nice comments people made about her, and, like most of us, she found it very uncomfortable.

It wasn't unusual for the person on the "hot seat" to cry, and Joe would encourage this emotion. He would force the tears to flow, and then get to the core of their cause. During these times, the room would get so thick with emotion that many others would cry too. All of us would look at ourselves as Karen, or someone like her, opened up her soul.

For the first two or three sessions, I held my "mud," which

meant I didn't open up or let anything said affect me. I was afraid. I didn't want anyone—especially Joe, Phil, or Rudy—to see the real me. I thought that if they did, they would all hate me. Since I hated myself, I believed that I was unlovable. I just knew that if I broke down, I would be rejected by even these drug addicts. But one day, at a moment when Phil was telling me how wonderful I was, my hypocritical heart began to crack, and I cried before the whole group.

Inside I was angry, almost on fire with rage. I felt cheated by God and by everyone I had ever known. I thought that no one had ever really cared about me, that they had only cared about using me. And I refused to let this anger seep out. I kept it hidden deeply inside. I was twenty-six years old, and no one really knew me. The saddest part of all was that I didn't know who I was, either. But even realizing this didn't cause me to break down completely. Although I cried, I kept most of my diamond-hard front, and I polished it regularly for several more sessions.

But eventually, little by little, I let out more of my emotions and faced more of the truth. As I did, I worked my way higher and higher in the program, leaving the teen stage and moving up to the young adult stage. It seemed that with each day I was given more freedom and less grief. When Rudy graduated, and they released him to the outer world, I suddenly realized that I was deeply in love with him. I needed him more than I did the program.

A few days after he left, he phoned me, and I was allowed to take his call.

"Lauren, how are you?"

"Rudy," I said, my voice unsteady, "I miss you so much."

"I miss you, too," he assured me. "But what are we going to do? You've got to stay there and graduate. It's important for you. Honey, it's very important!"

"I know, but I need you too," I answered. "I'm afraid you'll go back to using, or forget about me—or—or . . ."

"Lauren," he interrupted, "I love you, and some day we'll get married. You know, just like we talked about, and just like both of us have dreamed. We'll have the house, the picket fence, the whole shot, just like you've always wanted. I love you."

Crying, I whimpered, "I know, and I believe you, and I want to be happy and respectable someday, but more than anything, I want you in that life. I need you now!"

"Lauren," he then quietly asked, "will you marry me?"

"Of course," I answered. "When?"

"As soon as you graduate!" Even as he said it, I knew that I couldn't wait that long!

By this time I had served almost a full year, and my original sentence had been for only ninety days, so Jack Hale couldn't legally keep me there. I knew this and demanded that he let me go. I told both him and the staff that I just had to leave and be with Rudy. But they didn't let me go easily; they fought me every step of the way. But after I had cleared my release with my parole officer and had the court's permission, the program had no choice. I left Jack, saying, "Don't worry, I've learned my lesson. I'm not going to do drugs again. I'm clean, and I'm going to stay that way."

As I walked out the gate, I cried. I had given up a lot leaving the program early. One of the rules was that I could not communicate with anyone there unless I finished my full term. By checking out early, I had to leave friends who meant a great deal to me. All this hurt me deeply, but not enough to go back and stick it out until the end.

Because he wasn't a full-time resident at the hospital, the rule of shunning didn't apply to Papa Joe, a psychologist. He cared a great deal for Rudy and me, and we had grown to love him too. The day I walked away from the program, Joe offered his apartment to Rudy and me until we got on our feet. Then he went away for several days, leaving us alone.

Even though we didn't bother getting married, we celebrated as if we were on a honeymoon. We shared more tender moments than I had known in my whole life. We spent hours laughing at simple things, and many other quiet times just holding each other. I spent hours studying his long, delicate fingers as he played his guitar. Our nights were as tender as was his music. He made love to me with more concern and gentleness than anyone I had ever known.

Rudy and I would often talk and share our dreams. During these moments our glaring differences became evident. Since he was a Mexican, his culture and heritage were far different from mine. I loved his roots, and I wanted to know all about them, but they created barriers that were hard to breach. He had more talent and intelligence than any person I had ever met, and yet he also had an attitude that claimed, "the world owes me." I would tell him repeatedly that working hard was the only way to get ahead, and he would laugh and tell me that he would take what was owed him. He justified everything by saying that the white man had stolen his world from his father's people, and it was his to take back. Even during our periods of pure joy, my heart ached, knowing that this type of attitude was going to get Rudy in trouble again.

When Joe came home, the magical spell of Rudy's and my first few days ended. It was time for us to move on and rejoin the rest of the world.

First we stayed with Rudy's mother, Elvira. She was a delightful woman who made me feel like family right away. She would become a dear friend. But even her friendship wouldn't be able to change the path down which her son and I were already heading. After a few days of staying with his mother, we moved into a friend's apartment.

There, Rudy and I began to use drugs again. In one instant, it was as if a whole year of my life had been for nothing. The humiliation, the lectures, the work, and the pain had all flown out of my head in a second. Deep down I didn't want to be using; I wasn't ready to go back to my personal prison of highs and lows. But I wasn't strong enough yet to resist, nor did I feel that I had enough good reasons to stay drug-free. In today's expression, I couldn't "just say no."

I guess I was using simply because Rudy wanted me to, and I didn't want to lose him. Being with him made me feel good. He didn't ask me to be beautiful or give him children; he didn't ask me to become a prostitute or work for him. He just wanted me to be with him. He accepted me, and that is all it took to make me feel whole. After a few weeks of bliss, however, I began to notice differences that had seemed so insignificant just a few weeks before.

Three of his four brothers were on drugs, and none of them seemed to care much about nice homes, cars, or clothes. Advancing and becoming a success weren't a part of their mental outlook. Life was just something to take as it came, and, if it didn't offer much, that was fine. Rudy gravitated toward this concept too. My stories of white picket fences around a nice house started taking on a hollow ring. I was faced with the fact that I was going to have to give up either my dream of success and comfort or Rudy. I didn't want to do either.

A few months after walking away from the downstairs drug program, I began to feel a little sick. I thought it might be the flu or a reaction to some bad drugs, but when it didn't go away, I became concerned. When I missed my second straight period, it began to dawn on me that I was pregnant. I kept the news from Rudy until I was sure. Then when I finally told him about the baby, I also issued an ultimatum: Both of us had to stop using drugs. I told him that I wasn't going to allow my child to be raised in a drug-infested world. Rudy agreed.

For the next few days, things were fine. I quit cold and was so happy about being pregnant that I didn't even desire a fix. I thought Rudy had quit too, until one day I came home to the apartment where we had been staying and found him overdosed. After I made sure that he wasn't going to die, I decided it was time to do something for me and the baby.

The next day I packed my things and walked over to his mother's. I told her why I had to leave, and she understood. I also promised her that I would keep in touch with her and make sure she knew her grandchild. She hugged me and wished me well. With five dollars in my purse, I walked to the bus station and caught a Greyhound back to L.A. I cried all the way. I had wanted Rudy to be Mr. Perfect, but he couldn't be. No amount of waiting and hoping was ever going to change him, and knowing this hurt me deeply. With no mother, no husband, and no friends, I was again on my own. But this time, I was responsible for another human being—my own child.

Getting out at the downtown bus station, I walked the streets. Broke, hungry, alone, and not knowing anyone to whom I could turn, I made fifty dollars the old-fashioned way—on my back. Taking the money from the trick, I grabbed a bite to eat, then walked and cried some more. Eventually, I ended up at a street corner I knew well—Franklin and Vine. There, behind the walls of a huge two-story house called the Vinewood Center, was a halfway program for female parolees. After pausing a moment to think of somewhere else to go, I walked up the steps and rang the bell. The woman who greeted me was an old friend from jail.

Frankie grinned when she recognized me and asked, "What in the world are you doing here?"

"Oh, Frankie," I answered, "I'm pregnant, and I want to live. I'm clean; I promise. Do you know someplace I can stay?" Then I began to cry.

Frankie took me inside and got the house officer, Harriet Hoopengarner, a short, brown-haired, happy, and outgoing woman, who listened to my story. Nodding her head as if she understood, she asked, "Can I test you? And if I do, is it going to be clean?" I agreed to be tested, and when it came back clean, I received Harriet's permission to stay, but then I found out that her permission wasn't enough.

Gloria, my parole officer, didn't want me living with a bunch of cons. She fought the stay. I couldn't convince her that all was okay, so Harriet and I were forced to get a change of venue and a different parole officer who would go for the move. The courts assigned me to Harriet. Then, just when I thought everything was set, my past haunted me again. I was still on probation from the drug bust on the border, and my probation officer not only wanted me out of the halfway house, but also wanted me to have an abortion. She cited my record as evidence that I wouldn't be a fit mother. But Harriet intervened again, fighting in my behalf. Finally, after weeks of staying at the Vinewood Center on a day-to-day basis, never knowing what tomorrow might bring, not even knowing if I would be permitted to keep my baby, I was cleared to keep my baby, live at the Center legally, and as an extra bonus my probation was dropped. Now I belonged somewhere. But that didn't mean that my life was now simple. Too much from my past conspired to make my next few months difficult.

For starters, Rudy's and my relationship was constantly up and down like an amusement park ride. Sometimes we would have good visits at the Center, but, more often than not, he was either high or drunk, so we'd end up fighting. He would ask me to marry him, saying that this was the last time he'd ask, and I'd say no. Then on his next visit, he would ask again. I'd explain that I didn't want to marry a drug addict who had no "clean time" under his belt, and he would tell me he'd get clean. I could see that he was falling deeper into a pit of no return, but I kept hoping he would change. I should have known better.

My health, which had never been very good, turned on me too. On July 23, 1972, I began to notice a bit of bleeding, which in seemingly no time developed into major vaginal hemorrhaging. Suddenly I had gone from feeling wonderful and laughing to being in great pain and screaming for someone to help me. I had miscarried so many times before that I knew what was happening, and I couldn't believe that God was going to do this to me again. I wanted very badly to have this baby.

Harriet and Frankie rushed me to L.A. General, where doctors confirmed my fears. A quick examination proved to them that I had lost my baby. They promised me, however, that they would verify their conclusion through additional testing. They did blood and urine testing, then sent me home for bed rest. They assured me that they would call within a week to tell me what I needed to do next.

I was heartbroken, and for the next several days I did little but sleep and cry. I felt totally inadequate as a woman. I needed Rudy to give me his assurance that I was a real woman, but he wasn't around. Nothing I could do was right—at least, that was how I felt. It was probably fortunate that I was at Vinewood, or heaven knows what I might have used to try to pull myself back together or bury myself in a world of illusions. Thanks to being at the Center, I stayed clean.

A week later a nurse from the hospital called and casually informed me that the test indicated that I was still pregnant, that I hadn't miscarried. Slamming down the phone, I screamed so loud that all sixteen girls in the home, as well as all the parole officers, came running to see what was wrong now. When I blurted out the great news, they responded as if they had just learned of a miracle that had happened. We had a night of loving and crying. *I still had my baby*. I cried and thanked God for his mercy and his wonderful gift, and I really felt as if he heard me.

Rudy called a week later and asked me to marry him. Again I refused. I told him that I wouldn't raise our baby in a world of slum and drugs. He had to change before I would consider his proposal. He agreed to think about it, and I asked him to keep in touch. The next time he came by, he asked me to take a drive with him. We talked a great deal, and I showed him where my mother had lived when she died. I talked for awhile about how strange and sad her life had been. The talk drifted slowly from her to why I wouldn't marry him. I told Rudy straight out that I wouldn't allow my child to grow up in a home that wasn't normal and filled with the proper influences of love and warmth. A home with drugs couldn't have that, and until he got his act together, he wasn't going to make a good father or husband. This honest evaluation enraged him.

Rudy began to cuss and threaten me. "Lauren, if you won't marry me, then you won't have this baby. I'm not going to let you." I had never heard him talk this way before. He sounded cruel, almost crazy, a great deal like Eddie had sounded when he was angry with me. Then, out of nowhere, Rudy raised his fist and dug it into my stomach. Raising it again, he repeated his first blow. Doubled over in pain, I opened the passenger car door and ran out, and he got out and began to chase me. I hadn't made it five steps when he caught me, turned me around, looked in my eyes, and suddenly his rage disappeared. Tears filling his eyes, he muttered a quick apology, put me back in the car, and took me home. Still in a great deal of pain—both physical and emotional, I wept as he drove off. It didn't surprise me when he didn't call for a long time.

Now I had a stronger desire than I had ever had before to live and experience the fullness of life. In order to reach out and know more, I began to work with other parolees and law enforcement officers by going into high schools and colleges and talking about the effects of drugs. I was so effective at my volunteer work that I became the Center's model parolee. It was a drastic change from the woman who had bucked every kind of authority just one year before. Being pregnant made me feel needed, and that led me to do things that mattered.

I continued this work and lived in Vinewood until just before my delivery date. The Center wasn't equipped for children, so Frankie and I found an apartment. Brother Stanley, who was now dropping by almost every day to check on me, had been instrumental in helping us get the lease. It wasn't a large apartment, just two bedrooms and a bath, but we decorated it as best we could, looking forward to filling it with the sounds of a newborn. A shower from the girls in Vinewood, the men in another halfway house, and my new friends at the apartment, also helped prepare for the baby. But the shower supplied more than just many of my physical needs for the nursery—it also met a few spiritual needs.

When the invitations to the shower had been sent out, I decided to send one to my father. It had been eleven years since we had been in touch with each other, and, even though I knew that he wouldn't visit me, I wanted him to know that I was alive. When after a week I heard nothing, I wasn't surprised, but on the day of the shower, a card arrived with a fifty-dollar check inside. It was from my father's mother, my grandmother Gee Gee. Inside the card was a telephone number and a simple request, "Please call me."

For me it was one of those moments when time stood still.

I was going to get to talk to someone who had cared for me as a child. My times with her had been wonderful. However, knowing what had transpired between my father and me, knowing that his mother had to side with him, I was nervous. I wanted to talk to her again, but I didn't know what to expect. For all I knew, she might hate me.

I walked to a pay phone and deposited my dime. Waiting for a dial tone, I then slowly made my fingers dial the number. As I waited for her to answer, I said a short prayer: "Oh, Father God, if you really are there, please hear me now. Help me get through this conversation. Don't let me blow it. Help me say the right words, the words that she needs to hear. Please help me find the words that will keep the lines of communication open." Then, I heard someone pick up on the other end.

"Hello?"

"Gee Gee?"

"Yes," the soft voice answered. "Who is this?"

"This is your granddaughter, Lauren."

"How are you, dear?" she asked.

"I'm fine; how are you?"

"I'm fine too."

Neither of us spoke for a second, and then she added, "Why don't we get together for lunch?"

"I'd love to," I quickly answered.

"Well, can you give me directions as to where you are, and I'll come get you, say a week from today at noon?"

I gave Gee Gee directions to my place, then we said goodbye.

As the days passed, my anxiety over the upcoming visit intensified. I contacted Brother Stanley for help. For the first time, I spoke with him as a priest, sharing with him the whole story of my father's abuse.

"You see," I explained as I finished, "more than anything else in this whole world, I want to have this relationship. I know she is going to ask me about the accusations that Mother must have told her about, and I don't know how to answer her."

"You need to let the Lord guide you," Brother Stanley smiled. "And you need to be honest with her and yourself." He then led me in prayer.

Later that night, I prayed too. "Dear Lord, please vindicate me, for this time I know I am innocent. Please help me make a mature decision as to how to handle this. Please allow me not to be vengeful. And more than anything else, please allow me and my grandmother to be close again. I need her."

As the day arrived for her visit, I felt more on the spot than I had felt when the panel had asked me if Rudy and I had had sex. I felt that, no matter how I answered Gee Gee's question, she would convict and condemn me. But then I remembered Brother Stanley's words: "Have faith and let God be in charge."

Noon finally arrived. I hoped that my prettiest pink, blue, and white smock and matching slacks would meet with my grandmother's approval. I wanted her to like everything about me. You see, I still wondered just how much of me there was to like.

When she drove up, I almost didn't recognize her. She looked so old. It didn't dawn on me until I saw her that she was now eighty-five years old. I remembered her as much younger. As she got out of her car, immaculately dressed as usual, and walked quickly to my steps, I could see that she possessed all of her old pride and energy. Her white hair was still styled and perfectly in place, and she stood straight. I could see the energy in her brown eyes and the delicate beauty of her pale skin. It took every bit of my reserve not to rush out and hug her.

As I opened the door, she smiled, said hello, then patted my stomach. Laughing, she added, "Oh, big baby!" I grinned and nodded my head. Somewhere, down deep in my heart, I just knew that everything was going to be all right.

She took me to the Assistance League in Hollywood for lunch. I didn't stop talking from the moment we got there until it came time to order. I didn't want to give her a chance to ask *the* question. I was afraid that, if she did, this dream would suddenly become a nightmare. Gee Gee just smiled and nodded her head as I spoke, waiting for an opportunity to talk to me. Right after we ordered and before I had a chance to chatter on about my own affairs, she jumped in. With her hands on the table, a warm look in her face, she slowly began, "We won't ever discuss this again, but we need to talk about it now." Her eyes never leaving mine, she paused for a moment to think about her words, then she continued: "Is what you said about your father true?"

I froze. I wondered, *What do I say now?* And even though I didn't want to, I began to cry. In a voice that caught in my throat and was filled with the emotions of my soul, I answered: "Gee Gee, all I can say is that I forgive him."

She patted me on the hand and never brought up the subject again. She knew the truth. I was vindicated at last.

What Gee Gee wanted was peace in her family. She desired to see my father and me back together. If I had lied, she could have had this easily, but now she knew that it would be a tough goal to accomplish. Nevertheless, she had hope. I did not. Too much had happened—too much pain had been exchanged for any trust to be left. But I dreamed about a reunion and restoration anyway. And with her at my side, I had someone with whom I could share my dream.

That night, I couldn't sleep. I was just too excited about reestablishing my ties with Gee Gee. So I patted my tummy and talked to my baby. "You know, little one, today is the happiest day in my life. Today I have been reinstated with my family—at least one very important part of it. I want you to know and love Gee Gee as I do, and now you can. I also want you to be proud of me. I hope that I never do anything to make you ashamed of me. I pray that I don't bring reproach to you. I pray, my dear sweet child, that with or without your father, I will do justice by you. It may not mean anything to you now, but I love you. And I know that your daddy loves you too. He just doesn't have much time right now. He hasn't grown up yet. Someday, you will know him and love him as I do. I know you will. But today, you and I got back into my grandmother's life. I never believed it would happen. I never thought I would be so blessed, not after all the things I've done. But it happened, and I'm so glad."

My child kicked me, as if to say, "I'm happy too." At that moment, I began to believe that I could give this child all of the things I had missed.

Gee Gee helped me a great deal over the next few weeks. She bought me furniture for my apartment, helped me get baby things I didn't have, and never pressured me about marrying Rudy. More than anything else, she offered me love and all the time I wanted. I gladly accepted both. I needed her to counterbalance a disturbing problem in my life.

Even as my grandmother was calming me down and bringing me some measure of peace, Rudy was running around going crazy. He was either drunk or high every time he dropped by to see me, and he was no longer interested in marriage. He was having an affair with a married woman, living life as if there were no tomorrow, daring someone to catch him and send him back up the river. I couldn't believe that he had gone through the whole program and learned nothing. I tried to avoid him as much as I could, but I was driven to be with him too. I loved him, and I loved him so much that I constantly put myself at odds with my own best interests. The way he acted was bad for me and his child, but I still loved him enough to think he could change. I constantly rode a rough road of reality mixed with heavy doses of hope.

Between the good times with Gee Gee and the bad ones with Rudy, the last six months of my pregnancy passed quickly.

At about four in the morning, on January 7, 1973, I went into labor and entered the hospital. I was a terrible patient—crying, screaming, demanding to be attended to, and getting mad at anyone who tried to help me. To quiet me, my doctor kept giving me more medication. By the time I was ready to deliver, I was so relaxed that I couldn't even push. The doctor then had to go in and get the baby with forceps, which scarred my newborn boy. But even as medicated as I was, when I heard my baby's first cry, I felt a tremendous surge of joy. Then, just as my doctor told me that everything was fine, I passed out.

I woke up the next day, and when I asked to see my baby, everyone seemed to put me off. After several hours of asking and not getting a definitive response, I became frantic. I convinced myself that my baby boy had been stillborn. Grabbing a nurse, I screamed, "You told me that I had a boy, a healthy boy. If that's true, why can't I see him?"

The nurse just smiled and shook her head. She tried to assure me that everything was all right, but it did little good. With all of the other new mothers feeding their babies, I couldn't shake the thought that mine had died; otherwise, I would be feeding my baby too. Finally, I called my doctor and asked why I wasn't allowed to see my child.

"I have no idea," he explained. "Let me check on it, and I'll get right back to you."

I cried as I waited. I just knew the worst had happened. I just knew that, after all of my pain and trials, the cruelest joke of all was being played on me. Every bit of my faith was disappearing, and yet I was still praying as quickly and sincerely as I ever had.

After waiting for what seemed like an eternity, Dr. Copper, my physician, called me back and explained the situation to me. "Lauren, your baby is fine. Someone called here last night and told the staff that you were a drug addict. Because of this, they had your son put into isolation. I told them that you had been clean for at least seven months, and then I ordered them to release the baby to you. He will be there before you know it."

"Thank you, Doctor," I sighed as he hung up. And for the next few seconds I was so relieved. But then it hit me— somebody had exposed my past, someone had snitched. I wanted to find out who it was and get my revenge. I wondered if it was Rudy's new lover or maybe even Rudy himself. With my blood pressure rising fast, I was about to erupt when the door to my room opened and the nurse brought me my child. All at once, the whos and whys didn't matter; only the fact that my baby was here was of any significance. My son was in my arms, and I was truly glad that all those times I had tried to kill myself had failed. I now had a small hint of just how wonderful life could be. After putting Matthew Edward Chapin to my breast, I began to know what real love was.

After holding and feeding my baby, I called Rudy who had been unavailable the day before. A few hours later, he came by.

"Hi," he said, entering the room. One look told me he had been drinking. "So, where's the little rug rat?" Looking past me, he saw Matt in the bassinet, walked over, studied him for a moment, then carefully picked him up.

Watching him, I couldn't help but be proud of my great accomplishment. The son was the image of his father: hairline, olive skin, and the same hands that had held me spellbound the first weeks we were together.

Looking up for a moment, he asked, "What did you name him?"

"Matthew Edward Chapin," I slowly answered.

"You what?" he shot back.

"I named him after my family," I explained.

"I suppose you didn't even put me on the birth certificate," he snapped.

"Yes," I calmly answered. "Your name is there as the father, but I gave him my last name."

"That's just like you." His voice had now taken on an edge that indicated real rage. "Lauren, you are such a————. You always go for the kill."

"No," I softly responded. "That's not it. I believe that for a child to carry a name—just like for a wife to carry a name—there should be some honor in it. My dear, there is just not much honor in yours." I could tell my words had hurt him, and they had hurt me too. But they needed to be said, and I couldn't back down now. I had determined the right thing for Matt and would firmly hold to my resolve.

The room was silent for a few moments before Rudy displayed his own feelings. "Lauren, you always get your way. You'll probably raise him to be a white sissy!"

I didn't waste time in answering his charge. "Rudy, he's half

Mexican, and I'm proud of his heritage. But I won't raise him to have a false macho pride like yours. He's not going to grow up with a chip on his shoulder, thinking that the world owes him. He'll know that what he gets from life is what he puts into it. That's much more than I can say for you. You still don't know that."

"You are such a self-righteous————," he said with hostility. "Everything has got to be *your* way. Why can't you just relax and flow with the breeze?"

"Lord knows, Rudy, I'll love you to my grave, and I know you will love me that long too, but raising children is a great responsibility, and I don't want my child to be ashamed of me. I know I will make mistakes, but I pray they won't be so bad as to cause severe pain to his spirit. I want to be your wife, and I want to have you help me raise Matt, but you've got to prove to me that you can stay clean and make something of yourself."

"Lauren, if you really loved me, you'd marry me and help me through all of this. You'd trust me."

"How can I trust you? What have you shown me that indicates a foundation for trust?"

Rudy didn't answer my questions, he just put Matt down and left the hospital. He never knew how close I was to breaking down and dropping my fierce resistance. He also never knew just how much I really wanted to be his wife. But still, even as close as I was to crumbling, I looked at my baby and realized that for his sake I couldn't. Together, we would make it. We could find a place to live and grow and become the family I had dreamed about for so long. After crying for over an hour, filled with all kinds of emotions, I fell asleep. When I woke up, I called Gee Gee and told her about the baby.

Gee Gee was thrilled. After finding out all the particulars, she made a simple request: she asked me to call my father. Although I thought it was crazy, I followed her advice, looked up his number in the phone book, and caught him at work.

"Daddy," my voice was very shaky. "This is Lauren."

"Hello," he answered in a voice showing no emotion. I

stopped for a moment, realizing that this was the first time I had talked to him in over a decade. He sounded older, and this shocked me.

"Daddy," I continued, "I had a baby boy last night. His name is Matthew Edward."

"Congratulations," he replied. "What hospital are you in?"

After I gave him the hospital's name and address and the number of my room, he assured me that he would come to see my baby later that day.

I was nervous about seeing him, so nervous that my eyes hardly ever left the door, expecting each new visitor to be him and knowing that I had nothing to say that could heal our old wounds. When visiting hours ended, I finally turned out the lights to go to sleep, feeling a little disappointed but also feeling a great deal of relief.

The next morning I was released to go home, and, just before I picked up my baby, Dad walked into my room. It was such a shock to see his face that I froze. Neither of us said anything for several long moments. Instead, we just looked at each other, studying how we had changed.

He looked older, very much older than I thought he would. I didn't know that ten years could do that to a middle-aged man. He just didn't look or move like the person I had known. His step was slower and his hair much lighter. He didn't seem as strong. I wondered if he had changed in any other ways as well.

"Hello," he began in a tone that seemed almost formal. "Where's the boy?"

Before returning his greeting I called the nurse and asked her to bring my baby to me. As the next two or three minutes passed, Dad and I sat in awkward silence. But when my little bundle finally arrived, he began talking, not as much to me but to the baby.

"What is his name?" he inquired.

"Matthew Edward," I answered, wondering why he hadn't remembered from when I had told him yesterday. Then after another long period of silence, I added, "I got the Matthew from the Bible, the Edward after Uncle Edward, and of course Michael's middle name too."

Daddy nodded his head, then said to the child, "Matthew, you *are* beautiful."

Then, handing him back to me, he said goodbye and walked out the door. He didn't even bother to find out where I lived or take my telephone number. But as I held Matthew and looked into his beautiful eyes, I didn't much care. I had seen Dad, I had my grandmother back, I wasn't using drugs, and for the first time in years, I had a reason to live. And it was all because of a baby too small to even know how much he had already done.

"Oh, Matthew," I cooed, "it is time for a new start. I promise I will give it my all. Don't worry; I'll do my best for you." And how I tried!

For the first few weeks, I checked on my child every three minutes. If he whimpered, I picked him up. I convinced myself that, by devoting every second to him, I was being the world's best mother. Having been raised a Catholic, I knew that I needed to have Matthew baptized. I never really cared what happened to me, but I didn't want something to happen to my baby and have him wind up in hell. I called Brother Stanley. He assured me that, baptized or not Matt was already in the palm of God's hand, but that wasn't enough for me. So he took Matt, his godparents, Rick and Karen Messa, Gee Gee, Frankie, and me to St. Joseph's church, and I had my son baptized. I was thrilled.

The only events that dampened my first six weeks of motherhood were the visits from Rudy. He would come by, look at Matt, make some wisecrack, and then we would fight. When he left, I was always crying. He just couldn't be kind.

In many ways, I expected too much of him. I wanted him to get clean, get a job, and have an attitude change. But he was not going to do this. Neither did he sense any obligation to help support Matt. I told him that if he didn't help provide for Matt, he couldn't see him. But a few weeks later, I gave in and let him visit the baby again. It was an extremely frustrating and confusing situation, as Rudy and I stubbornly fought for our own way; with neither of us ever compromising.

Rudy wasn't the only distraction in my life. Billy, my brother, and I were seeing each other again, and he was using. I could tell that he was lonely and that he was heading down the same road that had almost killed me. But now that I really wanted to help him and be close to him, I couldn't get through to him. At night I prayed that he wouldn't overdose.

Frankie was backsliding too, and living with her was becoming a bad experience. She was drinking, smoking grass, and taking Valium. On top of this, she was pregnant, and her mood swings made her almost impossible to predict. She would gripe and get angry for no reason; then she would cry and beg forgiveness. The only thing that really kept me from going crazy was my baby.

I had never been around babies before becoming a mother, so I was often afraid that I was doing the wrong things. I read book after book, but I still didn't know what to do when my son would cry for hours at a time. I didn't know to whom to turn who could soothe my nerves and calm my fears. For the most part, however, Matthew looked and acted healthy.

Six weeks into his life, Matthew began losing weight. Then, whenever I nursed him, he began to throw up violently. I had never seen anything like it, but I tried not to get overly alarmed. I treated his problem like colic, but he didn't get any better—he just began to look weaker. I cried at night, praying that the next day he would wake up completely well. I even reread the books I had bought, believing that I was to blame for his poor condition. But nothing they suggested and nothing I did worked. Finally, on February 27, 1973, I became so concerned that I took him to the hospital's emergency room. After running a battery of tests, the doctors determined that he needed immediate surgery. He had an obstruction between his stomach and intestines that was causing him to starve to death.

As they wheeled him into surgery, I ran to the chapel. On my knees, I began to say every prayer I knew. I had to get through to God and convince him that he shouldn't take this baby. I knew that I would end up going crazy and dropping back into my old lifestyle if Matt died. For the next hour, I tried to show God that Matthew was my salvation, that this baby had gotten me back on the right track, and with his help I could stay there. I wanted and needed to give him all of the things in life I had missed. I promised God everything just to insure that he would let me keep one little life. Finally, in a moment of deep desperation, I made a rash promise: "God, if you give me my son back, I'll live my life for you." I felt horrible about that bargain. I just knew that it would mean I would spend my whole life never smiling, never having any fun, never getting to wear bright clothes, never going to parties, and never laughing again. I pictured myself living a Spartan existence, saying, "Praise the Lord" all the time. Nonetheless, I used my vow to try to persuade God to save my son.

An hour later, a nurse came into the chapel and told me that Matthew was out of surgery and going to be fine. I jumped to my feet, a smile running from ear to ear, and quickly forgot my promise. God wouldn't expect me to keep it anyway, or so I thought.

• Fifteen •

THE NEXT YEARS of my life were filled with great stability, at least when compared to my previous ones. I had gotten a job in a drug treatment program, and was doing well professionally, working with doctors in a confident manner. I had not returned to using hard drugs, and I had found a new roommate I really liked. To those around me, I appeared to have my life together. But if people had taken a moment to look under the surface, they would have seen signs of struggle. I was drinking a lot, smoking three packs of cigarettes a day, and smoking grass whenever it was offered to me. I didn't see how any of these things were wrong or could hurt me. After all, they weren't the hard stuff, and in my mind you had to be on heroin or the like to be an addict. I thought of myself as clean.

My roommate was a porno star named Barbara. She was generous, big-hearted, and loved Matt. What she did for a living didn't concern me. I knew a lot of people on the fringe of show business. I could rationalize what they were doing simply by believing that it was the only way for them to survive. No real sense of right or wrong directed my life. As

238

long as I couldn't see a way it directly hurt someone, I saw nothing wrong with someone doing whatever it took to maintain.

Besides Matt and my work, the only other constant in my life was Gee Gee, but she was getting older, and this worried me. I didn't want her to die, depriving me of the only mother figure I had and the only woman who had ever loved me for myself. She survived, living life as best she could, inwardly determined not to die until she reunited me with my father. At eighty-seven, Gee Gee was still a dreamer.

For her birthday that year, I wrote and sent her a poem. It expressed many of my heartfelt emotions:

It has been more than three years now since we first met.
That day we looked at each other, oh how we wept!
The years have gone too swiftly, too fast for us to know—
A grandmother—a granddaughter—so much love to sow.
You have brought to my life more love and understanding,
More hope and kindness with seemingly no ending.
I pray every night your dreams may come true,
To have your whole family truly love you!!
May the years to come, my Gee Gee dear,
Bring you peace of mind, good health, and cheer.
For the years have gone swiftly, too fast for us to know—
A grandmother—a granddaughter—so much love to sow.

A few weeks later, my neighbor and friend, Arzine, Matt, and I were driving down the Hollywood Freeway, headed home after a day out when a strange feeling came over me. It was almost like something reached out and grabbed me as we passed Forest Lawn Cemetery. Even though I had passed it on countless occasions, I hadn't been there since Mom's funeral; I simply hadn't seen a need. But this time a voice called out to me, asking me to get off the freeway and go and visit her grave. This voice from deep inside my soul was so assertive and so strong that I couldn't ignore it.

"Arzine," I asked, "would you like to help me look for my mother's grave?"

Shrugging her shoulders, she answered, "Sure, why not?"

I turned the car around and headed to the cemetery. As I drove up to the front gate, a guard stopped us and asked us if he could be of service. I told him why we had come, and then I asked him the location of Mother's grave. He didn't know, but he directed me to the main office. Once there, I recognized an old face.

"Aren't you Danny Richards—Mom's friend?" I asked as I walked up to the man.

"Well, Lauren," he smiled, "how are you, honey?"

"Fine," I replied, "and how are you?"

"Good!" As he answered, I noticed him looking at Matt.

"Danny, I want you to meet someone." Leading him back to where Matt was standing, I proudly announced, "This is my son, Matt." After a few minutes of catching him up on my life, I introduced Danny to Arzine and told him why we had come.

"Of course I know where she is," Danny answered. "I go to your mother's grave often. She was a wonderful friend to me and my family. I loved her a lot."

In the past when people had said what he had, I would have either gotten jealous or mad. But not today. Today I only smiled and tried to understand.

Danny drew a map explaining how to get to her grave. After a few more moments of small talk, I thanked him, took the map, and returned to the car. It took Arzine and me several minutes just to get to the area where Mom was buried. As I got out of the car, an irony hit me: all the graves in this region of the park were facing the Warner Brothers, Universal, and Burbank Studios. I thought Mom would have liked that—still being able to keep an eye on the people she had tried to charm for so long.

It took me almost another five minutes to find Mom's grave, which had no headstone, no flowers, only a number. I had to check the paper that Danny had given me just to make sure that I had the right grave. Convinced that it was, the three of us stared blankly at the barren ground. Soon bored, Arzine and Matt wandered off to look at some of the more impressive markers. When they left, I knelt in the grass and began to say the words softly that lay heavy on my heart.

"Mama, can you hear me? Mom, do you know that I'm here?" As I spoke, tears began to stream down my face. I so wanted to see my mother's face and know that my words were getting through.

"I don't know where you are, Mama. You left pretty suddenly. There were no goodbyes, no notes, just a cold departure. Did you know where I was at the time. Did you know that I was in jail again? Is that what caused your death? I hope not.

"I don't understand how you could have been the same mother to all three of us kids. None of us knew you in the same way. I wish it hadn't been that way. I wish I could have known the woman that Michael loved.

"I miss you, Mama. Do you know how many times I've cried out for you? Do you know how many times I've wanted to share something with you? Do you know that I'm now grown up and have a boy of my own?

"You'd like Matt. I wish you could see him. I'm giving him all the love I stored up but never gave to you and Dad. You see, he's my salvation. He's my whole life. I know now what you were talking about when you said that your children were an extension of yourself. They are. Sometimes they are even a reflection of ourselves. They show us our good and our bad sides. They even overpower us with their little victories. Mama, this child will know victories—big ones—and we will celebrate them together. I'm going to be there for him.

"Mama, I miss you. I really do miss you. It frightens me that I don't know where you are. The church says something about purgatory, but I don't believe in that. Are you in heaven, or are you in hell? It scares me to death to think that you might be in hell. No matter, I pray to God you can hear me now."

Pausing for a moment, I studied the all but unmarked plot,

pulled away a few weeds, wiped a tear from my cheek, and then tried to continue.

"Mama, I think I can forgive you now. I think I can forgive you for not being the mother I needed. I think I can forgive you for the humiliation and anger you so deeply stirred in me. I think I can forgive you for being so imperfect—just like me.

"There were so many times when I needed your gentle touch, so many times that I needed to feel your loving arms around me. The few times you put them around me just weren't enough. Inside of me a void grew, a void that only love can fill, and now Matt is finally filling this void.

"Oh, I hated you for not being able to show me you loved me! But now, now after all of this time, I am willing to release you. Mom, please forgive me for being a terrible daughter to you. I lied, stole, rebelled, hated. I made you grieve a lot. You weren't the mother I needed, and I certainly wasn't the daughter you needed. I guess we both got the raw end of the deal.

"But, Mom, I love you. It may be a little late, but I'm going to try to understand and forgive you."

As I got up from my knees, a strange kind of peace began to flow over me. I felt much like I had when I had been released from CRC. It was a freedom that made me feel almost reborn. I had released much of my hatred and scorn; I only wished I had been able to do it before my mother died. I prayed that Mom too felt this magical sense of liberation.

A few minutes later, Arzine, Matt, and I were once again headed home.

I have never gone back to the grave, nor do I see a time when I ever will. There just isn't a need. Mama's not there anymore. If I ever needed to realize that, my visit brought it home. The stop had also brought me a new understanding of myself.

With Mom's death now resolved and with me finally giving up that battle, only Rudy was left to contend with. He had moved up north; therefore, Matt and I saw him little. But because of my son, my relationship with Rudy remained an important part of me. Even if Rudy hadn't settled down, he had given me something that had made me feel needed and loved, and I appreciated that more than he would ever know. Our son was probably the only reason I was still alive. So, even though I didn't want anything to do with Rudy's lifestyle, I was thankful that he had come into my life, and secretly, I prayed that he would change radically and come home to us. However, just because I had a baby and was still hoping Rudy would be trustworthy and respectable, I wasn't without other male suitors.

I had a number of men in my life. Each meant something different to me. And I was crazy about each one, but only for a while. I hadn't hit a point at which I was attracting men who made commitments, nor did I really want to make one myself.

In 1976, I was thirty-one and beginning my second year working at the Tarzana Treatment Center. Jack Hale, my old partner and former head of the drug treatment program I participated in during my last stay in confinement, was one of the supervisors there. He had asked me to work as a counselor. I was doing well in my job, but my health, which had been good since I had kicked the heavy drugs almost five years before, was beginning to fail.

A parade of illnesses and medical traumas began when I got a bad case of hemorrhoids. I underwent surgery to solve the problem, but, while I was recovering at home, I continued to get weaker and weaker. Finally, thinking something else might be wrong, I called my doctor and returned for a follow-up examination. Within seconds of examining me, he dashed across the hall to a proctologist's office. He brought the physician back with him to look at me. This doctor was a small, Oriental man with a big smile and a heavy accent. He took one look at me, glanced at my file, and then spoke to me in a very serious tone.

"Miss Chapin, do want me to call ambulance?"

I looked back at him, shocked, and didn't respond. He continued: "You very sick. You go to hospital, get surgery, or die. Must move fast!"

Taking a moment to compose myself, I finally asked what

was wrong. He answered that I had a tremendous amount of internal bleeding and that it had to be stopped soon or I would bleed to death. Still in a state of shock, I suddenly became aware that I had to get Matthew at his day-care center.

"I can't have surgery! I don't have time. Besides, who will take care of my child?" I tried to beg off, but they wouldn't let me. Finally, I pleaded to be granted a few hours to get my home-life in order. The two doctors conferred on my request, and then agreed, but only if I took no more than two hours.

Picking Matt up, I dashed over to Arzine's home. Arzine was watching television when I got there. I dropped Matthew and the keys to my place in her lap. I tried to explain what was going on, and then I asked her to take care of my son. Nodding her head, she was still analyzing my rapid-fire explanations as I ran out her door and raced to get to the hospital.

Within hours I was in surgery, and then in another sixteen hours, I woke up. I was not prepared for what I witnessed upon coming out of my coma. My bottom was being held in the air by a set of pulleys. I felt like someone had violated me with a hot poker; my face was pressed against my pillow, and was completely immobile. Later, the Oriental doctor came in and told what had happened during the operation.

"Miss Chapin, your anal passage exploded. We take about ten feet your intestines and rebuilt your anal canal. You going to be in great pain, but given time, you be okay." I sure believed the pain part. Even when I had tried to cut off my wrist, it hadn't hurt this much.

For the next two weeks, they loaded me with painkillers and fed me intravenously. I remember very little of this time. Then, as they slowly brought me off the medication, I began to accept visits from my friends. Arzine sneaked in one night and asked me if I wanted anything special. I hadn't eaten any solid food in a long time; even though the doctors had told me that I couldn't eat for at least three or four more days, I requested a piece of chocolate. She left and came back with a two-pound box of See's candy. That night I ate it all. Three days later, the chocolate ripped out all my internal stitches. They had to do the whole job over again. Once again I paid a big price for not listening to the voice of authority and following the rules. I stayed in the hospital for another two days. Finally, however, I was released.

After a few weeks of recuperation at home, I returned to work. I was back to doing "intakes" (interviewing patients, filling out the required forms, and the like), assisting the physicians, and running errands to the lab. I liked being out of bed and back with my friends, but I still didn't feel right. I was having problems with food. I reacted strangely to all kinds of different foods, getting sick eating food that had never before turned my stomach. Each day I lost another pound, and I was becoming more and more run-down. I thought I had the flu, but when I consented to be tested, the doctors discovered that I had hepatitis, and put me in an isolated room at UCLA Medical Center for one month. Everyone who visited me, worked on me, fed me, dressed me, changed my bed, and gave me medicine wore a mask and gloves. By the time the month was over, I was almost a mental case. I had now been sick for four straight months, twice had almost died, and had been cut off from my son and work. I was lonely and stir crazy.

When I was finally released from the hospital, I was ordered to stay home for the next few months, and even as my strength rebuilt and I enjoyed playing with Matt, I still didn't feel as if I was completely over my surgery and illness. Nevertheless, by September, money was so tight that I had to return to work.

Within weeks of going back, I began experiencing constant headaches. I thought, as most people did, that they were probably brought on by my nerves. The throbbing, which began in the front of my head and would slowly form a circle to the back, often went on for days. Nothing I took killed it. I couldn't sleep, couldn't eat, and because I was always hungry and tired, I fussed at everyone. I was an unpleasant person to be around. Barbara caught most of my hostility, and she gave it back to me full force. Our home became a battleground. Neither of us wanted to be there.

The headaches became constant in November, and by

Christmas, I was afraid that I was either dying or going insane. I heard things, and I thought that I was becoming possessed by demons. But when no one could find the cause of my pain, I just assumed that I had a hidden tumor that was going to grow until my head exploded. The pain finally became so intense that I could not work at all. I would sit for hours, holding my head in my hands, pressing on it, trying to keep from screaming. I thought that I was going mad. I would even see things and people that I knew weren't there. I got friends to stay with me, to just talk to me, to try to keep me from going over the edge and doing something stupid. I didn't want to kill myself, but if I was left alone with the pain, I thought I might. For weeks the hammer-like pounding continued inside my skull.

Finally, on January 7, 1977, at 2:30 in the morning, a friend of mine pulled me off my bed. When he found me, I was screaming at the top of my lungs, holding my head, moaning something about dying. I scared him so badly that he drove me to the hospital.

Over the next few hours, I was given numerous tests. I passed in and out of lucidity, occasionally recognizing people, but usually unaware of where I was.

Once I looked up and saw my father. Certainly that had to be an illusion. I couldn't understand how he could have found out about this and become interested enough to drive down and check on me. But when I waited for his image to fade, it didn't. I grabbed for his hand, quietly saying, "I want to die, Daddy; please let me die so the pain will go away."

Taking my hand, my father quietly said, "You can't die. I won't let you." This was the first time we had touched in fifteen years.

As he held my hand, the doctors inserted a huge needle in my back for a spinal tap. Within minutes they diagnosed viral encephalitis. They immediately placed me on morphine, Valium, and a host of other drugs to fight the infection, kill the pain, and stop the swelling. For almost two months, I stayed in the hospital fighting off death. My family—what was left of it—actually gathered around me in support.

Finally, in March, I was released. I had no apartment, no money, and no place to go. My brother Michael and his wife Carolyn, who had taken charge of Matthew during this bout of illness, offered me a place in their home. They told me that they wanted to help me put my life back together.

When I got to their house, I was weak and drugged. I was hooked on so many different kinds of medication that every impulse and dependency that I had ever shaken came back to haunt me. I saw all the old monsters, had all the old nightmares, and went through all the old pain. But this time, Carolyn was there holding my hand. She was also there praying. The praying surprised me. I hadn't expected people praying for me, other than Brother Stanley, and he was supposed to—that was his job. But Carolyn and a host of her friends constantly prayed for me. She even read the Bible to me, and I often discussed it with her.

As I began to regain my strength, I started thinking about the things that made Carolyn so happy. She was so giving, so turned on by this force she called the Holy Spirit, that she needed no drugs, no affairs, no alcohol, and no cigarettes to pad her world and make it better. She was a truly content and peaceful human being. In a way I wanted what Carolyn had, but not badly enough to give up all the fun things that had been part of my life for so long. I decided that saying a prayer or two wasn't so bad, and I didn't mind turning to God when I was in trouble, but I didn't want to act like Jesus. That was just too confining. Instead, I took God on my terms. As long as he didn't get in my way, I'd say hello to him once in a while.

As soon as I could stand, and long before I should have, I hit the road visiting friends. The withdrawal symptoms I was having forced me to occasionally admit that I wasn't completely well yet. Once, while driving back from L.A. to Michael's home in Irvine, I had a seizure. I was in the middle of the freeway when it struck from out of nowhere. My perception narrowed and jumped out of focus. It was a miracle that I managed to drive to the shoulder of the road and stop the car without causing a wreck. A few minutes later, after partial vision returned, I found a phone and called Michael. He came and got me, and then lectured me all the way home about taking things too fast. My brother was playing the role of a parent, something he did almost all the time; it was the role Mom had assigned to him as a child, but it was thirty years too late to keep me out of trouble. I didn't listen to him any better than I had ever listened to anyone else.

By June, I was on my feet but still weak, very thin, and extremely pale. Except for lapses in my memory, I was beginning to feel pretty good. I was at least in good enough form to play with my son and party from time to time. I was also well enough to begin to understand that I couldn't live with my brother for much longer. I needed to get back on my own feet. I needed some kind of break. Of course, I hadn't really had one of those in a long time. So, I figured that nothing big was going to fall into my lap.

I was shocked when Michael's phone rang later in the month; on the other end was a young woman from a Hollywood studio requesting my whereabouts. It was like a call out of my past.

"She's right here," my brother informed her and handed the phone to me. "Hello?" I wondered who in the world was looking for me and how they found me at Michael's.

"Miss Chapin, could you hold just a moment? Al Ontaranto wants to talk to you."

As I waited, I thought about the name the woman had just said. It sounded familiar, but I didn't know why. So much of my life was misty and forgotten that I wondered when and if I had met him. Thinking as hard as I could, I still couldn't imagine who he was. I wasn't worried by this; after all, the statute of limitations had run out on most of the things I had done. Whoever he was, he probably wasn't going to give me bad news.

"Lauren, it is so good to find you," a man's pleasant voice interrupted my mental scanning.

I immediately thought, *He doesn't sound like any bill collector I've ever known*. After I said hello, he continued.

"We have been looking everywhere for you. Everybody at Columbia wondered where you are. We are planning this new movie, and I wanted to know if you would come down and talk to us about playing in it. You'd be picking up your old role of Kathy Anderson. We are thinking about doing a reunion movie. Would you be interested?"

Would I be interested? I couldn't wait. I would have driven to Columbia at that moment if they had wanted me to. I was knocked off my feet and as happy as I had been in years. Gathering my thoughts, I quickly inquired, "What about the others? Are they coming back?"

"Yes, Lauren. All of you are back. If it works out, it will be just like old times."

The rest of the conversation consisted of setting interview times and informing me of what I would need to bring. When I hung up, I felt a high like no drug had ever given me. I was flying. After twenty years—two full decades of wondering—I was going to get a chance to go home. Looking over at my brother and sister-in-law, I beamed, "They want me. I can't believe it. Columbia wants me again!"

• Sixteen •

AFTER BATTLING ILLNESS for over a year, I didn't exactly look like a television actress the day I went to Columbia to visit with the casting director. Even though I had worn as nice an outfit as I owned and carefully applied my makeup, I still didn't feel very confident. I weighed ninety-two pounds, was extremely pale, and hardly looked the part of Kathy Anderson grown up.

When I got to the studio, everyone stared. This began to unnerve me. Finally, one of the casting people mustered the courage to tell me, "You don't look like we expected." My heart fell. I didn't think I looked very good, but to be pointed at because of it crushed me. Just when I thought I would cry, he finished his observation. "We had heard that you were obese. We were thrilled to see you come in and not see rolls of fat falling off of you."

The thoughts of tears gave way to laughter. I may have been a lot of things that these people weren't expecting, but obese was not one of them. Knowing that this was creating the stir made me breathe easier. I could handle not being fat. But what about the state of my memory? I didn't know if I could remember enough to do the movie.

After several short interviews, I was offered the part of Kathy and a very good salary for my work. It would be the first time that I would ever do "Father Knows Best" and get my share of the money without fighting someone else for it. This, and knowing that I was just a few weeks away from seeing all the old crew again, thrilled me.

Irvine was too long a daily drive for the three weeks required to shoot the television movie, so Gee Gee offered to let me stay with her while we were filming. I agreed, and Michael and Carolyn took care of Matthew. I spent the days before the morning when I would walk back through the gates and face my old television family again reviewing my lines and cues. I wasn't memorizing anything very well, so when the time came for me to really go to work, I was terrified that I couldn't do it.

I was still scared a few hours later when a crew member escorted me to my dressing room. I was sure that Robert, Jane, Ellie, and Billy all knew about my stays in prison and my life as an addict. I wasn't sure how they would react. I wondered if they would even want to associate with me. As I opened the door to the dressing room, excitement and fear were fighting inside me. The extreme joy of returning was dimmed by my dread of the reactions of my costars. I was battling the demons of my past, facing all the horrible scenes in my life—until I looked into my room. Dozens of pink roses graced the room. From one of the flowers hung a small note. I pulled it off, opened the envelope, and read it. "Welcome back, Kitten. We all love you." Immediately, all my fears vanished. I couldn't wait to see the old gang and get back to work.

I had never been hugged so hard in my entire life. Robert, Jane, Ellie, Billy, and I all had a loving family reunion right on the set. We were all grinning, and it didn't seem to matter that seventeen years had passed or that each of us had taken different routes and done different things. There was still a very real sense of family that superceded all else. It felt so good. If only I could have been surrounded by such love and support in my real life—if only everyone could. I now realized at least part of what I had been searching for for so long.

It took us three weeks to film the *Father Knows Best Reunion*, and for each of us it was like slipping into a rediscovered pair of old comfortable shoes. It was so easy, because each of us cared not only about the work we were doing but also about each other. Every day, almost every minute, we would all be reminded of some moment from the past and would then share the memory. I had never felt as warm; it seemed like forever since I had felt as whole. When they turned out the lights on the last day of shooting, I knew that it really didn't matter if I ever acted again. What mattered was that I had been reconnected with the most stable influences of my childhood, and we still loved one another. I realized then that some things never change, and that certain feelings can't be stripped away from your heart no matter what happens to your body.

After filming, all of us went on tour, doing one talk show after another. We spent more time promoting what we had done than we did doing it. These times, when there were no scripts to study and no filming schedules to follow, were the most relaxed of all. It gave me a chance to share with all my costars what I had been through and how lucky I felt to have survived and gotten a chance to be with them again. I may have seemed mushy at times, but I knew that each of them felt as I did. When it was all over, leaving them and going back to Irvine was tough, but not as tough or painful as being forced out of Columbia so many years before.

I took the money I had made and moved with Matthew across the street from my brother. I had actually wanted to find a place in Hollywood, but I really didn't have anything to do, and the rent there was much higher than what I could afford, so I stayed in Irvine. I know that Michael and Carolyn were grateful that I did. They didn't want me to get involved with the old Hollywood crowd. Besides, they wanted to keep their close relationship with Matt.

After buying furniture and moving into my new home, I took

some of the money that was left and went to Hawaii. Although there were better ways to spend my earnings, I wanted to get away, and I felt I deserved the trip. Besides, I felt I needed to spend some time with my son.

When I returned to southern California, I found a job at a discount stock brokerage house giving out quotes on the phone. I had enjoyed my return engagement playing Kathy, but I knew that acting was still not a viable alternative for me. The doors just weren't going to open wide enough for me to make a living at it. I determined, therefore, that I would do whatever I could to get by and be satisfied with that. I was going to be happy and stay free, particularly free from drugs.

I made friends with almost everyone on my block. The people outside of my family with whom I became closest were Linda and Flint Mize, and Sharon and her two children. I loved spending time with both of these families. They let me be myself, and they enjoyed each moment of their lives. After wasting so much of my own, this was something I was determined to do too.

A few days after I moved into my house, my phone was installed by a tall, blond man named Bill. As he worked, we talked, and we found ourselves very interested in each other. A physical attraction just hung in the air, and we both eagerly breathed it in. Outgoing and manly, he later called me for a date, and we were soon seeing each other several times a week. Matt adored him, and after a while I lost count of the wonderful days and evenings we all shared.

One weekend, some friends of mine persuaded me to go with them to Norco to attend a bluegrass festival. I invited Bill to meet us there on Saturday. I was primed for a good time. I loved music, and I was so actively involved in activities that embraced energy and fun that this weekend should have been perfect. Unfortunately, I got sick. I wasn't bedridden, just queasy and under the weather. As the weekend ended, I entertained the idea that I might be pregnant. I didn't know how I could be. After all, I wasn't even supposed to be able to have Matt. But, when my stomach was still churning on

Monday, I decided to have a pregnancy test. It came back positive.

I was immediately shocked and concerned. Bill was married, and even though he and his wife had been separated for five years and she was living with another man, he still hoped that someday they could restore their relationship. From the time we began dating, he had explained that involvement in another serious relationship was not his goal. So I knew that he would not welcome news of my pregnancy. But I wouldn't have an abortion. With Matthew, I had learned what a miracle life was, and I wasn't going to snuff out a miracle before it began. I decided that the only way to be with Bill was straight and honest. I would tell him the situation, what I was going to do, and then see how he reacted. I called and invited him over. He had only been there for a few minutes when I broke the news.

"I'm pregnant," I said bluntly.

"Are you sure?" his shocked look proving to me that he had difficulty believing it.

"Yes," I nodded. "I am sure. I've been to the doctor and had a test."

"Oh," he answered.

"Listen, Bill, I know that our relationship is not the kind you build on. It's been nice, but I'm not going to hold you to anything. I know you still want to get back together with your wife, and I can't blame you. I'm going to have this baby, but that doesn't mean that I expect anything from you."

Letting my words sink in, he then asked, "Are you sure you want to keep it?"

"Yes," my reply was firm. "I don't know how I will make it, but I am going to have this child, and I'm going to love this baby, and I know that we will be okay. If you want, you can walk out now. I won't hold it against you. But if you want to stay, you are welcome. It's up to you."

Staring at me for a moment, he shrugged his shoulders and said, "Let me think about it for awhile." He then got up and left. I didn't know if I would ever see him again. But a few hours later, he called and said, "Let's go to dinner and celebrate the fact that you're pregnant and going to have my baby." I still knew that we didn't have a future, but at least I knew we could be friends. At the time, that was enough and I was happy. At least I wouldn't have to go through this pregnancy alone or battling the man who should have been sharing the precious moments with me.

As had happened with Matt, I began to hemorrhage badly around my third month. My neighbors, Linda and Flint, drove me to the emergency room, where I checked in, assured them that welfare would cover the bill, and was examined. The doctor told me that I had lost the child. He wanted to do a D and C without any further tests. My first reaction was to let him, but a voice inside me was screaming much more loudly to get a second opinion—to run a few more tests. Rather than sign the necessary papers, I called my own doctor in L.A., then had Linda and Flint drive me the sixty-five miles up there. After several different tests and examinations, Dr. Cooper assured me that I was fine, but he did want me to go home, get in bed, and basically stay there until the end of my term.

All the way home from the hospital, I pondered over how the first physician could have been so wrong. Then I remembered how his face had looked when I told him that welfare would be paying for my treatment. I concluded that he wanted to do an abortion because I was poor and worthless in his eyes. Perhaps I was paranoid, but I still wonder if he hadn't lied when he told me that I had miscarried. Thoughts of what he could have done still scare me.

Over the next few months, I spent most of my time in bed. I was smoking, drinking a little beer, and partying like always, but now just at home. To me this is what bed rest was all about. But even while I seemed oblivious to it, a large group of people, led mainly by my sister-in-law, was praying for me and coming by to talk to me about Jesus.

In all honesty, I didn't mind all the talk. Jesus was fine with me as long as he didn't ask me to give up anything I loved. If I could have a good time, I could go along with Jesus. But if he started to tell me how to live or that I had to go to church and share about him with others, then I didn't really want him. It was obvious to almost any Christian that I didn't understand a thing about what Carolyn or the Bible was saying, but I thought I did, and that was all that mattered to me. In my opinion, religion was shallow and easy. I thought that I was doing enough when Bill and I read a few verses in the Bible each day.

One day when I was feeling good, Gee Gee called and asked me to come for a visit. I jumped at the chance to get out of the house. For hours that day we sat and talked, and then out of the blue, she looked at me, touched me on the shoulder with her hand, and asked, "Do you think that I will go to heaven when I die?"

I was caught completely off guard and answered her the only way I knew how. "Gee Gee, don't be ridiculous. You aren't going to die for a long time." She wasn't put off by my answer, but she kept pushing ahead with earnest concern about her eternal fate.

"Lauren," she was looking at me directly in the eye and almost pleading as she asked, "do you think I will get to heaven?"

Looking down at the floor, I shrugged my shoulders and finally answered, "Of course. You have been a good person, and good people go to heaven." My answer seemed to satisfy my grandmother, but it would have been obvious to any real Christian that I didn't understand the key to salvation.

For the next few weeks, this conversation, the worried look on Gee Gee's face, and the answer I had given her would play back in my mind. The reality of heaven and hell had become intensely personal, and it worried me. I didn't understand it at the time, but I felt as if something—or someone—was pursuing me.

Matthew was working on me too, but his way was much more direct. Thanks to a bus ministry run by a Lutheran congregation, he was going to church every Sunday with Michael's children. Just like my mother, I thought that it was good for him to attend church, but I didn't see how my going with him could make any real difference in his or my life. *Kids need that sort of thing,* I kept telling myself, *but adults don't.* Whenever Matt would ask me to go with him, I would find an excuse to stay behind. Being pregnant, an excuse was always easy to find.

In order to make ends meet and have someone help with the chores, a girl named Linda and her boyfriend, Kirk, moved in with me. They were good kids, and we had fun playing games with Matt and talking together after he went to bed. Because they weren't Christians, I felt much more comfortable with them than I did with those who were praying for me. Over the last few months of my pregnancy, I passed time playing cards with them, as well as going over to Linda's and Flint's for conversation, refreshments, and lots of Yahtzee.

I had experienced false labor three times before I finally had the real thing. When I was ready to deliver, my friend and coach, Cindy Wilde, and I got caught in a traffic jam on the Hollywood Freeway. My water broke at four in the morning, and the traffic was so bad that we didn't get to the hospital until eight-thirty. I tried to call Bill, but I couldn't reach him. I did manage to find Gee Gee, though.

At eleven, I was told that it would be another four hours or so before I would deliver. But just ten minutes later I gave birth to Summer Ryann Elizabeth Healy-Chapin. My baby was a beautiful, seven-pound one-ounce, twenty-one-inch, healthy little girl. Twenty-four hours later we were both home.

Summer's birth created numerous changes in my life. I was still determined to be an even better mother than I had been with Matt, but having a daughter was different from having a son. Both were precious, but Matt had been easy. He had been "God's gift," and I knew how to take care of him, or at least I had now forgotten all the hard times we had had. But I was almost afraid to have a little girl; I was afraid that I'd be like my mom, and that we wouldn't get along. I had no role model for a healthy mother-daughter relationship, and I was frightened that I would do something to hurt Summer emotionally.

But, as I would later find out, God knew what he was doing; a daughter would prove to be just as wonderful as a son!

A week after Summer's birth, a week in which I lived with my fears and tasted so much new joy, my old friend Sheri and her daughter drove up from Palm Springs. We spent a wonderful day reliving our lives, laughing about stupid things that we had done and wondering how we had survived. We were still having a good time at supper when the telephone rang. I answered.

"Lauren, this is your father. I thought you'd like to know that your grandmother died today."

I was shocked, not only by the news, but by his cold, unaffected voice. I scarcely knew what to say, and all I managed was, "What happened?"

"She died in her sleep," he explained. "Some neighbors found her, and they called me. I took care of things from there."

I began to cry. I had lost my best friend, and she had died alone. She hadn't even had a chance to see her new granddaughter. I silently prayed, "Dear God, please take her to heaven." It scared me that I didn't know if he had.

Over the next week, Gee Gee's death affected me greatly. I couldn't sleep or eat for crying. Dad had refused to have a funeral, a memorial service, or even a family gathering. He simply had her remains cremated, and then went on as if she had never existed. He did not see the need to say goodbye to a person whom death had already claimed. I was extremely bitter over his coldness and his lack of respect, but I seemed to be the only one. No one else seemed to care. An old woman had died, and I was the only one who noticed. This thought hurt me almost as much as her death.

A few weeks later, Dad called again, this time informing me that Gee Gee had left me two thousand dollars, her 1963 Impala, which had only 14,000 miles on it, her diamond and sapphire ring, her desk, and an antique picture. He further explained that after his death my brothers and I would get all of the real estate property she had left in her will for us. This land was in Kansas. Gee Gee had purchased it so it could

provide income for her grandchildren and their children forever. It was never to be sold.

A month later, Dad came by and brought me Gee Gee's
dresses, a thousand dollars, and a ring. The ring was one I had
never seen, and it was missing a diamond.

As I studied it, I asked, "What happened to the ring?"

"What do you mean?" he responded.

"This isn't the ring she left me. What happened to it?"

"This is the ring that I have," Dad replied. "Now, sign this
paper."

"What happened to the money?"

"Well, your grandmother didn't leave Billy anything, so I
gave him half of your money and the car."

"You what?" I screamed. "You can't do that! She left them
to me. Billy will only destroy the car and either drink away or
shoot the money up in drugs. Gee Gee knew what she was
doing when she left these things to me to handle."

"As executor, I can do anything I want. Now, that's all you
get. Sign the paper."

When he left, I realized just how much I hated him. The next
few months didn't improve my feelings toward him; they only
grew worse. Dad sold all of Gee Gee's land and didn't tell any
of us. When I accidentally found out, I called and asked him
about it, and he replied, "Don't worry, you'll get your third
when I die. But I wouldn't hold my breath." I know he must
have laughed when I hung up.

I called Michael and tried to get him to go to an attorney with
me, but he didn't want to fight. He didn't think it would be
worth the pain. He was probably right.

Through his actions, Dad had attempted to erase Gee Gee's
life and memory. Even in the end, he thought of only himself.
While he tried to take away everything of value, he couldn't
take away her touch. I could still feel her hand and her love.
Losing her left me with a great spiritual void, but not as great
as it would have been if I had never had her at all. I thanked
God for the years we had shared.

Until Summer was six months old, whenever Matt had asked

me to go to church with him, I had told him that his sister was too young, adding, "God doesn't really want me there right now." But that didn't work anymore because Matt saw babies at his church all the time. Running out of excuses he would accept, I finally agreed to go with him.

I found the people there somewhat unfriendly and the service so formal that it reminded me of the church I had attended in my youth. When we got home, I told Matt that I didn't fit in at his church. He suggested we try another, and wouldn't take no for an answer. Reasoning with a six-year-old was next to impossible, so we tried a Catholic church. I didn't like it either. But Matt kept after me. Over the next eight weeks, we attended eight different churches, and I felt that all of them were a waste of time. I hoped that after eight attempts, Matt would give up, but he didn't. He desperately wanted to find a church that we could attend together.

Sharon, a young widow with two children who lived across the street from us, heard about our failed search and invited us to go the following Sunday to her church. I didn't want to walk through the doors of any church again, but, in an attempt to be polite, I asked her about it. She told me that her church was called the "Eagle's Nest," and it was nondenominational. That name meant something to me. I thought years before I had been in a bar that had used that name. At any rate, it didn't sound like my kind of place. Then Sharon really got my attention.

"Lauren, there is a single guy at my church who is so good looking that I think you would really like him."

I immediately thought, "*Oh, what the heck. We'll try it one more Sunday*. I knew this wasn't the right reason for going to church, but it was the best one I had been given in years.

On March 18, 1979, Sharon drove Matthew, Summer, and me to church. It took us ten minutes to travel to an old movie theater that had been converted into a place of worship. After we parked, Sharon and the kids hurried inside, but I stayed behind to smoke. I was now smoking more than three packs of cigarettes a day, and I knew that I couldn't make it through the whole service unless I lit up before I sat down. As I smoked, I watched the front door to see what kind of people I would be meeting.

For starters, unlike the other churches I had attended, these people were laughing and smiling as they got out of their cars and greeted one another. They seemed happy, and unlike the other places I had visited, these people were all carrying Bibles. There was a great deal of back-slapping and hugging too. There were even two ladies at the door who were greeting and hugging everyone who walked through. This made me very nervous. I didn't want to have to talk to these happy people, and I sure didn't want one of them hugging me. I began wishing that I had gone in with Sharon. Being alone made me feel like an open target.

I waited outside the building for five minutes, studying the situation and working on a plan to sneak by the two enthusiastic greeters. When I noticed a large group approaching the entrance, I made my way to the middle and squeezed through the door with them. I thought I was home free when, out of nowhere, a hand reached out and grabbed me. Suddenly, I was being pulled against the huge bosom of a large, stocky young girl, who as she hugged me enthusiastically wailed, "Praise the Lord! It is so good to have you with us, sister." I thought I was going to die! After several seconds of exuberant hugging, she released me, and then proudly and loudly introduced herself. "I'm Brenda Scott, but most folks just call me by my Indian name, Princess Blue Skies."

One quick look at her face told me that she wasn't kidding. She had dark eyes, high cheekbones and a noble, native American Indian look. Her smile covered the whole lower half of her face, and she looked like she was going to explode and hug me again if I didn't move on quickly. Nodding my head, I kind of stuttered, "Nice to meet you ah—ah—ah—Brenda. My name is Lauren."

"I am so glad you are here, Lauren," she was almost shouting, and I had no doubt that everyone in the general area could hear every word she was saying. I wanted to hide, but

Brenda was putting me in the spotlight, and there was no place to run. This was not fun, nor did I think it should be happening in a church. Again I nodded at the woman, and then quickly turned and walked toward the old auditorium.

Before I could enter the main part of the building, I noticed a crowd standing around a derelict man. Obviously he was a reject from Skid Row, and my eyes quickly examined him and his filth. He repelled me, but the people who were gathered around him were very loving and accepting. As I continued to stare at the man, I thought, *I wouldn't touch you with a ten-foot pole!* Then, even though he wasn't talking, I heard him speak to me, "I know how bad I look, young lady, but today I met Jesus, and my sins were washed away. I was cleaned by His blood! What's your story?" Frightened, I quickly turned away and ran toward the auditorium.

Upon entering, I saw all kinds of braces, casts, wheelchairs, and crutches hanging from the walls. On the stage I noticed a piano, an organ, a synthesizer, drums, horns, and a group of singers. The room was quickly filling up, and there were so many people roaming around that I began to wonder if I could find Matt, Summer, and Sharon.

Then the music began. It sounded more like a jam session than a church, and I immediately liked it.

Still looking for Sharon and my kids and trying to look inconspicuous, I was grabbed by the arm by a man who said, "Here's a seat, sister." The next thing I knew, I was sitting in the chair—but not for long, because soon everyone was on their feet, clapping their hands and singing.

Only black churches play music like this, I thought. *What is it doing in a white church?*

Focused on the front of the auditorium, I saw the words to the songs being flashed on a huge screen above the stage. Before long, I loosened up and joined in, clapping my hands and singing along. For an hour, we flowed with the music, an hour in which I didn't think of a cigarette once. I was too caught up in the music for anything else to matter. Then, as the singing and music stopped, I knew the mood would quickly change, so I prepared myself for a fifteen-minute lecture by the priest or minister or whatever he was called.

All of a sudden, a little Omar Sharif look-alike appeared on stage and began to preach. *My God!* I thought. *This is the man Sharon wanted me to meet.*

The fifteen-minute, boring lecture I had expected turned into a riveting, hard-hitting, one-and-a-half hour sermon. I don't recall what he said, but I do remember that every word young Pastor Gary Greenwald said struck my apathetic heart like a fiery dart. I was moved beyond understanding. With my whole being, I felt an incredible need to know the person he was speaking about—Jesus Christ. But years of hurt and rebellion had hardened me almost beyond penetration. I knew I needed him, but I fiercely fought the pull on my soul.

Then the pastor ended his sermon with an invitation for all who needed Jesus in their lives to accept him. Pastor Greenwald didn't realize it, but his invitation seemed directed right at me.

"There is a young woman here today. She has been known and loved by millions. She has experienced the desire to die because of the torment in her life caused by drugs and alcohol. Fearful of never being loved and afraid to give the love she so desperately needed, she is lost. She has run and run, and now there is nowhere else to hide.

"Jesus is speaking to you this morning. He wants to heal those memories, those disappointments, those sins you have done in the dark of night. Like the prodigal child, it is time to come home."

As he talked on, my life moved across the screen of my mind, and I thought, *Oh, god, I'm so unworthy of you. I'm ashamed of my actions and my thoughts. How can you ever receive or forgive me?* My ears interrupted my thoughts as they tuned in to Pastor Greenwald's words.

"Young lady, man has let you down. Man has not forgiven you because he is unable to. But my Jesus, he is more than able! Let him forgive you."

Once he finished speaking, the pastor asked those in the

audience who needed Jesus to signify their need by raising their hand. Mine was the first one up. Then he asked those who had raised their hand to come forward and stand before the congregation. I didn't want everyone there to know I was a sinner, but my legs, apparently with a mind of their own, moved me out of my chair and into the aisle. The next thing I knew I was standing in front of Pastor Greenwald with tears streaming down my face—tears that flowed from the depth of my soul. As each tear fell, a chain of bondage fell with it, until I felt a heavy burden being lifted from my shoulders. I had never realized that it was ever there. Between deep sobs, I repeated what is called the sinner's prayer.

When I finally looked up, wiping the tears away, I no longer saw the young pastor—only Jesus. And I heard him say to me, "Welcome home, Lauren. I have waited thirty-three years for you."

Matt ran up and wrapped his little arms around me, hugging me harder than he ever had before. An indescribable sense of love, tenderness, and unconditional acceptance filled my being. I knew that my life would never be the same. I had found my Father—the One I had been searching for all my life. And I realized then, as I do now, that my Father really does know best.

• Conclusion •

My story doesn't end here. Quite the contrary, on March 18, 1979, I experienced and accepted a life-changing challenge: to let Jesus come into my heart and be the Lord over my life. Throughout the years since, I have conquered mountains and struggled through valleys. God's mercy and infinite patience have helped me overcome a three-pack-a-day cigarette habit and the abuse of chemicals of any sort. He has taught me how to walk in his love and forgiveness.

Of course, the "old Lauren" pops up once in a while—the one who was deeply insecure, the one who was beaten and rejected only to learn mistrust from that, the one who felt bitterness and confusion over what her parents and so-called friends did to her. But as I have laid all of these heartaches at the feet of Jesus, he has been faithful to care for me, to heal me, and to love me despite all of my faults. Through him, I am learning to love myself, even as he loves me—unconditionally.

About the Author

Lauren Chapin is as popular today as she was in the 50s and 60s thanks to the syndication of her television series, *Father Knows Best*. Lauren is active on the speaker's circuit, talking about drugs, alcohol, child abuse, and her Christian faith. A singer, and mother of two, she makes her home in Texas.

If you would like Lauren to come speak in your community, write her at P.O. Box 922, Killeen, Texas, 76540.